"An extraordinary feat: To encompass the dynamic, creatively unsettling and pluralist tensions *between* the schools of psychoanalysis and depth psychology, and also *within* each of the main schools in one volume. The Editors have briefed their authors perfectly, and the authors have risen to the occasion. It is a mine of information, both reliable and challenging. Could stimulate an international road show of conferences based on the book. The field needed this, and it will hugely benefit the widest possible range of practitioners, those in training, and those engaged with the area."

– **Andrew Samuels**, Professor of Analytical Psychology, University of Essex, UK; Former Chair, UK Counsel for Psychotherapy

"This timely book will surprise people outside of psychoanalysis who think that nothing much has changed in it since the pioneering work of Freud, and it will broaden the perspectives of those within the field who have kept abreast of just one or another 'school'. Psychoanalysis still remains the richest and most rewarding firmament of ideas about the lived life of the mind."

– **Mark Solms**, Research Chair, IPA; Science Director, APsaA

"*Innovations in Psychoanalysis* is an outstanding, singularly unique contribution to the psychoanalytic literature. Astute, scholarly, fresh, Govrin and Mills have brought together a most impressive and eclectic group of psychoanalytic voices. Here, in one volume, are the most important developments in psychoanalysis today."

– **Galit Atlas, PhD**, NYU Postdoctoral Program for Psychotherapy & Psychoanalysis; author of *The Enigma of Desire*

Innovations in Psychoanalysis

From its very inception, psychoanalysis has been a discipline encompassing two contradictory tendencies. This dualistic tendency – tradition alongside disenchantment and the will to improve knowledge – is likely responsible for psychoanalysis's powerful capacity to survive. In *Innovations in Psychoanalysis: Originality, Development, Progress*, Aner Govrin and Jon Mills bring together the most eminent and diverse psychoanalysts to reflect upon the evolution, vitality, and richness of psychoanalysis today.

Psychoanalysis is undergoing significant transformations involving the entire spectrum of disciplinary differences. This book illuminates these transformations, importantly revealing the innovations in technique, the evolving understanding of theory within existing schools of thought, the need for empirical resurgence, innovations in infant research, neuropsychoanalysis, in the development of new interventions and methods of treatment, and in philosophical and metatheoretical paradigms. Uniquely bringing together psychoanalysts representing different fields of expertise, the contributors answer two questions in this collection of ground-breaking essays: "What are the most important developments in psychoanalysis today?" and "What impact has your chosen perspective had on conducting psychoanalytic treatment?" Their thought-provoking and challenging answers are essential for anyone who wants to fully understand the field of psychoanalysis in our changing, current world.

Innovations in Psychoanalysis brings a whole array of differing schools of thought in dialogue with one another and will be of interest to psychoanalysts, psychologists, psychotherapists, philosophers, and historians of the behavioral sciences worldwide.

Aner Govrin, PhD, is a clinical psychologist and director of the doctoral program in Psychoanalysis and Hermeneutics in the Department of Hermeneutics and Cultural Studies at Bar-Ilan University. Author of many publications in psychoanalysis and ethics, he maintains a private practice in Tel Aviv and is a member of the Tel Aviv Institute for Contemporary Psychoanalysis.

Jon Mills, PsyD, PhD, ABPP, is a philosopher, psychoanalyst, and clinical psychologist. He is a faculty member in the postgraduate programs in psychoanalysis and psychotherapy, Gordon F. Derner School of Psychology at Adelphi University; is Emeritus Professor of Psychology and Psychoanalysis at Adler Graduate Professional School, Toronto; and is the author of numerous works in psychoanalysis, philosophy, and cultural studies. He runs a mental health corporation in Ontario, Canada.

PHILOSOPHY & PSYCHOANALYSIS BOOK SERIES
Series Editor
Jon Mills

Philosophy & Psychoanalysis is dedicated to current developments and cutting-edge research in the philosophical sciences, phenomenology, hermeneutics, existentialism, logic, semiotics, cultural studies, social criticism, and the humanities that engage and enrich psychoanalytic thought through philosophical rigor. With the philosophical turn in psychoanalysis comes a new era of theoretical research that revisits past paradigms while invigorating new approaches to theoretical, historical, contemporary, and applied psychoanalysis. No subject or discipline is immune from psychoanalytic reflection within a philosophical context including psychology, sociology, anthropology, politics, the arts, religion, science, culture, physics, and the nature of morality. Philosophical approaches to psychoanalysis may stimulate new areas of knowledge that have conceptual and applied value beyond the consulting room reflective of greater society at large. In the spirit of pluralism, *Philosophy & Psychoanalysis* is open to any theoretical school in philosophy and psychoanalysis that offers novel, scholarly, and important insights in the way we come to understand our world.

Titles in this series:

Ethics and Attachment
How We Make Moral Judgments
Aner Govrin

Jung and Philosophy
Edited by Jon Mills

Innovations in Psychoanalysis
Originality, Development, Progress
Edited by Aner Govrin and Jon Mills

For more information about this series, please visit: www.routledge.com/Philosophy-&-Psychoanalysis-Book-Series/book-series

Innovations in Psychoanalysis

Originality, Development, Progress

Edited by
Aner Govrin and Jon Mills

LONDON AND NEW YORK

First published 2020
by Routledge
2 Park Square, Milton Park, Abingdon, Oxon OX14 4RN

and by Routledge
52 Vanderbilt Avenue, New York, NY 10017

Routledge is an imprint of the Taylor & Francis Group, an informa business

© 2020 selection and editorial matter, Aner Govrin and Jon Mills; individual chapters, the contributors

The right of Aner Govrin and Jon Mills to be identified as the authors of the editorial material, and of the authors for their individual chapters, has been asserted in accordance with sections 77 and 78 of the Copyright, Designs and Patents Act 1988.

All rights reserved. No part of this book may be reprinted or reproduced or utilised in any form or by any electronic, mechanical, or other means, now known or hereafter invented, including photocopying and recording, or in any information storage or retrieval system, without permission in writing from the publishers.

Trademark notice: Product or corporate names may be trademarks or registered trademarks, and are used only for identification and explanation without intent to infringe.

British Library Cataloguing-in-Publication Data
A catalogue record for this book is available from the British Library

Library of Congress Cataloging-in-Publication Data
A catalog record for this book has been requested

ISBN: 978-0-367-40861-9 (hbk)
ISBN: 978-0-367-40862-6 (pbk)
ISBN: 978-0-367-80956-0 (ebk)

Typeset in Times New Roman
by Apex CoVantage, LLC

Contents

About the contributors   ix

Introduction   1
ANER GOVRIN AND JON MILLS

1 **Contemporary Freudian theory: perspectives on synthetic ego functions and the paradox of punishment fantasies**   11
STEPHEN J. MILLER

2 **The most innovative ideas in psychoanalysis: a Kleinian approach**   39
RACHEL B. BLASS

3 **Cultural complexes in the psyche of individuals and groups: revisioning analytical psychology from within**   52
THOMAS SINGER

4 **The subject in the age of world-formation (*mondialisation*): advances in Lacanian theory from the Québec Group**   75
JEFFREY S. LIBRETT

5 **Existential psychoanalysis: the role of freedom in the clinical encounter**   100
M. GUY THOMPSON

6 **Moving forward: new findings on the right brain and their implications for psychoanalysis**   119
ALLAN N. SCHORE

7	**The impact of the interpersonal innovations on contemporary psychoanalysis** IRWIN HIRSCH	137
8	**Relational self-psychology: a contemporary self-psychological approach to the practice of psychoanalysis** ESTELLE SHANE	153
9	**Relational psychoanalysis: origins, scope, and recent innovations** STEVEN KUCHUCK	172
10	**Phenomenology speaks: from intersubjectivity to the ethical turn** DONNA M. ORANGE	191
11	**Self-medication, anaclitic and introjective personality styles, drug of choice, and the treatment of people with substance use disorders: theoretical and clinical implications of the empirical research** WILLIAM H. GOTTDIENER	208
12	**Bodies and screen relations: moving treatment from wishful thinking to informed decision-making** GILLIAN ISAACS RUSSELL AND TODD ESSIG	228
	Appendix	250
	Index	252

About the contributors

Rachel B. Blass, PhD, is a training and supervising analyst at the Israel Psychoanalytic Society, a member of the British Psychoanalytical Society, and formerly a professor of psychoanalysis in leading universities both in the UK and in Israel. She is on the board of the *International Journal of Psychoanalysis*, where she is the editor of the "Controversies" section. She is currently in private practice in Jerusalem. She has published a book and over 80 articles which elucidate the foundations of psychoanalysis and their role in contemporary analytic thinking and practice, offers close study of Freud's texts and the evolution of his ideas (especially regarding the notion of truth), and clarifies how Kleinian psychoanalysis grounds and advances these ideas. She has lectured, taught, supervised, and offered clinical seminars in many countries, and her writings have been translated into 15 languages.

Todd Essig, PhD, is a training and supervising psychoanalyst and faculty at the William Alanson White Institutes. He served on the editorial boards for *Contemporary Psychoanalysis* and the *Journal of the American Psychoanalytic Association* and recently co-edited (along with Gillian Isaacs Russell) a special issue in *Psychoanalytic Perspectives* on technology. For 16 years, until 2009, he was Director and Founder of The Psychoanalytic Connection (psychoanalysis.net), becoming widely known as a pioneer in the innovative uses of information technologies for mental health professionals. He currently writes "Managing Mental Wealth" for *Forbes*, where he writes about the intersection of emerging technoculture, mental health, and building a good life. His clinical practice is in New York City, where he treats individuals and couples, almost all of whom come to his office.

William H. Gottdiener, PhD, is a licensed clinical psychologist, psychoanalyst, and tenured full professor of psychology at John Jay College of Criminal Justice of the City University of New York (CUNY). Dr. Gottdiener received his PhD in clinical psychology from The New School for Social Research, and he completed a National Institute on Drug Abuse postdoctoral research fellowship. He is the Director of the John Jay College Addiction Studies Program. In addition, he is a faculty member and supervisor in the psychoanalytic training program of the Washington Square Institute in New York City. He has published over 40 articles and book chapters and is on the editorial boards of the journals *Addiction Research and Theory* and *Psychoanalytic Psychology*. He is an APA fellow in the divisions of addictions, clinical psychology, general psychology, and psychoanalysis, a fellow of the International Psychoanalytic Association, and was honored by the APA division of psychoanalysis with its prestigious Research and Scholarship Award in 2015.

Aner Govrin, PhD, is a clinical psychologist and on the faculty of the Department of Hermeneutics and Cultural Studies at Bar-Ilan University, where he is the Director of an academic doctoral program, Psychoanalysis and Hermeneutics, for mental health workers. He maintains a private practice in Tel Aviv and is a member of the Tel Aviv Institute for Contemporary Psychoanalysis. Govrin has authored numerous publications, including four books: *Between Abstinence and Seduction – The Analysis of American Psychoanalysis* (Hebrew, 2004); *Conversations with Michael Eigen* (Karnac, 2007); *Conservative and Radical Perspectives on Psychoanalytic Knowledge: The Fascinated and the Disenchanted* (Routledge, 2016); and *Ethics and Attachment: How we Make Moral Judgments* (Routledge, 2018).

Irwin Hirsch, PhD, is a faculty, supervisor, and former director of the Manhattan Institute for Psychoanalysis, distinguished visiting faculty, William Alanson White Institute, clinical adjunct professor of psychology and supervisor, Postgraduate Program in Psychotherapy and Psychoanalysis, Adelphi University, clinical adjunct professor of psychology and supervisor, Postdoctoral Program in Psychotherapy and Psychoanalysis, New York University, and faculty and supervisor, National Training Program, National Institute for the Psychotherapies. He serves on the editorial boards of *Contemporary Psychoanalysis*, *Psychoanalytic Dialogues*, and *Psychoanalytic Perspectives*, and is author of over 80 publications, including four books: the Goethe Award winning, *Coasting in the Countertransference: Conflicts of Self-Interest between Analyst and Patient* (Routledge, 2007); *The Interpersonal Tradition: The Origins of Psychoanalytic Subjectivity* (Routledge, 2015); co-edited with Donnel Stern, *The Interpersonal Perspective in Psychoanalysis, 1960s-1990s: Rethinking Transference & Countertransference* (Routledge, 2017); and also co-edited with Donnell Stern, *Further Developments in Interpersonal Psychoanalysis, 1980s-2010s: Evolving Interest in the Analyst's Subjectivity* (Routledge, 2018).

Steven Kuchuck, DSW, is Editor-in-Chief of *Psychoanalytic Perspectives*, Co-Editor of Routledge Relational Perspectives Book Series, President of the International Association for Relational Psychoanalysis and Psychotherapy, and a board member, supervisor, and faculty at the National Institute for the Psychotherapies (NIP), faculty/supervisor at the NIP National Training Program, the Stephen Mitchell Relational Study Center, and the Institute for Relational Psychoanalysis of Philadelphia, as well as other institutes. Dr. Kuchuck's writing focuses primarily on the analyst's subjectivity, and in 2015 and 2016, he won the Gradiva Award for best edited books: *Clinical Implications of the Psychoanalyst's Life Experience: When the Personal Becomes Professional* and *The Legacy of Sándor Ferenczi: From Ghost to Ancestor* (co-edited with Adrienne Harris).

Jeffrey S. Librett, PhD, is Professor of German at the University of Oregon. He is the author of *The Rhetoric of Cultural Dialogue: Jews and Germans from Moses Mendelssohn to Richard Wagner and Beyond* (Stanford University Press, 2000), *Orientalism and the Figure of the Jew* (Fordham University Press, 2015), and numerous essays on literature, philosophy, literary theory, and psychoanalysis. He has translated Jean-Luc Nancy's *The Sense of the World* (1997) and *Of the Sublime: Presence in Question*, by Michel Deguy et al. (1993), and he is Editor of *Konturen*, an online journal for German studies and theory. In addition, he is also founding Editor of *Metalepsis: Journal of the American Board and Academy of Psychoanalysis*. He is currently working on a book provisionally titled *Anxiety's Modes: Phenomenology, Neuroscience, Psychoanalysis*. In the clinical domain, he is an analyst of the Freudian School of Quebec and works at Options Counseling and Family Services and in private practice in Eugene, Oregon.

Stephen J. Miller, PhD, ABPP, is a training and supervisory analyst with the Psychoanalytic Institute of Northern California (PINC) and a member of the International Psychoanalytic Association. He is a former president of The American Board and Academy of Psychoanalysis; a former president of The Academy of Psychoanalysis; a former president and founding member of The Oklahoma Society for Psychoanalytic Studies; and a former secretary and board member of Section I of Division 39: Psychoanalysis. of the American Psychological Association. He has written and presented extensively, primarily on the topic of punishment anxiety. He teaches and practices psychoanalysis, psychotherapy, and psychoanalytically-informed couples therapy in Oklahoma City.

Jon Mills, PsyD, PhD, ABPP, is a philosopher, psychoanalyst, and clinical psychologist. He is a faculty member in the postgraduate programs in psychoanalysis and psychotherapy, Gordon F. Derner School of Psychology at Adelphi University; is a Emeritus Professor of Psychology and Psychoanalysis at Adler Graduate Professional School in Toronto; and runs a mental health corporation in Ontario, Canada. Recipient of numerous awards for his scholarship, including four Gradiva Awards, he is the author and/or editor of 22 books in psychoanalysis, philosophy, psychology, and cultural studies, including *Inventing God* (Routledge, 2017); *Underworlds* (Routledge, 2014); *Conundrums: A Critique of Contemporary Psychoanalysis* (Routledge, 2012); *Origins: On the Genesis of Psychic Reality* (McGill-Queens University Press, 2010); *Treating Attachment Pathology* (Rowman & Littlefield, 2005); *The Unconscious Abyss: Hegel's Anticipation of Psychoanalysis* (State University of New York Press, 2002); and *The Ontology of Prejudice* (Rodopi, 1997).

Donna M. Orange, PhD, PsyD, is educated in philosophy, clinical psychology, and psychoanalysis, teaches at the New York University Postdoc Program and the Institute for the Psychoanalytic Study of Subjectivity, New York, as well as conducts private study groups. Her recent books include *Thinking for Clinicians: Philosophical Resources for Contemporary Psychoanalysis and the Humanistic Psychotherapies* (Routledge, 2010), *The Suffering Stranger: Hermeneutics for Everyday Clinical Practice* (Routledge, 2011), *Nourishing the Inner Life of Clinicians and Humanitarians: The Ethical Turn in Psychoanalysis*

(Routledge, 2016), and *Climate Justice, Psychoanalysis, and Radical Ethics* (Routledge, 2017).

Gillian Isaacs Russell, PhD, is a UK-trained psychoanalyst. She is a member of the American Psychoanalytic Association, the International Psychoanalytical Association, British Psychoanalytic Council, and the British Psychotherapy Foundation. She has served on the editorial board of the *British Journal of Psychotherapy*, as Book Reviews Editor, and is now a member of the reviewing panel. She co-edited a special technology and psychoanalysis issue of *Psychoanalytic Perspectives* with Todd Essig. Her book, *Screen Relations: The Limits of Computer-Mediated Psychoanalysis and Psychotherapy*, was published by Karnac Books in 2015. Dr. Russell is internationally known as a lecturer, author, consultant, and researcher. She speaks and teaches on technology and its impact on intimate human relationships, particularly in psychoanalytic treatment. She currently practices in Boulder, Colorado.

Allan N. Schore, PhD, is on the clinical faculty of the Department of Psychiatry and Biobehavioral Sciences, UCLA David Geffen School of Medicine. He is author of six seminal volumes, including *The Science of the Art of Psychotherapy* (Norton, 2012), and most recently *Right Brain Psychotherapy* (Norton, 2019) and *The Development of the Unconscious Mind* (Norton, 2019), as well as numerous articles and chapters. He is past editor of the acclaimed *Norton Series on Interpersonal Neurobiology*, and a reviewer or on the editorial staff of more than 45 journals across a number of scientific and clinical disciplines, and has had a private practice in psychotherapy for over four decades.

Estelle Shane, PhD, is a founding member, member of the Board of Directors, faculty member, and training and supervising analyst, The Institute for Contemporary Psychoanalysis, Los Angeles; faculty member and training and supervising analyst, The New Center for Psychoanalysis, Los Angeles; past president and council member, International Association of Psychoanalytic Self Psychology; adjunct faculty, UCLA Department of Psychiatry, Los Angeles; consulting editor, *Psychoanalytic Inquiry*; editorial board, *Self and Context*; author of numerous publications; and co-author (with M. Shane and M. Gales) of *Intimate Attachments: A Developmental Systems Self Psychology* (Routledge, 1997).

Thomas Singer, MD, is a psychiatrist and Jungian analyst in private practice in San Francisco. He is the editor of a series of books that explore cultural complexes in different parts of the world, including Australia, *Placing Psyche* (Spring, 2011), Latin America, *Listening to Latin America* (Spring, 2012), Europe, *Europe's Many Souls* (Spring, 2016), and North America. *The Cultural Complex* (Brunner-Routledge, 2004). He is currently working on a book about cultural complexes in Asia. In addition, he has edited *Psyche and the City*, *The Vision Thing*, co-edited the Ancient Greece Modern Psyche series and co-authored *A Fan's Guide to Baseball Fever*. Dr. Singer currently serves as the President of National ARAS, which explores symbolic imagery from around the world. His most recent chapters include "Trump and the American Selfie" in *A Clear and Present Danger* and "Trump and the American Collective Psyche" in *The Dangerous Case of Donald Trump*.

M. Guy Thompson, PhD, received his psychoanalytic training from R. D. Laing and associates at the Philadelphia Association in London, and his PhD in Clinical Psychology from The Wright Institute, Berkeley. He is a personal and supervising analyst and faculty member, Psychoanalytic Institute of Northern California, and adjunct professor at the California Institute of Integral Studies, San Francisco. Dr. Thompson is also the Founder and Director of Free Association, Inc., a not-for-profit organization devoted to the relief of severe psychopathology, and the author of numerous journal articles, book chapters, and reviews on psychoanalysis, phenomenology, and schizophrenia. His most recent books include *The Legacy of R. D. Laing: An Appraisal of His Contemporary Relevance* (Routledge, 2015) and *The Death of Desire: An Existential Study in Sanity and Madness*, 2nd Edition (Routledge, 2016). Dr. Thompson serves on the editorial boards of numerous professional journals, including *Psychoanalytic Psychology*, the *Journal of Phenomenological Psychology*, the *Journal of European Psychoanalysis*, and the *Journal of Existential Analysis*. He has lectured extensively throughout the United States, Canada, Mexico, Great Britain, Spain, and Australia. Dr. Thompson practices existential psychoanalysis in San Francisco and lives in Marin County, CA (www.mguythompson.com).

Introduction

Aner Govrin and Jon Mills

Psychoanalysis is internally divided: declared a science, hermeneutics, a theory of mind and culture, a clinical treatment, a general method of observation regarding human phenomena, even a *Weltanschauung*; we can neither find agreement nor consensus. Here we may observe a fundamental split in its identity. In its insistence on being viewed as a science, it has embraced naturalism, rationalism, and empiricism, while other proponents champion psychoanalysis as a psychological theory of subjectivity and human dynamics, which in turn inform clinical method and cultural critique. As apologists are busy attempting to lend scientific credibility to the discipline – from empirical research in attachment to neuroscience, traditionalists maintain their narrow focus (and subsequent insularity) by staying devout to their own school's self-enchantment, opposed to rival disillusioned perspectives that threaten them (Govrin, 2016). In this way, group loyalty quells dissent and internal critique by preaching to the choir, of which there are many congregations. Yet there are independent thinkers within contemporary times that have stimulated a renewal of intellectual energies by turning to philosophy, a trend that is likely to spark an appreciation for novel concepts typically not addressed by psychoanalysis, albeit ones based on a return to past ideas.

The history of psychoanalytic knowledge is an extremely tangled one, including a plethora of factors and phenomena along the axes of time and space. Any attempt to outline the innovations in this domain will have to tread a narrow, dialectical line between two opposing directions. On the one hand, there will be the exposure of a dynamic of change in therapeutic approaches, the rise and fall of theoretical models, and the development of new therapeutic techniques. On the other, there is the fact that there has not been all that much change in the influence of mainstream psychoanalytic theory (i.e. Freud, Bion, Lacan, Klein, Winnicott, Kohut, and others). Innovation has mainly come via interpretive extensions.

Very few analysts have tried to envision the future of psychoanalysis as a whole outside of their narrow identification with their own tribe. Those who have made the attempt have advocated for pluralism (Samuels, 1989), comparative integration (Willock, 2007), unity of theory (Rangell, 2007), consilience between schools (Valone, 2005), a return to classical models (Chessick, 2007), or a radical rejection for postmodern paradigms (Mills, 2012). Although attention has been paid to the internal conflicts, schisms, and marginalization that has occurred in the organizational life of psychoanalysis itself (Eisold, 2018; Stepansky, 2009), very view solutions are in sight. When it comes to overall progress, Axelrod, Naso, and Rosenberg (2018) cogently show how psychoanalysis has mismanaged its own profession and largely failed to identify its own impediments to progress, hence contributing to our contemporary crisis of devaluation and rejection by the mainstream culture. They argue for, and begin to outline, a profession-wide vision for growth, advancement, and improvement in order to combat demoralization and revitalize the future of our profession. This current project complements and extends their vision of rehabilitative efforts through the continued need for innovation, development, originality, creativity, and systemic progression.

Critics of psychoanalysis comment negatively on psychoanalysts' tendency to dwell on the past. As Bornstein and Masling (1998) note: "A geneticist of 1900 could not sustain a conversation with a contemporary geneticist, but Freud would have no trouble recognizing the psychoanalysis of 1997 or reading a modern psychoanalytic journal" (pp. xviii–xix). According to Bornstein (2001), psychoanalysis lacks any innovative quality. Uncurious about the extra-analytical scientific world, and communicating only among each other, psychoanalysts don't often expose themselves to alternative theories that might enrich their knowledge.

But one might take a different angle: science, literature, and philosophy are unlike technology, medicine, or economics. Change, in them, happens at a different, much slower pace. When we use this slower yardstick, psychoanalysis can be seen to change, nevertheless.

Psychoanalysis is more like philosophy than like science. While scientific theories in use decades ago will have given way to more novel theories, philosophical theories going back to antiquity, for instance, still continue to inspire, drawing interest among contemporary philosophers.

University departments of philosophy around the world teach work that hails from long ago – from ancient Greek philosophy to the philosophy of the modern age – Spinoza, Kant, Mill, Hume, Hegel, and Nietzsche, to mention but a few. These philosophers continue being read because the depth of their insights transcends historical periods, and their relevance does not diminish.

And this is not just the case for philosophy; the same goes for literature. Royal Netz (2016) provides an illustration from the field of papyrology. In 1896, in Egypt, thousands of decaying papyrus scrolls were discovered. Scholars were excited: new texts and new books in the literature of ancient Greece were about to be discovered, they believed, and the study of antiquity was about to undergo a great upheaval. Here and there, indeed, an ancient papyrus carrying a hitherto unknown text was found (a poem by Sappho, for instance). But such incidents were rare. By far the most discovered scrolls were manuscripts of texts we already knew: the same Plato again and the same Homer. The scholars' hope that our ancient forefathers knew other writers than the ones who were copied onto parchment in the Middle Ages proved vain. Monks in medieval Constantinople chose to copy the very same texts that had been copied on papyrus, in Egypt, a millennium earlier. It transpired that literary taste does not tend to change nor renew. Sophocles, Aeschylus, and Euripides were Athens' most popular playwrights even in their own life times. And they remained so for the next 2500 years. Conceptualizations concerning the psyche also do not lose their relevance rapidly. Truths of this type go on being discovered by one generation after another. This type of innovation might be captured by the notion of wisdom, which casts a new light on mental life. And much like in the case of philosophy, these ideas become the source of inspiration for new ideas, which in turn will multiply.

Any analyst who describes the inner life in a new way exposes his or her innovation to the weight of their predecessors' descriptions in the course of transforming them. The tradition keeps appearing like a shadow that follows the innovation wherever it goes. T. S. Eliot wrote: "The poem which is absolutely original is absolutely bad; it is, in the bad sense, 'subjective,' with no relation to the world to which it appeals" (Pound, 1934, p. x). And yet, the 12 chapters of this book demonstrate that change is ever-present in psychoanalysis. Members of the professional communities inspired by Melanie Klein or Heinz Kohut do not work in the same way as their predecessors; the relational approach, with its notions of mutuality and intersubjectivity, and its postmodern affinities, suggests a radically different view of therapeutic relations; and new, active communities – like infant research or neuropsychoanalysis – propose to expand and enrich psychoanalytic insight by linking it to other, non-analytic fields of knowledge. Even our understanding of fundamental psychoanalytic concepts such as the unconscious, interpretation, object relations, transference, and countertransference is currently more varied and expansive than it originally was. And, of course, technology with its dazzling progress has also sneaked into the clinic.

Innovations across the psychoanalytic domain

Within today's climate of comparative psychoanalysis and pluralism, we envisioned this project as a forum to allow for all the major psychoanalytic schools to have a voice. We partially accomplished this goal, as it can be debated what constitutes a school, historical movement, tradition, and contemporary offshoots, not to mention redirecting shifts in emphasis and critical horizons of emerging perspectives and political platforms that dominate our attention or come on the scene at any given moment. If the field of psychoanalysis is to evolve, it must expand its scope of reference and be willing to engage in critique. This is why critique among differing schools and internal debate within one's own theoretical orientation allows for innovations to arise and flourish.

We begin with the contemporary Freudians and modern conflict theory. In Chapter 1, Stephen J. Miller argues that the single most important development in contemporary Freudian theory is its emphasis on the dynamics of intrapsychic conflict. Compromise formations represent a synthesis of the components of intrapsychic conflict, which comprise all conscious and unconscious mental activity. Conscious experience is a result of complexes of compromise formations that permit the translation of a mental phenomenon from primary process to secondary process form. Fundamental to this process is the development of self- and object-representations, defining superego functions. The consolidation of these self- and object-representations requires a synthesis, such that systems of prohibitions/ideals are relatively coherent and internally consistent. Failures of this synthetic process yield paradoxical discontinuities in superego functions. Illustrative clinical material is presented to articulate how unconscious punishment fantasies operate.

In Chapter 2, Rachel B. Blass champions innovations in contemporary Kleinian theory. Here she describes important developments from the perspective of a Kleinian approach, which has originated and evolved in London, where it continues to thrive. At the heart of this approach is the idea that psychoanalysis is a process of coming to know or integrating unconscious phantasy as encountered in the analytic relationship. After clarifying the meaning of this idea, the author goes on to examine its implications for how analytic treatment is conducted, referring both to the analytic setting and to matters of technique. She then turns to address the question of the major developments in contemporary psychoanalysis, distinguishing between developments from within this Kleinian approach and those that have emerged from the broader analytic field. The latter include neuropsychoanalysis and the adoption of one or more of the following clinical stances: evidence-based; focused on trauma or other environmental causes; postmodern and eclectic. The author argues that while developments from within the Kleinian approach advance the analytic process of coming to know unconscious phantasy, those of broader fields adopt attitudes to the nature of psychic reality and the possibility of its discovery that, in effect, inhibit it.

In Chapter 3, Thomas Singer examines developments in post-Jungian thought. Building on disillusionment with an over-reliance on archetypes to explain social and political phenomena in the psyche of individuals and groups, an innovative renovation of traditional Jungian theory emerged. It began with Joseph Henderson postulating a middle zone of the unconscious – the cultural unconscious – which sits between the personal and collective unconscious. It further posits that cultural complexes are the foundational building blocks for the contents of the cultural unconscious. Examples of the activity of cultural complexes are investigated. The first explores the case of an individual with a potent cultural complex that deeply influenced his inner and outer life for his first 40 years. The second explores a cultural complex occurring at the level of the group or collective psyche in the United States during the era of Donald Trump.

The Lacanian school has become quite influential, particularly in academe, but contemporary developments remain largely unobserved unless you are intimately identified with that theoretical orientation. In Chapter 4, Jeffrey S. Librett presents some of the advances in Lacanian theory that have been developed in recent years by Willy Apollon, Danielle Bergeron, Lucie Cantin, and other analysts and scholars at the Freudian School of

Québec, as well as the interdisciplinary clinical and research group from which it sprang. These advances involve: first, an extension of Lacan's primarily linguistic notion of the symbolic order into a more fully articulated ethno-psychoanalytic understanding of the unconscious subject in its cultural-civilizational surroundings; and second, an application of this extended theory to the analysis of the disruptions and re-constellations that accompany economic globalization and of the profound effects of these developments on individual subjects today. He begins with a discussion of the notion of "world-formation," in terms of which Apollon and the Québec group summarize the political, socio-cultural, and psychic effects of globalization. Then he describes the structure of the subject of the unconscious, as they conceive it, in relation to language, culture, and civilization. Third, Librett sketches some of the clinical implications of the resultant notion of the subject of culture in the age of world-formation for an analytic approach to understanding adolescence today. Finally, he considers the role of the aesthetic realm for adolescents and for analytic treatment in the current conjuncture.

When Freud, Jung, Klein, and Lacan were active competitors in establishing and expanding the psychoanalytic movement, the presence and interpenetration of phenomenology and existentialism were equally dominating contemporary philosophy and hence simultaneously influencing psychoanalysis. M. Guy Thompson's chapter examines the concept of existential psychoanalysis by situating it at the interface between the existential philosophical tradition and postmodernism. To this end, he compares and contrasts some of the themes from the existential tradition that were incorporated into the relational perspective, with one glaring omission: the role of freedom in the psychoanalytic endeavor. Here he has largely relied on Jean-Paul Sartre's critique of Freud, thereby exposing the inherent problematic of the psychoanalytic conception of the unconscious: the problem of a lie without a liar. The specifically clinical innovation of Sartre's "existential psychoanalysis" is situated in the existential conception of freedom, which deconstructs the conventional conception of the unconscious process by personalizing it, which is to say, replacing the unconscious with the concept of intentionality. Thompson's chapter concludes with a critique of the concept of change, replacing it with the notion of becoming.

Brain laterality research on hemispheric asymmetry is now experiencing a resurgence in neuroscience. This rapidly expanding field is describing the functional and structural differences between the left and right brains, and thereby between a conscious "left mind" and an unconscious "right mind." Allan N. Schore presents his own model of hemispheric asymmetry, first articulated in 1994, and continues to articulate how the right brain is centrally involved in not only the *intrapsychic* unconscious processing and self-regulation of emotions and social information, but also in the *interpersonal* communication and interactive regulation of emotion by a right brain *relational* unconscious, via right brain-to-right brain nonverbal communications of face, voice, and gesture. In his work, he describes the implications of recent discoveries of the right brain for both theoretical and clinical psychoanalysis and suggests that the expanding connections between psychoanalysis and neuroscience can generate innovative future directions for the field.

Before neuropsychoanalysis, self-psychology, and contemporary relational theory, the interpersonal tradition set the stage for innovation and progression. Both early and subsequent interpersonal writing has reflected the first and most thorough effort, certainly in the United States, to move away from hegemonic conceptions of an endogenous drive-defense way of explaining the essences of human development, replacing this with the focus on the history of exogenous relationships with others and with culture, and the internalization of these relationships, as a more pragmatic way to understand how each individual develops into the person they have become. In his chapter, Irwin Hirsch shows how this innovative perspective further evolved into the view that each unique psychoanalyst also brings his personal idiosyncrasy into his work and in a parallel way with interpersonal conceptions of human development: both subjective co-participants cannot help but exert unconscious influence on one another. In the context of these once radical innovations, psychoanalysis can no longer be viewed as a relationship between an objective scientist-therapist and a subjective patient, and in corollary, a relationship between a sick and distorting patient and a healthy and totally clear thinking analyst. This ethos has led to a distinct levelling of hierarchy between patient and analyst – seen now still as an asymmetrical relationship, albeit one between two flawed subjectivities. Examination of the interaction between patient and observing-participant therapist invariably reflects parallels with ways that each patient engages in repetitive and recurring internalized patterns in extra-transference and earlier childhood relational configurations. The examinations of these repeatedly patterned modes of engagement that get lived-out in the transference-countertransference matrix become a vehicle for increased awareness of how patients unconsciously shape their lives to conform to the familiar and familial past, while opening the possibility of engaging in new and hopefully internalized dimensions of being with the significant others, starting with the co-participating analyst.

In Chapter 8, Estelle Shane introduces her vision of contemporary relational theory, which encompasses relational and interpersonal theories, Stolorow and collaborators' intersubjective systems theory, Coburn's complexity theory, and Beebe and Lachmann's dyadic systems theory. The expansiveness of relational self-psychology itself is then described, first in terms of its origins in Kohut's self-psychology, along with the alterations in Kohut's formulations Shane has made based on our contemporary understanding. After she introduces concepts from relational and interpersonal theories, relational self-psychology's capacity to encompass ideas drawn from other related disciplines is described, including attachment theory, infant research, existential epistemological philosophy, systems theory, evolutionary biology, and neurobiological studies, and most particularly, Gerald Edelman's global brain theory of consciousness. Shane believes it is this very integration of theories around contemporary thought that allows for and constitutes the most important developments in psychoanalysis today. Furthermore, she believes that the introduction of brain-based psychoanalysis, with the contributions that such non-linear, process thinking affords, offers the promise of a new, stronger, more individualized psychoanalytic treatment.

As one of the leading proponents of the relational school, Steven Kuchuck's chapter begins with an overview of the distinction between small r and big R relational psychoanalysis. The author explores reasons why Relational psychoanalysis is often difficult to define, delineates key themes within the perspective, and introduces founding as well as more contemporary authors along with their contributions. The newest Relational ideas about clinical implications of the analyst's subjectivity, deliberate self-disclosure, and "silent-disclosure" are reviewed. New thinking about enactment, psychotherapy integration and trauma treatment, race, gender, and sexuality – among other concepts – are considered. The chapter closes with a Relational model for how psychoanalysis might stay relevant and evolve rather than stagnate through applying Karl Popper's notion of critical rationalism, the contention that scientific knowledge grows not by accumulating supporting evidence but by subjecting one's beliefs to severe criticism.

In Chapter 10, Donna M. Orange revisits her intersubjectivity model in the context of the ethical turn in psychoanalysis. Though phenomenology itself has a long history now in continental philosophy, its robust presence in psychoanalysis is truly new and challenges the certainties that have formed a psychoanalytic bedrock from the outset. Chief among these we must consider the view that pathology resides in the patient who brings it to the psychoanalyst for diagnosis and cure. Intersubjectivity theory, in its phenomenological form, is a contextualism holding that psychological trouble forms, develops, and may be healed only in intersubjective fields formed from two or more experiential worlds interweaving.

In the next chapter, William H. Gottdiener reviews research on the self-medication hypothesis of addictive disorders. The self-medication hypothesis is a psychoanalytic model of addictions, and it argues that most people who develop an addiction do so in response to early childhood traumas. Alcohol and other drugs, and even behavioral addictions such as gambling, are engaged in to cope with dysphoria that arose from past traumas. In addition, the self-medication hypothesis argues that people develop preferences for classes of drugs because those drugs best help ameliorate their psychological suffering. Gottdiener provides an argument that a person's drug of choice is linked to their personality style. People with an introjective or anaclitic personality style have preferences for different types of drugs. In addition, there are clinical implications, based on psychoanalytic research, that result from knowing the patient's personality style.

In our final chapter, Gillian Isaacs Russell and Todd Essig examine the clinical horizons of technology in psychoanalytic treatment. Innovation in psychoanalysis and technology moves beyond the empty seductions of technologically mediated remote treatments. Instead, it places the radical differences between local therapy and remote therapy, including the inevitable losses and limitations distance requires, at the center of clinical decision-making. To understand these differences, the concepts of "affordance" and "presence" are discussed and placed in both technological and psychoanalytic contexts. Differences in clinical processes in local and remote treatment are examined, including those in the facilitating environment, in free-floating attention and reverie, in memory, in the introduction of a "technological unconscious," and in the potential for regression. The consequences for practice made by these differences are discussed, including recommendations for whether and how to offer remote treatment.

Taken as a whole, innovation in all the psychoanalytic schools shows the vibrancy and ingenuity of the profession in the twenty-first century. It furthermore shows the plurality across the psychoanalytic domain, with modes of overlap in theory, research, and praxis despite harboring differences and redirecting shifts in theoretical, clinical, and applied approaches and methodology. With increasing tolerance for competing differences between psychoanalytic traditions, we hope this book will breach and intersect cross-disciplinary boundaries and stimulate future interdisciplinary dialogue.

References

Axelrod, S. D., Naso, R. C., & Rosenberg, L. M. (2018). *Progress in psychoanalysis: Envisioning the future of the profession.* London: Routledge.

Bornstein, R. F. (2001). The impending death of psychoanalysis. *Psychoanalytic Psychology, 18*(1), 3–20. doi:10.1037/0736-9735.18.1.2

Bornstein, R. F., & Masling, J. M. (1998). Empirical investigations of events within the analytic hour. In R. F. Bornstein & J. M. Masling (Eds.), *Empirical studies of the therapeutic hour* (pp. xv–xxxiv). Washington, DC: American Psychological Association.

Chessick, R. D. (2007). *The future of psychoanalysis.* Albany: SUNY Press.

Eisold, K. (2018). *The organizational life of psychoanalysis: Conflicts, dilemmas, and the future of the profession.* London: Routledge.

Govrin, A. (2016). *Conservative and radical perspectives on psychoanalytic knowledge: The fascinated and the disenchanted.* New York, NY: Routledge.

Mills, J. (2012). *Conundrums: A critique of contemporary psychoanalysis.* New York, NY: Routledge.

Netz, R. (2016). Some reflections on the illusion of literary fame. *Ho! Literary Magazine (Hebrew), 14,* 191–203.

Pound, E. (1934). *Selected poems* (Ed. and Intro. T. S. Eliot). London: Faber & Faber Ltd.

Rangell, L. (2007). *The road to unity in psychoanalytic theory.* Lanham, MD: Jason Aronson.

Samuels, A. (1989). *The plural psyche.* London and New York, NY: Routledge.

Stepansky, P. E. (2009). *Psychoanalysis at the margins.* New York, NY: Other Press.

Valone, K. (2005). Consilient psychoanalysis. *Psychoanalytic Psychology, 22*(2), 189–206.

Willock, B. (2007). *Comparative-integrative psychoanalysis.* New York, NY: Analytic Press.

Chapter 1

Contemporary Freudian theory
Perspectives on synthetic ego functions and the paradox of punishment fantasies

Stephen J. Miller

From the perspective of classical psychoanalysis, the most innovative issue in the last 40 years has been its focus on intra-psychic conflict. In this capacity, no one has been a more significant contributor than Charles Brenner (1984, 2006). In his revision of Freud's (1923) structural model, Brenner's components of intra-psychic conflict (wishes, defense, superego functions, and the negotiation of dysphoric affects) have altered the understanding of basic psychoanalytic concepts, making possible new and novel understandings of psychopathology and personality development. For the purposes of this present chapter, Brenner's compromise formation model permitted my identification of drive satisfactions implicit in punishment fantasies (Miller, 2004a, 2004b, 2008) and enhanced the appreciation of attendant resistances.

However, in my view, compromise formation theory does not adequately speak to issues of synthesis of mental trends comprised of vast complexes of compromise formations as is necessary in the integration of personality. It also largely accounts for issues of consciousness/unconsciousness only in terms of the selection of compromise formations. In this chapter, I argue in favor of some sort of mental agency, such as Freud's (1923) structural ego. I also attempt to demonstrate that aspects of Freud's metapsychology continue to be efficacious and essential for the understanding of psychopathology and personality development.

Internalization and the paradox of punishment fantasies

Punishment fantasies enlist punitive experiences, fanciful and actual, in the drama of forbidden desires, prohibition, and punishment. The internalized amalgamation of contributions of one's self and the other into self- and object-representations enhances one's capacity to control oneself even in the absence of the prohibiting other. The severity of these punishment fantasies, their consistency with other expectations and prohibitions, the degree to which they effectively restrain action, and the degree to which they promote or encumber adaptation to reality (Hartman, 1958) are measures of psychopathology. They maintain an intimate relationship with the forbidden (although largely unconscious and symbolically expressed) while at the same time preserving contact with propriety, safety, security, and love. In this sense, they form a bridge between the conflicted and the security it threatens to destroy.

In these internalizations, there is often a certain layering of experience in which self-representations closer to consciousness are seen as rebelling against the demands of the object-representation, but, paradoxically, at a deeper level this rebellion is accomplished in such a way as to comply with the very demands and perceived prohibitions of the object. This dynamic is evident in every patient we see. The young man who as a boy wanted to pursue his own desires felt dominated and controlled by his father. Now he rebels against any demand made upon him, but he rebels in such a way that he is unable to achieve his own aspirations. A woman patient felt constantly criticized by her self-absorbed mother and longs for a loving mutual relationship in her contemporary life. Yet she vehemently criticizes her husband for any slight breech in empathic attunement, inducing his sensitized counter-criticism, a wish for revenge, and emotional distance.

Case study: initial indications of synthetic failures

One can see this dynamic quite dramatically enacted by a patient with obsessive-compulsive disorder. In his rituals, manifestations of both forbidden desires and self-punishment were evident. For example, he spent hours ritually brushing his teeth, forcing the toothbrush against his teeth and gums until they bled, and then felt compelled to rinse his mouth in a patterned manner, making sure to empty his mouth of every trace of toothpaste.

As a child, his fantasy of being an Oedipal victor was both overstimulated and disappointed. His father, a victim of polio, had an atrophied leg and suffered from post-polio fatigue. The patient and his mother shared their contempt for the father's "laziness" in his need for rest. Simultaneously he felt a terrible sense of guilt, reinforced by his father's Catholicism, which he felt was forbidding of his hostile and sexual fantasies and desires.

Both parents provided powerful shaping influences for the cruelty of his conscience and ego-ideal. His father was a rather passive and remote man who was obviously dominated by his critical wife. A rare subject of assertion was father's insistence of the family's devotion to the Catholic Church, with its severity, perceived anti-sexuality, and threats of damnation. A shaping influence for his ego-ideal was his controlling mother, with her disdain for father, which provided a threat that the patient could be next if he failed to live up to her expectations.

He had an older brother who was idealized in the family. His mother repeatedly implored him to aspire to be like the brother. He was enraged at not being the prized one in her eyes but also guilty and fearful of his competitive rage towards his brother.

In early adolescence, he had repeated homosexual experiences with neighborhood boys, crystallizing a "solution" to his conflicts. Initially he only told me that the boys performed fellatio on him while he enjoyed a sense of sadistic dominance over them. They assumed the role of the forbidden woman, while he turned the tables on his rivals, dominating and emasculating them. Only later in the analysis did I discover that he also performed fellatio on them, enjoying a perceived shameful sense of passive, receptive submission.

The guilty, shameful, but irresistible sado-masochistic fantasy was disguised and enacted in this seemingly incomprehensible tooth-brushing ritual, painfully repeated twice daily. In this ritual, he played both the dominating sadist, forcing the toothbrush/penis into the mouth of his submissive victim, and the submissive victim himself. Both forbidden desires and terrible guilt and shame were represented, while ownership of perceived forbidden and dangerous impulses was disavowed.

Internalizations of *both* the sadistic aggressor and the helpless victim were represented. Closer to consciousness was a desexualized identification with the helpless victim, but his internalization of the forbidden sadist was also represented as an object-representation who cruelly forced himself on the helpless self-representation. He consciously felt unfairly victimized by these terrible rituals/fantasies, having successfully disconnected both his vengeful, erotized sadism and his erotized masochistic longing from consciousness. He was compelled to seek these forbidden pleasures through the circumscribed channels of this and other ritualized enactments.

We can infer the intra-psychic situation prior to the development of the self- and object-representations enacted in this obsessive-compulsive symptom. There must have been a time when he was much more conscious of both his own rivalry, sadism, and wish for revenge as well as his tender longing for father's love. The prize for being the special one with respect to his mother's love brought him into sharp conflict with his rivals – his father and brother. This rivalry was invested into his erotic impulses, with mother presumably the object, resulting in intense feelings of sadism, directed at his rivals. Yet the seductive promise of mother's love forced him to renounce his longing for father's love, replacing it with the guilty, heartsick rivalry.

In his perceived victimization, he transformed his erotic wish for father's love into a fantasy of attack and intimidation. On this opposing side of the conflict, he desperately loved his father and brother and longed to take in their power, protection, and love. He felt pity for his father's impairment, and a sense of magical responsibility for it, his terrible guilt coming from his conviction that his sadistic rivalry had injured his father: "I loved Dad, I really did and I felt sorry for him in his polio, because he had polio. . . . Now I would say, 'Mother why don't you just leave Dad alone?' I think of how hard it must have been for Dad to deal with that".

The strivings for father's love were represented even more clearly in yet another obsessive-compulsive ritual involving the fear of contamination. He feared being contaminated by things he ate or with which he had contact. He feared that he would become "intoxicated or crazy", representing being "taken over" by his masochistic sexual and aggressive wishes. He wanted to remain "pure, deserving God's (the Father's) love", beatific, desexualized, and disconnected from the conflicted longing for his actual father.

Of course, these rituals too compromised his aggressive hostile wishes towards father (in the form of a reaction formation), but the former was frequently more available in his associations. For example, he had great anxiety regarding taking pills. He became alarmed at any slight blemish on the pill and felt compelled to reject it. He regularly associated the blemish with sperm, leading back to his fellatio memories and related fantasies. In one session, he stated, "I'm thinking of pill-taking last night. I had a clear association between the pill-taking and the sexual side of it. As I was looking at the pill I had my old OCD problem of getting stuck. I thought 'You're breathing heavily' and I remembered the sexual escapades of my youth. I remembered breathing like that with the boys when we'd engage in sexual escapades. I had that thought and then I wasn't stuck! I just went ahead and took the pill".

These two opposing poles of the conflict must have generated enormous and intolerable levels of anxiety, guilt, shame, and rage. The resulting self- and object-representations imbued in the tooth-brushing ritual and the array of other obsessive-compulsive symptoms functioned as a "solution" of sorts to his conflict. *Yet in this solution, in this failed synthetic process, conflicting derivatives were fundamentally not reconciled or integrated. Instead they were consciously disavowed and compulsively enacted.*

With respect to heterosexual wishes, instead of "owning" his perceived dangerous, competitive sadistic impulses, he was the victim of them. He moved from torturer to the tortured, from victimizer to the victim. The intolerable, erotized sadistic fantasy was symbolically condensed and displaced into the act of brushing his teeth, but in this ritual he did not experience himself as the perpetrator; instead, he was the victim. In the reversal of self and object, his forbidden erotic and sadistic wishes and guilt (manifested in the act of atonement) were disguised but represented. In the symptom compromise, he satisfied his forbidden wishes and paid the price, over and over again on a daily basis.

Simultaneously, with respect to homosexual Oedipal wishes, he assumed the role of the dominated victim. The perceived shameful, passive-receptive homosexual wishes were replaced by a sense of attack and victimization. A sense of agency with respect to these conflicted wishes was replaced by a dominated and helpless self-representation at the mercy of a cruel object.

These self- and object-representations worked in a reciprocal and complimentary manner, both being necessary in order to satisfy his forbidden desires and feelings of guilt and shame. This arrangement was necessary in order to achieve satisfaction of his forbidden desires (comprising the un-integrated Oedipal poles) without experiencing intolerable levels of anxiety, guilt, and shame. It allowed him to preserve and satisfy his forbidden desires while optimally delimiting his exposure to pain.

His punishment fantasy was manifestly apparent in a feeling of panic, which ensued whenever he failed to follow the dictates of his compulsive rituals. A balance between enjoyment of his forbidden wishes and his severe punishment anxiety was maintained in those compromise formations. Deviation from them threatened the eruption of both the forbidden wishes and his terrible punishment anxiety into consciousness.

Rituals such as these, embodying the drama of prohibition and forbidden desire, largely took the place of a life lived. All aspirations, all activity, all relationships remained subservient to the limitations imposed by these rituals and their attendant anxiety. In this displaced and condensed form, they unconsciously preserved the forbidden pleasures and fantastical dangers of childhood while simultaneously comprising the bars of the cell in which he existed.

The role of secondary process in synthetic functions

A perspective on the synthetic process can be observed in the translation of mental phenomena from primary process to secondary process. The fluidity of a mental phenomenon ("mobile cathexis"; Freud, 1900) in primary process thinking (e.g., a penis is a toothbrush) results in an obscuring of reality such that the distinction between reality and fantasy is blurred. The process of converting primary process mental phenomenon to secondary process involves this process of synthesis, the integration of one's impulses and one's judgment, as well as one's sense of propriety and morality, all in light of one's developmental experiences. This process transforms a mental phenomenon from a primitive state of relative disintegration to greater integration. Mental phenomena are transformed from a state of relative unconsciousness to a state of relative consciousness.

Unconscious mental phenomena are characterized by an ill-defined power, unfocused ideation and affect, pressing for conscious expression. Achieving consciousness involves the representation of things in an increasingly defined and definite form. The translation from unconsciousness to consciousness is analogous to the focusing of a lens of a camera. It moves from a state of unfocused obscurity to that of the sharply defined. Yet this focus includes an alteration of the original objects of observation. The individual ingredients are transformed into the finished cake of conscious symbolic representation.

The most conflicted aspects of impulses and superego injunctions require maximal distortion and encryption. Conscious derivatives of both drives and prohibitions must be incorporated into the fabric of one's mental life in an internally consistent and cohesive manner. At the same time, there is the economic question of the extent to which the consciously recognized derivatives of impulse and prohibition adequately satisfy both the drives and prohibitions from which they were derived.

In this process, there is a defining of the reality of things, the achievement of a definite sense of things, permitting the discrimination between thought and action. A sense of one's desires and their consequences is altered and clarified. With increasing integration, the distinction between thinking something and actually doing something in the world becomes clearer and more distinct.

In the process of achieving consciousness, mental phenomena are increasingly symbolically represented. They are conceptualized. In attaining consciousness, not only do they become represented in conscious ideation and memory, but they also must be integrated into the fabric of one's personality and the demands of reality. They must fit in with one's aspirations, talents, values, and sense of propriety. Derivatives highly charged with guilt and shame are especially difficult, as they produce extreme conflict, resulting in anxiety and depressive affect.

Much is to be learned from an example of a failure of the synthetic process. In our obsessional man's tooth-brushing ritual, for example, we saw that he had very limited ability to permit conscious gratification of his sadistic, competitive impulses or his passive-receptive homosexual wishes. In this ritual, as in a child's play, he vacillated between sadistically forcing the toothbrush/penis into his victim's mouth and being himself the victim of that aggression (and defending against the homosexual wish). Agency, in terms of both aggression and homosexual wishes, was permitted to achieve only very modest and incomplete secondary process form. The conflicted impulses were largely not conceptualized and had neither context in his life's story nor avenues for adaptive gratification.

The primary channel to consciousness for both his aggression and the homosexual wishes involved himself as the victim, the recipient of the aggression. Neither his powerful wishes to defeat nor adaptive derivates (healthy competition, positive self-esteem, confidence) were permitted the significant conscious conceptualization that is secondary process thinking. Likewise, adaptive derivatives of the homosexual wishes (e.g., wishes to please, to be loved, to be taken care of) were permitted only very limited adaptive representation.

Freud (1900) noted that contradictory impulses comfortably co-exist in the unconscious. This is obviously not true of conscious mental activity, which requires both some level of acceptance and integration such that one's mental life is relatively consistent and cohesive. When our patient's sadistic feelings were first interpreted, for example, he could barely stand to hear it. He would wince and become disorganized in trying to talk about such thoughts and experiences. When he began talking about his youthful homosexual indulgences and contemporary wishes, he experienced almost unbearable feelings of mortification.

Parenthetically, our therapeutic goal, of course, was to render such wishes mundane. This process involved assisting him in reality testing, in analysis of conflicted wishes and superego injunctions, as well as assisting him in cohesively integrating the disparate poles of his desires. This effort required continued discriminations between thought and behavior, in and outside the transference. It required him to recognize the difference between his infantile narcissistic fantasies of sadistically defeating and replacing father and actually injuring him.

It also required him to recognize and discriminate his tender erotic wishes to be dominated and loved by father. It necessitated not just awareness of his homosexual wishes but both placing them in the context of his life's story and reality testing (such that recognition of such desire was not equated with the magical loss of his heterosexuality). The therapeutic task required him to reconcile these diametrically opposing wishes and to achieve some adaptive synthesis of derivatives of them.

The task was to assist the patient in using his signal anxiety (Freud, 1926; Sterba, 1934; Fenichel, 1945) and depressive affect (Brenner, 1982) to flag conflict. Therapeutic action involved helping him to use what he learned in the analysis to, himself, conceptualize his impulses and punishment anxiety instead of automatically resorting to his symptoms and thus promoting active ego mastery of the conflicts.

Returning to the dynamics implicit in his tooth-brushing ritual, we assume it had a biphasic character. Initially he was driven to seek the unarticulated, amorphous, and disguised pleasure of both the sadistic sexual gratification and the homosexual wishes. Yet he had no conscious sense of such desires. Such wishes were not consciously recognized, as they were absolutely at odds with that which was permitted consciousness. In the second phase, the channel to consciousness took the form of identification with the victim, with its attendant pain, suffering, and atonement. The suffering was permitted some level of consciousness, but only in the form of primary process thinking, violating consciousness in an incomprehensible and non-contextualized form.

As will be further explicated in the next section of this chapter, there was a dramatic transmutation in self- and object-representations, as reflected in this ritual. With respect to the heterosexual Oedipal wishes, in the original object-relational configuration, the nascent self included an intense, hostile, competitive sense. The original object representation included a sense of father as weak, lazy, and inadequate. Yet, presumably following the consolidation of the internalization of the forbidding father-representation, the patient's self-representation had been transformed to include a sense of himself as a weak, terrorized, and defective victim. The object (as reflected in his obsessions, which he treated as an alien presence within him) had been transformed to include a cruel, terrorizing victimizer.

The conflicted hostile, sadistic, and competitive sense had been redirected from hostility with agency, directed towards the object, to that same hostile, sadistic, and competitive sense, without agency, directed towards the self. The route to "enjoyment" of the hostile competitive sense required a sense of a cruel object imposing this hostility on a helpless, victimized self.

With respect to the homosexual wishes, again, agency regarding these conflicted wishes was altered. Instead of taking ownership for the conflicted wishes, they were disguised and represented as something painfully forced upon the patient by a cruel object. *There is a convergence of motives resulting in the cruel object-representation and the helpless self-representation.* Such self- and object-representations redirect perceived dangerous hostility while also offering disguised sources of satisfaction of his homosexual wishes.

This synthetic activity involves **not just** a compromise formation between the forces of drives, defense, negotiation of dysphoric affect, and superego injunctions (Brenner, 1982). Rather it represents the *convergence of complexes of compromise formations (and potential compromise formations)*, all of which serve related functions. Such synthetic activity maintains a dynamic equilibrium. While manifesting some variability, the fundamental organization is determined by the need to integrate divergent wishes and their attendant punishment fantasies, as evidenced by our patient's failed ability to integrate heterosexual and homosexual trends.

Self- and object-representations comprising the superego

For post-1923 Freud, the structure of the mind associated with a sense of morality is an archaic aspect of the ego, the superego. Prohibition of desire is achieved through internalized self- and object-representations designed to contain one's impulses. The sense of prohibition is immensely exaggerated by the projection of one's own hostility onto the prohibitive object, rendering the subsequently internalized object exponentially more severe and dangerous (Abraham, 1927; Klein, 1975a). Both desires and unconscious superego functions are also subject to the encrypting processes of displacement, condensation, and symbolization, resulting in one's desire and prohibition being subject to infinite derivative forms.

The superego is the product of compromise formations, resulting in self- and object-representations which function in a complementary manner. Aspects of the prohibitive other are incorporated into self-representations. Aspects of the nascent self are attributed to object-representations. Self- and object-representations, which function in a reciprocal manner, are designed to allow for the satisfaction of one's impulses in a sharply defined manner as well as distinguishing both one's prohibitions and ideals.

If the object-relational configurations and potential configurations which comprise the superego are to be adaptive, they must perform a host of functions. Most obviously, they must maintain a dynamic equilibrium between satisfaction of impulses and prohibition. They must provide for the satisfaction of impulses while at the same time protecting one from overwhelming conscious feelings of shame and guilt anxiety and depressive affect (Brenner, 1982, 1994).

At more subtle levels, such object-relational configurations must also perform synthetic functions. They must promote the integration and reconciliation of conflicting trends and do so in a way that is both internally consistent and fits into the fabric of one's personality. Internal consistency within the superego is important if conflict is to be minimized. Such consistency is increasingly possible to the extent that impulses and prohibitions/ideals (and their relationships with each other) are subject to secondary process thinking, as it opens up multiple and less conflictual channels to consciousness. Additionally, the extent to which prohibitions and ideals conflict with one another is one measure of internal conflict.

When we discuss internalized parental personality characteristics, most especially unconscious parental personality characteristics, we are obviously in a highly speculative realm. Remembered aspects of parents and inferences derived from such memories and from personality characteristics of the parents are obviously highly distorted by the patient's defensive structure. The internalizations that comprise the self- and object-representations are a function of the delicate interplay of the child's impulses, his defensive efforts, and the parental impulses, defensive style, and superego structure.

To some extent, however, these internalizations follow the contours of parental drives, ego and superego functions, conscious and unconscious. Clearly the extent to which drive derivatives and prohibitions are permitted to assume the ideational clarity of secondary process thinking relates to what is permitted by the parents. Additionally, the child's burgeoning conscience and ego-ideal are quite vulnerable to the effects of parental acceptance, projections (Ferenczi, 1933), as well as conscious and unconscious parental ideals (Johnson, 1949; Johnson & Szurek, 1952).

The child may be pressured to identify with disavowed parental projections (Ferenczi, 1933) or to play transferential roles. Impulses denied by parents may be difficult for the child to conceptualize, especially when they are associated with shame and guilt. Desired but unconscious and prohibited parental impulses may also structure the child's ego-ideal. Internalized parental prohibitions and ideals may not simply conflict with the child's impulses; they may also conflict with both the demands of reality and other of the parents' and/or the child's internalized ideals and prohibition. Parental conflicts may be induced into the child, who subsequently internalizes the conflict.

I am reminded of a case years ago when I was the Clinical Director of an adolescent residential treatment facility. A young woman patient was admitted due to severe impulse control problems, primarily involving extreme and dangerous promiscuity. The intake interview was concluded, the girl went onto the unit, and her parents went home. Several hours later, the mother returned, stating that she had forgotten to leave clean underwear for the girl. She gave the milieu staff panties and emblazoned on the butt was "Sexy Thing". Like the cliché ethics committee who is "forced" to watch every frame of the pornographic movie in order to properly criticize it, the mother projected her unconscious wishes for unlimited sexual gratification onto her daughter while condemning her for it.

Returning to our patient, the actual relationships with his father and mother supplied shaping influences in the development of his superego. On the one hand, his father was interpersonally quite passive, nondemonstrative, and obviously dominated by the patient's mother. Our patient's hostile, competitive feelings were all the more unbridled and intensified by the disappointment of his affectional wishes towards his rather emotionally unavailable father.

His father was a devote Catholic and uncharacteristically insisted that the family subscribe to the Catholic faith. His mother was a convert and reluctantly tolerated the role of Catholicism in the family life. Our patient recalled his father attempting to convince him to become a priest and mother adamantly challenging his father's attempts. The patient also recalled his own secret defiance of the priests, with a refusal to engage in confession primarily due to a dread of exposure of his masturbatory and homosexual activity.

These phenomena supplied the raw material for his subsequent severe conscience. His own competitive hostility towards his somewhat distant and seemingly inadequate rival was projected upon his father. This, in light of his defiance of the perceived threatening church, produced severe object-representations which, when internalized, supplied the basis for his severe and tyrannical conscience. Unconsciously, his conscience threatened and opposed his heterosexual Oedipal ambitions while refusing his wishes for a loving father.

Conflict over longing for father's love was further accentuated by the mother's dominant personality and her devaluation of father. Not only did her dominance render her, in many ways, a more attractive identificatory object, her devaluation of father also supplied an implicit threat against seeking his love. Consequently, the identification with father was further stunted, and the identification with the devaluing mother was reinforced.

Real conflict was thus built into his conscience and ego-ideal. The wish to take in father's love, power, and authority was opposed by his perceived forbidding mother, with whom he largely identified, yielding self-representations which were likewise devaluing and critical of father. Such self-representations rendered him quite vulnerable to feelings of shame in response to conscious wishes for father's love. This greatly complicated the developmental task of identifying with father and encouraged his sham Oedipal fantasy with respect to mother (Chasseguet-Smirgel, 1985).

Due to the intra-psychic conflict in each of his parents, in the parents' marriage a fault line was established, which further complicated our patient's adaptive integration of maternal internalizations with the paternal. On his father's side, his father was not only very inhibited with respect to his aggression but also modeled an equation between passive receptive wishes and degradation and humiliation. His mother assumed a dominant role, not only devaluing and humiliating her passive husband but also subtly encouraging this attitude on the part of her son. It is further assumed that conflict with respect to both passive-receptive wishes and adaptive uses of aggression was shared by both parents. One begins to see the outlines of the ensuing problem in developing self- and object-representations that permitted an adaptive integration of the heterosexual and homosexual Oedipal poles.

Adaptation to reality demands the development of self- and object-representations, designed to contain and direct these over-stimulated and restricted wishes. His father's unstated hostility, immensely intensified by the boy's projections of his own hostility, was associated with the wrath of the Catholic church, yielding threats of damnation and promoting his identification with his passive, emasculated father. At the same time, such an identification united him with the father whose love he longed for while desexualizing such wishes in the identificatory process.

However, further complicating the situation was both the mother's unacknowledged insistence of his sadistic rivalry with father and her own equation between longing for father's love and feelings of shame. There was at once an unstated and presumably unconscious demand from the mother that he join her in her attack upon the father and that he deny and forego his longing for father's love. Again, all of this occurred in a context in which both parents were quite inhibited from direct ownership and expression of hostility, which was largely denied but enacted.

Thus the parental fault line, internalized by the child, effectively prevented the development of internally consistent and synthetic internalizations that contained and adaptively redirected his Oedipal impulses. *In order to achieve a conscious and adaptive synthesis, the self- and object-representations comprising the superego must permit derivatives channels into consciousness that allow for reconciliation of conflicting wishes and prohibitions.* Our obsessive-compulsive patient was unable to achieve an adaptive integration of derivatives of heterosexual and homosexual wishes and their attendant prohibitions. Again, we assumed that particularly the overstimulation of heterosexual Oedipal fantasies, due both to his father's limitations and his mother's seductiveness, and related prohibitions greatly complicated the integrative task Consequently, little solution was available except a symptom compromise.

Symptoms, as Freud stated in 1900, involve the intrusion of primary process material into consciousness. Symptomatic behavior and discontinuities of the superego are not properly encrypted into secondary process thinking and are not integrated into one's personality. Yet for our patient, greater integration would involve taking ownership of impulses that provoked profound feelings of guilt and shame. Thus he only vaguely consciously recognized his competitive, hostile wishes, his passive, receptive wishes, or their attendant prohibitions. Instead he simply experienced the tyranny of his rituals and the perceived dangers of losing control.

A consequence of integration is flexibility in one's mental life. This patient's lack of integration of these conflicting and conflicted wishes resulted in his being increasingly under the desperate control of his symptoms. Stimulation of these conflicting wishes resulted in reinvestment in these rigid, stereotyped, and formulaic enactments.

The paradox of punishment fantasies and their alteration

With this, we approach the possibility of understanding the paradoxical nature of punishment fantasies and of understanding some components necessary for the modification and alteration of the effects of such fantasies. Such fantasies originate out of conflict with objects clearly more powerful than one's self and objects on whom one depends. Consequently, we attempt to minimize such conflict and defend against it through the process of internalization.

In this internalization process, we take on aspects of the object as self-representations (identifications) while attributing parts of the nascent self to objects, resulting in object-representations. The fantastic dramas between such self- and object-representations open up channels through which one's forbidden desires and one's fears of punishment find expression. *With respect to the superego, this process of developing self- and object-representations (Jacobson, 1964), which regulate and define the expression of impulses, is a fundamental and critical aspect of moving from primary process to secondary process thinking.*

Internalizations comprising the superego include contributions from drives, modified by the history of one's experiences with prohibitive others. The drives are defensively modified by projection and internalization, yielding object-relational configurations which are informed by one's sense of propriety, one's judgment, and the demands of reality. These object-relational configurations offer drive discharge pathways. Object-relational configurations intrinsic to an individual represent a system of well-worn compromise formations in which some sort of balance between the impulses, reality demands, and one's sense of propriety is established and maintained.

However, the object relations comprising the internalizations of the superego do not represent a monolithic structure. Rather, they are comprised of a complicated network of related object-relational configurations and potential configurations pertaining to different facets of the conflicted drives and their attendant punishment fantasies. Some internalized object-relational configurations are more severe than others, some more adaptive than others, etc.

In part, the severity may represent the developmental levels of the internalizations, with the earlier being more severe. It also relates to one's developmental experiences of the danger situations of childhood (Freud, 1926; Brenner, 1982) (abandonment/annihilation; loss of love; castration resulting in experiences of guilt anxiety), real and imagined. Regardless, this severity is a function of some drive derivatives being more successfully encrypted than others and therefore less severely prohibited, requiring less severe object-relational configurations.

Synthetic functions refer to the ego's capacities to reconcile the conflicting forces implicit in the stimulation of potential drive satisfactions, prohibitions and ideals, the dictates of reality, the history of one's development through the danger situations of childhood, and the intensity of internal demands. The constituents of this synthetic process are constantly changing and determining the nature and severity of object-relational configurations required in order to maintain a dynamic equilibrium between enjoyment of impulses and prohibition in any moment in time. To some extent, such synthetic functions are organic processes, with one's history of object relations, fanciful and actual, the malleable clay out of which one sculpts contemporary object relations.

Somewhat different object-relational configurations can be activated and constructed in different moments in time. In one moment, one may be less or more prone to seek more or less adaptive forms of satisfaction. One may be more or less prone to adaptively respond to possible sources of satisfaction in the world. One may be less or more motivated to seek specific satisfactions based on the intensity of one's desires. One may be less or more capable of tolerating the fantasized dangers associated with impulses. One may be less or more able to tolerate compromise formations that are more or less adaptive in the world, even though a more adaptive compromise may offer a less complete satisfaction of the drive in question. As we shall see later, our obsessional patient's capacities for synthetic ego functions were quite compromised, necessitating his falling back on the patterned discharge pathways supplied by his symptoms despite their costs to his adaptive functions.

The actual subjective experiences of punishment anxiety remain remarkably similar. The conscious ideational content of such fantasies is typically quite concrete, while the affect is profound and intensifying to the extent that one fails to renounce or transform forbidden gratification into an acceptable form. Our patient evidences this when he reports that he fears he will "become a drunken impulsive madman", "he will die", or "he will go to hell" if he does not comply with his compulsive rituals. This punishment anxiety is largely disconnected from the larger drama of his forbidden impulses and punishment for them, resulting in a disorienting loss of context and meaning. His compulsive rituals represent a disguised but acceptable balance between his forbidden impulses and prohibition; yet one which was consciously incomprehensible to the patient himself.

Optimally the transmutations of self and object which comprise the superego are achieved in such a way that the impulses find optimal satisfaction, minimal pain, and, simultaneously, are adaptive to functioning in the world. No such solutions are without conflict. However, gross evidence of conflict between one's impulses and the forbidden, which compromise adaptive functioning, indicates that the encryption of the conflicting forces and the subsequent synthetic processes are inadequate for the effective translation of primary process into secondary process in an adaptive manner.

One problem associated with the development of adaptive compromises is that of fixations in drive development. I am not referring to a regression to earlier psychosexual stages. Instead, I am emphasizing something similar to what Freud (1917, p. 348) referred to as "adhesiveness of the libido" or what Rothstein (1980) called "shaping influences". Over-stimulation or traumatic deprivation of infantile drives can result in fixation, creating difficulty in developing more adaptive self- and object- representational configurations. Such fixated impulses are repressed and, as such, dissociated from consciousness, rendering them unable to be significantly satisfied consciously (Freud, 1909).

Our obsessive-compulsive man, for example, had very intense overstimulation of his Oedipal fantasies due to his father's physical deficits, his mother's condemnation of his father, and her enlisting the patient into her devaluation of father. This, from the perspective of the patient as a child, seemed to confirm his Oedipal fantasy of being preferred to his father, greatly increasing his enjoyment of his Oedipal rivalry. Consequently, there is a real pull towards situations in life which seem to satisfy feelings associated with these fantasies, while simultaneously an equally strong superego injunction forbids such guilty pleasures. At the same time, such overstimulation resulted in a forced renunciation of homosexual Oedipal wishes and limited his capacity to develop satisfying derivatives.

These fixations lead him to be hypersensitive to situations in life that offer the possibility of perceived satisfaction of these polar and intense drives. With the intensity of these desires, there was a certain pressure to unconsciously view all life situations in terms of the potential satisfactions that they offered these specific wishes (Arlow, 1969a, 1969b; Miller, 2004b, 2008). At the same time, these forbidden wishes were associated with his developmental experiences of the danger situations of childhood, which evoked equally strong punishment anxiety. Such persistent and rigid demands and their attendant punishment fears create intensity that is difficult to manage in an adaptive and realistic manner.

For example, the patient had an appointment with his urologist, who performed a testicular examination. His doctor completed the examination and told him there was no gross evidence of pathology. My patient implored him to repeat the exam, stating that he was convinced he had a tumor. The physician reexamined him and again stated that he did not see any evidence of a tumor. My patient then again implored him to repeat the examination. At this point the doctor apparently sensed the patient's unconscious motivation, told him to get dressed, that the exam was over. The patient barely got out the door before he barged back into the office and desperately beseeched the doctor to reexamine him. He placed his physician in an extremely uncomfortable position, provoking his doctor into refusing to treat him.

The strength of the patient's unconscious homosexual impulses and unconscious hostility resulted in the impairment of his ego functions, emerging symptomatically in his unfounded anxiety that he had testicular cancer. The conflicted wishes emerged in a dramatic impairment in reality testing, flooding him with feelings of shame and humiliation and inducing his urologist to fire him.

One can see why, in order to regulate his contact with reality, he was eventually compelled to divert such pleasures and temptations into the channels of his obsessive rituals, which maintained some sort of balance between his divergent and forbidden pleasures and atonement through suffering. These rituals divert desires and punishment into a contained world, while enormously restricting his adaptive functioning. The pleasure achieved remains largely unconscious, while the need for self-punishment remains quite conscious.

Further complicating the transition from primary process to secondary process thinking is the fact that contradictions are entirely acceptable at an unconscious level. Primary process does not require the type of realistic organization that secondary process thinking does. Both the intensity and polarity of his ambivalence towards his father, for example, would require much more complex and sophisticated self- and object-configurations in order to achieve an integrated and adaptive representation in secondary process thinking.

In a developmental sequence without the need to bridge such intense divergence, subsequent identifications with a more realistic and loving father would soften the earlier and more severe representations of the cruel father. However, with our obsessive-compulsive man, the intensely fixated desires and their attendant prohibitions achieved only fairly rigid channels of compromise formation – primarily those of the obsessive rituals. The rivers of desires, with attendant prohibitions, were channeled into these specific streambeds. His ego had very limited power to manage these impulses/anxieties in a more fluid, creative, and adaptive manner.

The patient's conscious experience was largely organized around strivings to be excessively proper, often expressed in a manner that others experienced as utterly exasperating and controlling. This dynamic can be seen as a manifestation of Freud's (1917) much maligned concepts of fixation and temporal regression (to an anal level of organization). The concepts of fixation and regression (to an earlier psychosexual level of organization) have been criticized as both inaccurate and formulaic (Dowling, 2004;

Gilmore & Meersand, 2014). They are seen as implying a sort of psychic "time machine that dials back to re-create the past" (Gilmore & Meersand, 2014, p. 324) in the face of conflict, returning the individual, in a wholesale manner, to a prior level of psychic organization.

It is not arguable that such views of fixation and regression are inaccurate and fail to acknowledge the fact of the individual's maintenance of dynamic equilibrium in the face of the experience of an ever-changing present. In my view, it also represents a misreading of Freud (1917); see Lectures XXII and XXIII), who clearly identified three interrelated factors in drive development as necessary etiological factors for the development of neuroses – frustration of satisfaction, fixation and regression, and conflict.

Further, Freud (1917) clearly stated that in fixation and regression, outmoded objects and aims have not been given up completely; they are retained in fantasied satisfaction. These persistent memory traces of real and imagined satisfactions represent the timelessness of the unconscious (Freud, 1900). Regression to fixated impulses and their derivatives involves the revitalization of these (more archaic) fantasied forms of satisfaction in the face of conflict, which compromises more contemporary forms of satisfaction.

Our patient's regression was obviously highly selective, with his organization around propriety and defiance clearly in response to the more profoundly conflicted Oedipal issues. His mother had discovered his childhood homosexual adventures. In my patient's view, this resulted in his fall from grace, a loss of her love, and a failure of his Oedipal ambitions. His propriety and the attendant fantasies of being mother's special love represented a quest for recovery of her love and an undoing of his perceived dangerous sexual and aggressive wishes. His rebellion against mother's admonitions and his Oedipal aggression were regressively condensed into his passive aggressive behavior, which was so often incredibly frustrating to others.

Now, returning to the paradox of punishment fantasies: the key to this riddle is in the fact that such discontinuities in consciousness belie complex, poorly integrated, and hidden stories of forbidden desires and barely contained punishments. As such, they represent an incomplete synthetic process, one that fails to achieve adaptive functions in reality. The intense resistances that patients manifest to exploring such discontinuities reveal their fears that pulling at the thread of such discontinuities threatens to open a Pandora's box, liberating terrible desires with terrifying consequences.

Countertransference and the analysis of a resistance

Before concluding, I want to discuss the analysis of an interesting transference/countertransference enactment with our patient which was responsible for the maintenance of a fundamental and important resistance. The first year and one-half of treatment appeared to evidence an active working alliance (Greenson, 1967). In the sway of a positive transference/countertransference, he received and made use of my interpretations, resulting in a dramatic diminution in anxiety, accompanied by the development of significant insight into both his psychopathology and personality structure. The treatment itself had an interesting and hopeful ambiance and seemed to be progressing well.

Quite subtly, however, this progression came to a halt, and a retrogression began to take its place. The change in the transference was implicit, particularly in the way in which he failed to use the analytic material, which I, rather unsuccessfully, attempted to make explicit (such that the transference was more analyzable). I, however, experienced a not quite conscious sense of devaluation, with corresponding resentment.

He would *exaggerate* minor concerns and distort their meanings in such a way as to undo our previous achievements, carefully maintaining a diminution of anxiety to a more tolerable level of suffering which he stubbornly maintained. His obsession with minor discoloration of the lettering on his pills "may have, *in the past*, been related to his homosexual fantasies. Now, however, in view of the obvious stains, they represented a *real and present* danger, a legitimate health concern". In another obsession, "his health was jeopardized by a possible infection of an ingrown toenail (which he had caused with his 'treatments'), which might result in developing gangrene and requiring amputation". This time he was not symbolically castrating himself, resulting in his anxiety. Instead, "this was a *real* danger". In yet another, "He worked *so hard* that he had no time for anything else. He couldn't travel or even exercise because he had too many towels to wash and dry".

He overtly resisted my calling attention to his exaggerations and attempted to justify them. My attempts to enlist his rational ego (Greenson, 1967) in observation of his enforced suffering resulted in a vain attempt on his part to prove the reality of his assertions. He fought my attempts at helping him to process this, acting as if I was attempting to *take something valuable away from him*.

We thus engaged in this transference/countertransference enactment, which ebbed and flowed for many months. I began to think about this process occurring between the two of us, and I noticed that he would often experience a quality of relief when he finally *"submitted"* to my assertions.

I thought about this from various angles – as a superego resistance involving a fear of his conscience should he experience a diminution in his suffering (Freud, 1926); as a masochistic fantasy in which I would "dominate him against his will and he would, having been over-powered, finally relent"; or as a competitive rivalry in which he defeated me by defeating my efforts to treat him. While I felt that my interpretations were accurate, they did not result in his relinquishing the enactment, nor in his attempts to take his need to suffer more seriously. I knew I was missing something and went "back to the drawing board", examining the interaction between us but, this time, also in observation of my contributions.

As I listened to myself, I realized that my interpretations were expressed with an angry quality of feeling. I had felt my analytic potency devalued and dismantled by him. In my unconsciously angry tone, I had unwittingly encouraged a defensive sadomasochistic arrangement between us. At this point, I will take a brief detour, focusing on aspects of psychoanalytic theory and, then, on my own psychodynamics and their contribution to the enactment. I will then attempt to demonstrate how, in treatment stalemates, we often unconsciously collude with the patient, sharing a defensive strategy, which permit unconscious satisfaction of disavowed impulses (shared by both) and thus contributes to impasses in treatment.

This is an area which has preoccupied my clinical thinking for almost 40 years now. I was first introduced to this area by Keith A. Horton, M.D., a mentor by whom I had the good fortune to be supervised in a parallel process supervision. I was in charge of an adolescent inpatient service and was continually confronted with impulse control disordered kids who regressively replaced unconscious and conflicted erotic and competitive impulses with interpersonal conflict. To the degree to which they activated my own unconscious and unintegrated conflicts, I would continue to be intractably drawn into the interpersonal conflict. However, when my own conflicts were properly analyzed in the supervision, defensive iterations of my intra-psychic conflicts would be transformed into a profoundly sensitive therapeutic instrument. I would not only recognize the patients' defenses with far greater depth and acuity but also appreciate the underlying conflicts and be in a much more powerful position to effectively help them recognize and integrate these conflicts in the transference.

Certainly, this issue is not a new area of thought. It was clearly talked about even by Freud. For example, take the way in which he discussed the Wolf Man's infantile tempter-tantrums as masochistic seductions (Freud, 1918, p. 28). This entire issue of induction was emphasized by Klein (1975b). The use of countertransference as a therapeutic tool was, of course, elaborated by Heinrich Racker (1968), who, in the eyes of many, remains the gold standard; with the type of countertransference reported here an example of "complementary countertransference". The use of one's countertransference as a therapeutic instrument had been earlier emphasized by Reik (1949). I discussed aspects of my thinking regarding the induction of one's conscience in significant interpersonal relationships as a way of achieving and regulating pleasure from disavowed impulses (Miller, 2008).

I am emphasizing here that as the analyst approaches material which is, in identification with the patient, conflicted for the analyst, the more likely the analyst will be to unconsciously fall back on regressive defensive measures. As we will see, in my case, this regression was stimulated despite my having worked and reworked these issues (of conflict between competitive and passive, receptive wishes) over many years – in years of supervision, personal analysis, and self-analysis.

This is just a restatement of Freud's (1914, 1918) idea that no position that the libido has occupied is ever completely abandoned. This serves to endorse Brenner's (1982) discussion of Freud's (1914) concept of working through, in which Brenner argued that nothing is "worked through". Rather we work "with" intra-psychic conflict and its vicissitudes, permitting insight which, hopefully, allows us to use signal affects to call up the work of the analysis and offer more adaptive ways of dealing with the conflict (see also Sterba, 1934).

Returning to myself and the impasse with my patient, during my childhood I had always felt envious of my successful older brother. I felt that he and my father had a special bond in light of his unique talents and successes. I felt myself to be on eternally the "East of Eden", and an angry and disappointed sense now gets activated in the face of my own failures, limitations, and disappointments. *Yet this sense also screens my conflicts between competitive and passive, receptive wishes, effectively insulating me from both, but at great cost.* Given this thumbnail sketch of aspects of my psychopathology and personality structure, let's look again at the interaction between my patient and I which led to our stalemate. However, this time, let's put a spotlight on *both* of us.

The patient began making quite naïve and provocative statements, refusing to use our work and, in fact, undoing our achievements. While ostensibly and, I think accurately, I saw this as an enacted transference resistance and began to analyze it as such, in my unconsciously angry tone, I undercut the efficacy of the analysis in my patient's eyes. Not only did my angry tone undermine the perception of safety in the relationship, but, perhaps more significantly, it provided him with sources of regressive, sadomasochistic satisfactions (Brenner, 1959). In my hostility, I offered sources of unconscious satisfaction in which we vacillated between the conflicted passive, receptive, and hostile competitive wishes, permitting both to remain unconscious.

Interestingly, I *rationalized my behavior just as he did!* I remember having said to myself, "This is the sort of provocative behavior that everyone feels with this guy", which was accurate. However, in my unstated enactment, I unconsciously added, "Therefore it is acceptable and reasonable for me to enact my anger rather than to analyze his defensive provocation".

The structure of my rationalization being conflated with an unconscious defensive justification was identical with his; "This time my irrational fear is *real* and I don't need to analyze it". We shared this defensive activity in which a rationalization was used to justify an enactment. At a still deeper level, with respect to the conflicted competitive and passive-receptive wishes, the experience of conflict between the wish to defeat a rival and to receive the love of a man was channeled into a sense of disappointment and hostility by both of us. We colluded with respect to both the shared defense and the achievement of unconscious gratifications in the enactment.

With my understanding of these dynamics as I analyzed this man, I was more aware of the nuances in our interaction. The transference was clearer to me. I felt I was more sensitive to the manifestation of conflicting impulses, defenses, and affects. Importantly, I was more comfortable in my identification with him.

In this identification, I tolerated greater sensitivity to both the intense demands of his wishes to defeat me and his longing for my love and help. Perhaps more importantly, I had an awareness of his difficulty in integrating these seemingly incompatible demands; an awareness of the plight of his enfeebled ego with its anxiety signals intensifying to panic proportions (Fenichel, 1945) and initiating desperate defensive measures.

Interestingly, as we continued to focus on manifestations of these two opposing trends, the rigidity of his conflict ever so slightly softened. He reported a different sense of his father (which I took to be an off-target transference as well). He reported, "I can feel him with me sometimes". He had memories of attempts by his father to be loving – to take him for soft drinks or attempt to please him in other ways. He was regretful that he was not more accepting of his father's overtures.

It was then that something surprising began to surface. Related to this, I have mentioned already that I always felt that I was missing something in my understanding of him. His thoughts repeatedly went back to his experiences with the priests. He talked of laying in the back seat of the car, looking out the back window, and feeling sick to his stomach as they approached the church every Sunday. (Again, I am compressing the work of many months into a few paragraphs. The actual progression of the work was far less neat and infinitely more confusing than that which is presented here.)

He told me of the Catholic rituals and his violations of them. One confesses one's sins to the priest, implicitly vowing to abandon one's sinfulness. As God's representative, the priest demands an act of penance, usually a recitation of a series of prayers, sometimes accompanied by the counting of the beads of the rosary; all of which entitles one to God's grace and redemption, as represented in taking Holy Communion. In this symbolic taking in of the "body and blood of Christ", one has taken in the God, who, in His suffering, takes one's sins as His own and expiates them.

My patient refused confession but he, nonetheless, *took communion*. He refused to tell the priest of his secret, sinful masturbation or his homosexual adventures. Seeking the priest's absolution in his mind meant to abandon his "sinfulness". It represented castration, the talionic punishment for his illicit erotic adventures. His wish for father's love was associated with both the loss of his special position with mother and his potency – the loss of his maleness – and, as such, it had to be avoided at all costs.

In his secret blasphemy, he deceptively *assumed the role of the priest* and, in this cosmic act of betrayal, again illicitly appropriated the role of the father. He repeated his Oedipal fantasy, defeating the father and taking father's place with mother (in her contempt for Catholicism). This time, however, he usurped the role of the priest and in this act of desecration, sought to achieve his special position with God himself.

Suffering and renunciation of pleasure thus now become his acts of expiation, but now with himself in the role of *both* the priest and the penitent. Rather than demanding the trivial prayers of the priests, he largely renounces all pleasure in life and replaces it with self-imposed suffering, again demonstrating his superiority to them. In his obsessional counting, he creates his own rosary and his own punishment, his own ritual. In his own suffering and deprivation, he provides his own satisfaction, *self and object are one*. The narcissistic goal of omnipotent satisfaction of wishes is complete (Freud, 1914).

The sense that *something valuable was being taken away from him* and his resistance to embracing my help suddenly makes sense, as does the fantasy that he must *submit* or *be forced against his will* to receive my help/love. He does not *claim* the desire for father's love. It only can be had in its disguised, regressive form as something forced upon him. He thus retains his fantasied superiority over father and his implicit position as an Oedipal victor. He realizes the negative satisfaction only through this mock "defeat", its implicit desire denied.

More remarkable still is the achievement of narcissistic satisfaction. He choreographs his own satisfaction without tolerating the inevitable disappointments and helplessness implicit in the human condition. In fact, in the attainment of his special position with God, suffering and renunciation of pleasure themselves are the currency with which he purchases the illusion of omnipotence. He worries and suffers that he might have prostate cancer. In the doctor's announcement that he doesn't, his suffering is confirmed as efficacious. His suffering is confirmed as an antidote to fate itself. Worry equals expiation, equals God's grace, equals control over the dangers of fate.

The difficulty of the therapeutic task was thus visible. Freud's (1895, p. 305) statement that "analysis turns hysterical suffering into ordinary human misery" seemed a dubious satisfaction in comparison to omnipotence. Not only did his symptoms offer satisfaction to these non-integrated Oedipal poles (replacing the need for acceptance and integration of derivatives of the original desires), but also they permitted the illusion of omnipotent control over the ravages of fate itself. These, then, were the obstacles which confronted the therapy, and in reworking them, we, as always, had to accept the partial successes achievable with psychoanalysis.

Conclusions

I have attempted to demonstrate the continued efficacy of Freudian theory, emphasizing the contemporary innovative focus on conflict theory, especially Charles Brenner's compromise formation theory. I have emphasized Brenner's ubiquitous constituents of compromise formations but have challenged Brenner's failure to adequately account for issues of synthetic ego functions, consciousness/unconsciousness, and his critique of the concepts of primary and secondary process thinking. I have attempted to make a case for some sort of mental agency, such as Freud's structural ego, which explicates these functions. Finally, I have included a section on transference/countertransference to both present additional theoretical material and to give a sense of the analytic process.

References

Abraham, K. (1911). Notes on psycho-analytical investigation and treatment of manic-depressive insanity and allied conditions. In *Selected papers on psychoanalysis*. London: Hogarth Press, 1927.

Arlow, J. (1969a). Unconscious fantasy and disturbance and disturbance of conscious experience. *Psychoanalytic Quarterly, 38*(1), 1–27.

Arlow, J. (1969b). Fantasy, memory, and reality testing. *Psychoanalytic Quarterly, 38*(1), 28–51.

Brenner, C. (1959). The masochistic character: Genesis and treatment. *Journal of the American Psychoanalytic Association, 7*, 19–226.

Brenner, C. (1973). *An elementary textbook of psychoanalysis* (2nd ed.). New York, NY: International University Press.

Brenner, C. (1982). *The mind in conflict*. Madison: International University Press.

Brenner, C. (1984). Working through 1918 through 1984. *Psychoanalytic Quarterly, 56*, 88–108.

Brenner, C. (1994). The mind in conflict and compromise formation. *Journal of Clinical Psychoanalysis, 13*, 473–488.

Brenner, C. (2006). *Psychoanalysis or mind and meaning.* New York, NY: The Psychoanalytic Quarterly, Inc.

Chasseguet-Smirgel, J. (1985). *The ego-ideal.* New York, NY: W. W. Norton & Co., Inc.

Dowling, S. (2004). A reconsideration of the concept of regression. *The Psychoanalytic Study of the Child, 59*, 191–210.

Fenichel, O. (1945). *The psychoanalytic theory of neuroses.* New York, NY: W. W. Norton & Co., Inc.

Ferenczi, S. (1933). Confusion of tongues between the adult and the child: The language of tenderness and of passion. In *Final contributions to the problems and methods of psycho-analysis* (pp. 156–167). New York, NY: Brunner and Mazel, 1980.

Freud, S. (1895). Studies in Hysteria. *S.E.*, 2.

Freud, S. (1896). Further remarks on the neuro-psychosis of defence. *S.E.*, 3.

Freud, S. (1900). The interpretation of dreams. *S.E.*, 4.

Freud, S. (1909). Five Lectures on Psychoanalysis. *S.E.*, 11.

Freud, S. (1914). On narcissism: An introduction. *S.E.*, 14.

Freud, S. (1917). Mourning and melancholia. *S.E.*, 13.

Freud, S. (1918). From the history of an infantile neurosis.

Freud, S. (1923). The ego and the id. *S.E.*, 19.

Freud, S. (1926). Inhibition, symptoms and anxiety. *S.E.*, 20.

Gilmore, K. J., & Meersand, P. (2014). *Normal child and adolescent development: A psychodynamic primer.* New York, NY: American Psychiatric Publishing.

Greenson, R. R. (1967). *The technique and practice of psychoanalysis, Volume I.* New York, NY: International Universities Press, Inc.

Hartman, H. (1958). *Ego psychology and the problem of adaptation* (D. Rapaport, Trans.). New York, NY: International University Press.

Jacobson, E. (1964). *The self and the object world.* Madison: International Universities Press, Inc.

Johnson, A. (1949). Sanctions for superego lacunae in adolescents. In K. R. Eissler (Ed.), *Searchlights on delinquency.* New York, NY: International Universities Press, Inc.

Johnson, A. M., & Szurek, S. A. (1952). The genesis of antisocial acting out in children and adults. *Psychoanalytic Quarterly*, 323–343.

Klein, M. (1975a). On identification. In *Envy, gratitude, and other works: 1946–1963.* New York: Delacorte Press.

Klein, M. (1975b). Theoretical conclusions regarding the emotional life of children. In *Envy, gratitude, and other works: 1946–1963.* New York: Delacorte Press.

Miller, S. J. (2004a). Relationships with the punisher. *Psychoanalytic Psychology, 26*, 482–416.

Miller, S. J. (2004b). Reality and conflict in punishment fantasies. *Psychoanalytic Psychology, 91*, 1–22.

Miller, S. J. (2008). Punishment fantasies and the construction of reality. *Psychoanalytic Psychology, 25*(2), 295–308.

Racker, H. (1968). *Transference and countertransference.* New York, NY: International University Press, Inc.

Reik, T. (1949). *Listening with the third ear: The inner experience of a psychoanalyst.* New York, NY: Farrar, Straus and Company.

Rothstein, A. (1980). The Narcissistic Pursuit of Perfection. New York: International Universities Press.

Sterba, R. (1934). The fate of the ego in analytic therapy. *International Journal of Psycho-Analysis, 15*, 117–126.

Chapter 2

The most innovative ideas in psychoanalysis
A Kleinian approach

Rachel B. Blass

My view of psychoanalysis

I come to address the questions posed by the editors of this book from a Kleinian perspective as this perspective is understood and practiced in London or as what I have referred to as a traditional Freudian-Kleinian perspective (Blass, 2011, 2016). Put very simply and briefly, from this perspective psychoanalysis is about integrating unconscious phantasy; that is, coming to know parts of the mind,[1] of our inner world, of our inner object relations, which we have split off because we do not want to know about them. These phantasies are about our loves and perceived needs, our hates, our longings, greediness, and envy, our desires and our destructiveness when we think that they are not met, our fears and anxieties, expected punishments for the harm which we feel we have caused, our sense of guilt, our belief and disbelief in the possibilities of forgiveness and reparation and many other dimensions of the basic conflict between love and hate, life and death, that lies at the very foundation of the human predicament.

Splitting off parts of ourselves is harmful to ourselves and to our relationship with reality and is a source of suffering. For example, because of our love of an object we may find our destructive relationship to that object unbearable; the idea of having (in our mind) harmed the object who is regarded by us as good and beloved may arouse devastating guilt or fear of retribution. As a consequence, we may deny the destructiveness – on a certain level not knowing or acknowledging its active presence in us. This, however, does not make it disappear. It continues to play a latent, unconscious role. The destructiveness may, in phantasy, be projected outward into the world, into others; the world then comes to be experienced as an unfairly destructive and persecutory place – a defensive move which at the same time allows for punishment felt to be deserved for our destructiveness (which, on some level, we still know about), and which now also includes the destructiveness inherent to the very act of projection (which makes a good object into a bad one). Alternatively, the difficult situation may be dealt with by denying the love of the attacked object or denying the guilt. We may then feel that our destructiveness is justified, but the world becomes a loveless and boring place. In all such possibilities, both ourselves and the world become distorted. Moreover, the mental efforts they involve (e.g., the denial, splitting and projection) may also leave us tired and our thinking processes impaired. We become unproductive, uncreative. Indeed, we are spared some distress – guilt and anxiety; this is why we do this. But a serious price is paid.

The psychoanalytic process of knowing or integrating the split off parts is possible despite the fact that it entails encountering and acknowledging precisely that which we wish not to because of the existence of a fundamental human desire to see reality as it is, to embrace truth in ourselves and others, to love – which depends on knowing the other and ourselves realistically. These are the most direct expressions of the life instinct. The analytic situation provides a context in which this instinct can better come to the fore, and the forces working against it can be met differently than when we deal with them on their own. The fact is that the reality of our inner predicaments is, as a rule, not as bad or as hopeless as it is unconsciously felt to be. To return to the example, our phantasies of having harmed beloved objects may in our inner world be felt by us to be completely unforgivable. We may feel that were the objects to know what we have done, they would no longer love us, they would cut all ties with us and leave us to die and rightly so. The pain of our guilt is unbearable. It may seem that the only solution available, the only way to go on living, is through some form of splitting off parts of ourselves, denying what we know, projecting the destructiveness into others, telling ourselves that we are so good that we would have never harmed an object or that our objects relate to us so perfectly that there would never be a reason to harm them, and even if we tried, they would be immune to our attacks, etc. But the fact may be that our attacks on the object are not as devastating as they seem; that good and forgiving objects within us may still be resurrected; that if we can feel the guilt and acknowledge our harmfulness, if we can feel sorrow over it, then our mind can also be freed to experience the love of our objects. Hope then can take the place of despair, and reality, even if painful, can be better tolerated.

The analytic situation facilitates this kind of opening to the inner world that ultimately allows for integration mainly through the interpretation of transference. This notion is often misunderstood. When I speak of transference, what I have in mind is the living out in reality of the inner world, the dynamics of unconscious phantasies, of our inner object relations. This happens all the time – not only in analysis. Our unconscious phantasies always underlie and determine the meanings of our experiences and actions. But in analysis, the analyst relates to the transference in ways that differ from what happens with it in any other relationship, and consequently it assumes a special role. For example, we can imagine a patient whose inner world is dominated by denied envy of his maternal object and her procreative and nourishing capacities. This will have a pervasive influence on his life, e.g., on whether he can allow himself to be creative, how he feels when he is or isn't creative, how he relates to women and the nature of his relationships with them, etc. The patient who I have in mind, a successful businessman, was having numerous extra-marital affairs with married women. It could be seen that the specific nature of his success and his affairs, the meaning of them to him, was driven and shaped by an effort to have confirmed that he had procreative abilities that surpassed those of his maternal object – his dependence on her and his envy of her being unbearable to him. This unconscious dynamic was lived out, projected into the world all the time and found expression also in an exceptionally high self-evaluation of his attractiveness, in the quality of his depression when he felt rejected, and in an apparent absence of concern for all the women in his life whom he supposedly loved, which only thinly veiled strong feelings of guilt in regard to them. In his analysis, too, the patient lived the same inner world, transferred it, so to speak, there too; for example, repeatedly seeking to create situations that would allow him to feel that the analyst (a woman) recognized that his maternal qualities were superior to hers, so that he could go on denying his envy of what he felt she (as the maternal object) had and he lacked. While in his ongoing life, the patient's "transference" received concrete responses, which he would then interpret in light of his inner world, in the analysis he met with something else. Instead of responding (positively or negatively) to the patient's demands of her to be and act in certain ways, instead of correcting his misperceptions of reality, the analyst tried to understand them, to grasp what they mean in the patient's inner world and to make this understanding accessible to him on a deep inner level. For instance, through what the patient said and did in the course of the analytic hours, the analyst could, at times, feel a pressure put on her by the patient to confide in him, and was met with an invasive degrading stance on his part when she did not do so. It was clear that she was then meant to feel worthless. She did not act on what the patient was doing, but rather tried to understand it and interpret it, i.e., convey the understanding in a live and immediate way to the patient, e.g., relating to his feeling that out of her envy she is denying his superior nurturing capacities and that, in turn, he will feed her anyway because she needs him so badly. What he, in phantasy, does with this interpretation is also something to be interpreted (e.g., spit it out, swallow it but deny its nourishing qualities).

This immediate kind of interpretation does not, as it is sometimes depicted, inform the patient of his dynamics, explain them to him so that he could through conscious reflection on his situation act more realistically and responsibly in the service of his best interests. Not that this kind of information and explanation could not sometimes have a positive impact on one's life. But it is not the positive impact that analysis, as I understand it, seeks. Conscious knowing about what one fears, denies and splits off does not in itself change the fears, denials and splits, and it is this change that analysis aims for. This change takes place as the unconscious dynamics, the phantasies, are directly engaged in the analytic relationship. The analyst's interpretation of what the patient feels the analyst is doing to him, and he to her, is something that can immediately resonate with what's going on in the unconscious mind and in this way open the mind to experience and, in this sense, know or integrate these parts of the mind. In this case, the patient would directly feel his envy and its intrapsychic source, he would struggle with the sense of limitation and frustration that it implies and the sorrow and guilt with which these are associated. The denied parts would become known in the sense that they would become integral to who he is and how he acts and feels in the world. This knowledge does not make the person consciously wiser about himself, but rather transforms who he is.

In line with this focus on the interpretation of the immediate unconscious dynamics that find expression in the transference, it should be emphasized that the analytic concern with transference as described here is not a concern with past events or actual people, but rather with the patient's contemporary, motivated state of mind; with his unconscious stories which shape how he thinks, feels and acts. If, for example, the patient feels that the analyst is enviously punishing him, the question then is how and why the patient's unconscious phantasies shape this experience of the relationship with the analyst – not which event of the past is being repeated. Indeed, the feeling of being punished and the broader range of phantasies associated with it first occurred at a certain point in time and may have been a response to certain actual events. But the analytic concern is not with the physical facts of the events per se, but with the phantasies that make all events psychical (Blass, 2017a).

It should be added that I practice psychoanalysis of the kind that I have described here not because some empirical finding has shown that it is the treatment that helps patients most, but rather because I maintain that coming in touch with one's unconscious self and reality in this specific live way of encounter is an inherently good thing to do. It is the desirable kind of change that psychoanalysis can offer. In fact, it is what analytic change means. People may want other things; often patients and therapists seek the most efficient form of psychological relief: They would like to be happy and free of symptoms as fast as possible and supposedly don't care how (as though happiness can be separated from the means to its attainment [Blass, 2003]). They would like advice on decisions they face or on how to improve their relationships at work or at home. They would like to have a friend who would be willing to empathically hear them out, etc. The analyst may be capable of supplying some of these wants and needs and, in principle, it may be good for the patient to have them fulfilled. (Clearly, having friends is helpful to one's wellbeing.) But from my perspective, the analyst would have to refrain from doing so. It's my understanding that to provide the kind of change that analysis allows for requires that the analytic stance of interpretation of the transference be consistently maintained.

And now to the questions posed:

"What impact has your chosen perspective had on conducting psychoanalytic treatment?"

It should be apparent from this description of my view of psychoanalysis that it is largely determined by what it means to conduct psychoanalysis. As I explained, for me to conduct analysis is to interpret what is going on unconsciously as this is encountered in the transference. However, there are several factors that facilitate this process. Among these are having a high frequency of meetings per week (normally five times per week). This creates a secure framework for the threatening unconscious parts of the mind to emerge and be interpreted. For the patient to come in contact with such explosive material and then to be left with them on one's own places a great demand on the patient and may either increase the patient's need for defensive denial and splitting or lead the analyst to set limits on what he interprets.

The use of the couch also facilitates the analytic process. Face to face seating arrangements invite attentiveness to reality, including the analyst's physical cues. Limited possibility for this kind of attention, as well as the horizontal posture, leaves more room for the free play of the unconscious. It also leaves the analyst freer to attend to the patient and to himself, not having to be concerned with the physical cues he (the analyst) is conveying.

In addition, consistently maintaining the analytic stance of interpretation of what's transpiring in the transference in the immediate sense that I have described here has various practical implications (see Blass, 2017a). These include always interpreting in terms of what's going on between patient and analyst (even when the patient discusses life events and other people); interpreting without trying to rationally convince the patient of the validity of the interpretation by explaining how one arrived at it; interpreting without conveying through intonation that what the patient phantasizes doesn't correspond to how things really are; and interpreting what's happening in the present moment. That is, interpretations do not state generalizations regarding how the patient tends to be or the nature of his fears regarding the future (e.g., "you fear that if you get angry people won't love you"), but how he is in the present moment with the analyst (e.g., "you see me as refusing to understand you after you now attacked what I said"). Interpretation is truly in the "here and now" of the patient's unconscious inner world as it emerges in the relationship to the analyst.

"What are the most important developments in psychoanalysis today?"

In thinking about the important developments in psychoanalysis today, I distinguish between developments that have taken place within the Kleinian approach to which I adhere and those of the broader field of psychoanalysis. As will become apparent, in my view, the latter developments do not actually take psychoanalysis forward.

Within my approach, innovation refers to an ongoing process of evolution since the time of Klein herself, ever-growing insight into the foundational Freudian and Kleinian ideas as they find expression in the clinical situation. This has included a growing understanding of various kinds of unconscious phantasies and their meanings and motives, with a special focus on how these phantasies impact our thinking processes and particularly how they do so within the analytic relationship. In this context, advances in our understanding of the phantasy of projective identification is most notable (Bion, 1957; Joseph, 1987; Segal, 1957; and Rosenfeld, 1952). We now better understand how, in projecting in this way, we fear retribution from the object into whom we project, or we fear losing parts of ourselves in that object and how we do in fact lose them. The various phantasies that we have regarding the thinking process itself have also come to be more elaborate. This includes the phantasies of thinking as acts of digestion or of intercourse; and in turn, not thinking as acts of "attacks on linking" (Bion, 1959) or of going into a "psychic retreat" (Steiner, 1993). There have also been new insights into how to interpret in ways that best allow for these phantasies to be grasped or integrated by the patient, e.g., through growing awareness to different aspects of the "here and now" of the analytic process that could be interpreted and deeper understanding of the role of the analyst's countertransference within that process (Bion, 1962; Feldman, 2009; Joseph, 1989; Segal, 1997; Steiner, 1994; see Blass, 2011). Others have developed an appreciation of various specific constellations of phantasies that find expression as specific kinds of disorders, e.g., hysterical (Britton, 1999), manic (Segal, 1981), perverse (Joseph, 1971), narcissistic (Rosenfeld, 1964), etc. These developments are innovative in the sense that they creatively enrich and deepen our analytic understanding and practice.

Looking at the broader analytic field, the major developments as I see them are of another order. I consider there to be five such major developments: (1) A concern with neuroscientific correlates of what is presented analytically (i.e., neuropsychoanalysis); (2) the demand for our clinical practice to be "evidence-based", demonstrated to be effective through general empirical research; (3) an increasing focus on explanations of the patient's predicament in terms of environmental causes – traumas and early parental deficits; (4) the adoption of a certain postmodern/intersubjective position, whereby there is no given psychic truth to be discovered and (5) the adoption of an eclectic stance, according to which different analytic approaches could be integrated. However, as I have argued in a series of papers, all of these developments undermine the practice of psychoanalysis as I understand it (Blass, 2006; Blass, 2015; Blass, 2016; Blass, 2017b; Blass & Carmeli, 2007, 2015). Let me explain why.

Learning about neuroscientific correlates of human experience can never contribute to the understanding of individual experience, the meanings the individual conveys at a given moment, the specific set of phantasies that shape his way of being. In fact, it interferes with such understanding. Just as the study of the chemistry of the paint of a work of art, without which it would not exist, does not contribute to the understanding of the meanings of that work of art, so information regarding the neurological correlates of human experience does not allow us to understand the person on a level of psychological meaning, the level which is relevant to psychoanalysis as I understand it. Moreover, to think that the biological level could be informative of meaning is not only misguided but also perverts how we consider the analytic task. This is because the kind of psychological correlates that neuroscience can refer to are on the level of functions, not contents. We may be able to make generalizations regarding the biological correlates of fear, but not correlates of specific contents, e.g., fear of spiders in contrast to fear of bees. Therefore, not only could neuroscience never tell us about the meanings of a fear of spiders in a specific patient, but also if one adopts the idea that what neuroscience has to say is important, one begins to take a general and function-oriented approach to the patient, an approach that is concerned with the fact of the patient's fear rather than with its specific contents and, in turn, with the specific meanings with which the fear is associated.

The demand that our clinical practices be grounded in the findings of empirical research, the so-called evidence-based approach, suffers from related limitations. The kind of research and evidence that is sought is of the kind that would allow for prediction. Based on this research, it might be suggested that a certain kind of intervention is likely to be helpful to a certain kind of patient, or even that certain kinds of statements or actions by the patient likely imply that certain events or memories or ideas are active in the patient. And, indeed, this kind of research may be helpful if someone must gamble on what something might mean or what would bring about the greatest change. Relying on predictive data of this kind might then be relevant. But if what one has to offer is only the kind of psychoanalytic understanding that I do, then relying on such generalizations rather than the specific and infinitely richer details of what my patient presents would be misguided. To return to the painting analogy: It could be the case that having a lot of yellow in a painting has been found to be associated with the painting being thought to express happy themes. I may rely on this if I had to bet on what a painting is expressing based only on information regarding its colors. But if I actually have access to the painting and could study it in detail, then this information would be irrelevant to me. It might be that in the totality of this specific painting, yellow does not at all express happiness or lead to an overall sense of it. In analogy, the generalizations of empirical research can distract the analyst from discerning what is finding expression in the individual analytic patient. Moreover, just as guessing what a painting expresses on the basis of predictive data is not the same as understanding it on the basis of observing it in detail, so the nature of understanding is fundamentally different when it emerges from listening to the specific details of what the patient is expressing in the analytic encounter, rather than the study of predictive data. As I have argued earlier, it is only in the former case and, moreover, only with the active involvement of unconscious phantasy in the transference, that interpretation could be mutative.

Of course, psychoanalysis as I practice it, too, relies on models which have emerged on the basis of clinical experience. But, these models don't inform and predict in the way that evidence-based models do. Rather they (e.g., regarding ideas on love and hate and guilt) open us to consider different ways in which what is specifically going on in the patient might be listened to.

The third development of the broader field of psychoanalysis in recent years, the focus on environmental causes of the patient's predicament, is detrimental to my view of psychoanalysis for other reasons – ones simpler to explain. Clearly, who we are is shaped in part by what we have experienced. Both Freud and Klein repeatedly take note of this. At the same time, the concern of psychoanalysis, as I see it, is not with environmental factors per se, whether these are conceived of in terms of traumatic experiences or parental deficits of various kinds. Events don't shape the mind, only the meanings ascribed to them do, and psychoanalysis as I see it is precisely concerned with such meanings as they find expression in unconscious phantasy. The patient may describe his mother as having been absent, but rather than being concerned with the impact of the mother's absence per se, we would be concerned with the meaning of this idea of her absence (e.g., that in his phantasy the patient feels that she recognized that he's bad, or that she feels that she could leave him because he's so self-sufficient, or that she is expressing the patient's own harmfulness, which he has projected into her). And here too, it may be seen that the focus on the environmental level is not only irrelevant but potentially harmful. It takes the place of a focus on the understanding of internal meanings; it supports projection rather than integration of what's projected and is often accompanied by the analyst assuming a corrective environmental role that interferes with the interpretation of the transference.

The postmodern/intersubjective turn that has gained force in recent years, the fourth development that I've noted, basically asserts that there is no actual objective truth to be discovered because the analytic situation is a "neocreation" determined by the interplay of the subjectivities of both analyst and patient (Greenberg, 2018). As such, it completely does away with the main aim of analysis as I understand it – coming to know or integrating actually split off parts of the self. While it may be argued that this turn doesn't *necessarily* influence the practice of analysis, only its understanding on some meta level of reflection, it may be seen that this meta level of reflection shapes the analyst's attitude and the way he attends to the patient and consequently his ability to maintain the analytic situation and interpret it. An analyst who listens to his patients and engages with their difficult transferences in the effort to uncover painful realities regarding actually split off parts listens, engages and understands differently and with a different kind of dedication than one who sees this as a kind of fictional exercise, aimed perhaps at creating more benevolent or flexible self-narratives. In fact, were a patient to seriously adopt this postmodern perspective in relation to himself within his analysis, a Kleinian analyst would tend to see this as a defensive maneuver. I would imagine that a postmodern analyst, in contrast, would have to paradoxically regard this (at least in part) as he regards his own adoption of this position – namely, as a move towards a truer vision of reality.

The last major development, the adoption of an eclectic stance, according to which different analytic approaches could and should be integrated, opposes psychoanalysis as I understand it for both theoretical and practical reasons. From my perspective, foundational analytic theories regarding human nature are to be regarded as true for all human beings. They will be revised and developed on the basis of experience; and they will be applied to the understanding of the uniqueness of each individual patient.

But analytic theories as descriptions of aspects of human nature that are of concern to psychoanalysis aren't the kind of thing that are true or useful for some patients some of the time, while for others, other kinds of theories apply (Blass, 2018). One may hold a very broad theory, but one cannot hold contradictory assumptions and shift between them depending on the patient. For example, with time, analytic theory may come to deeper understandings of Oedipal conflict, and its specific forms and roles may vary from patient to patient, but one couldn't hold both a Freudian view of Oedipal conflict and an opposing Kohutian one, sometimes applying one and sometimes the other.

As to the problems of this eclectic stance in terms of practice, I have argued for the necessity of my analytic approach being consistently applied. For example, an analyst who sometimes chooses to actively take on idealized roles projected by the patient cannot relate to the transference and interpret it in the way prescribed by my approach.

Conclusion

It is interesting to note that while the first three major developments in the broader field of psychoanalysis that I have mentioned here involve a growing concern with material reality – biology, demonstrable empirical evidence and actual trauma, the last two emphasize that reality is either unknowable or exceptionally flexible. I would suggest that both these directions, although diametrically opposed, are responses to the difficulty of contending with psychic truth. As described earlier, psychic truth is so complex and multifaceted, such a source of pain and guilt, that we would rather not know it and distrust and doubt what we do know and rightly so. But traditional psychoanalysis of the Freudian-Kleinian kind that I have described in this chapter also recognizes that coming to know psychic truth, with all the difficulties this involves, is the grounds of our ability to fully live and love. Therefore, rather than limit psychic truth to material facts or deny its existence altogether, it sets as its objective the attainment or integration of such truth, explores the difficulties in doing so, demonstrates how this is possible nevertheless through the process of understanding that emerges in the lived experience of the analytic encounter and steadily works towards the deepening of this process. To my mind, it is only through this kind of work that psychoanalysis could truly develop.

Note

1 When referring to the aim of psychoanalysis, I will use both the terms "integrating" and "knowing", often in succession, to express a process in which the person becomes linked or relinked to what is known. It is an act of knowledge that is integrative rather than directly intellectual, but does not involve an active step of synthesis on the part of the analyst.

References

Bion, W. R. (1957). Differentiation of the psychotic from the non-psychotic personalities. *International Journal of Psychoanalysis*, *38*, 266–275.

Bion, W. R. (1959). Attacks on linking. *International Journal of Psychoanalysis*, *40*, 308–315.

Bion, W. R. (1962). *Learning from experience*. London: Karnac.

Blass, R. B. (2003). On ethical issues at the foundation of the debate over the goals of psychoanalysis. *International Journal of Psychoanalysis*, *84*, 929–944.

Blass, R. B. (2006). Introduction to "*Tradition and Truth in Psychoanalysis*". *The American Imago*, *63*, 253–260.

Blass, R. B. (2011). On the immediacy of unconscious truth: Understanding Betty Joseph's "here and now" through comparison with alternative views of it outside of and within Kleinian thinking. *International Journal of Psychoanalysis*, *92*, 1137–1157.

Blass, R. B. (2015). Psychoanalytic theories as efforts to grasp the true (not fictional) nature of human reality: Commentary on Greenberg. *Journal of the American Psychoanalytic Association*, *63*, 47–63.

Blass, R. B. (2016). The quest for truth as the foundation of psychoanalytic practice: A traditional, Freudian-Kleinian perspective. *Psychoanalytic Quarterly*, *85*, 305–337.

Blass, R. B. (2017a). Reflections on Klein's radical notion of phantasy and its implications for analytic practice. *International Journal of Psychoanalysis*, *98*, 841–859.

Blass, R. B. (2017b). Committed to a single model and open to reality. *Journal of the American Psychoanalytic Association*, *65*, 845–858.

Blass, R. B. (2018). The teaching of Klein: Some guidelines for opening students to the heart of Kleinian thinking and practice. In K. Long & P. Garvey (Eds.), *The Kleinian tradition* (pp. 73–90). London: Karnac Press.

Blass, R. B., & Carmeli, Z. (2007). The case against neuropsychoanalysis: On fallacies underlying psychoanalysis' latest scientific trend and its negative impact on psychoanalytic discourse. *International Journal of Psychoanalysis*, *88*, 19–40.

Blass, R. B., & Carmeli, Z. (2015). Further evidence for the case against neuropsychoanalysis: How Yovell, Solms, and Fotopoulou's response to our critique confirms the irrelevance and harmfulness to psychoanalysis of the contemporary neuroscientific trend. *International Journal of Psychoanalysis*, *96*, 1555–1573.

Britton, R. (1999). Getting in on the act: The hysterical solution. *International Journal of Psychoanalysis*, *80*, 1–14.

Greenberg, J. (2018). Comments on "*Lectures on Technique by Melanie Klein*". *International Journal of Psychoanalysis*, *99*.

Feldman, M. (2009). *Doubt, conviction and the analytic process*. London: Routledge.

Joseph, B. (1971). A clinical contribution to the analysis of a perversion. In *Selected papers of Betty Joseph, 1989* (pp. 51–66). London: Routledge.

Joseph, B. (1987). Projective identification: Some clinical aspects. In *Psychic equilibrium and psychic change: Selected papers of Betty Joseph, 1989* (pp. 168–180). Routledge: London.

Joseph, B. (1989). *Selected papers of Betty Joseph*. London: Routledge.

Rosenfeld, H. (1952). Notes on the psycho-analysis of the super-ego conflict of an acute schizophrenic patient. *International Journal of Psychoanalysis*, *33*, 111–131.

Rosenfeld, H. (1964). On the psychopathology of narcissism: A clinical approach. *International Journal of Psychoanalysis*, *45*, 332–337.

Segal, H. (1957). Notes on symbol formation. *International Journal of Psychoanalysis*, *38*, 391–397.

Segal, H. (1997). The uses and abuses of countertransference In. *Psychoanalysis, literature and war* (pp. 111–119). London: Routledge.

Segal, H. (1981). Manic reparation. In *The work of Hanna Segal* (pp. 147–158). London: Free Association.

Steiner, J. (1993). *Psychic retreats*. London: Routledge.

Steiner, J. (1994). Patient-centered and analyst-centered interpretations: Some implications of Containment and countertransference. *Psychoanalytic Inquiry*, *14*, 406–422.

Chapter 3

Cultural complexes in the psyche of individuals and groups

Revisioning analytical psychology from within

Thomas Singer

> "This dualistic tendency – fascination and observance of tradition alongside disenchantment and the will to improve knowledge – is likely responsible for psychoanalysis's powerful capacity to survive."
> – Editors

I might rewrite this sentence to say, "If psychoanalysis is to survive, it must balance in creative tension the honouring of its traditions alongside the capacity to tolerate disenchantment and the will to improve knowledge." Few traditions can remain static and survive. And yet without tradition, there is nothing to build on and grow from. As a Jungian psychoanalyst, I spent years finding my way into a working knowledge and comfort with my tradition. At the same time, I became increasingly aware of ways in which I thought the tradition was limited and even ossified. Paradoxically, I found myself returning to Jung's original insights and theoretical work on complex theory as a way of finding a renewal in the tradition. In this chapter, I will describe that journey of a return to and extension of Jung's original complex theory as a way to grow, renew and transform the tradition from within. Several innovative steps have been at the heart of this renewal and transformation, and I will present how these layers of innovation unfolded in the following order, which is, of course, somewhat schematic in outline:

1. The first step of innovation: tradition and disillusionment
2. The second step of innovation: Joseph Henderson's notion of the cultural unconscious
3. The third step of innovation: the notion of cultural complexes
4. The fourth step of innovation: applying the new theory of cultural complexes to the psyche of an individual

5 The fifth step of innovation: applying the new theory of cultural complexes to the psyche of a nation

Disillusionment

As a young medical student in the midst of an American cultural revolution between 1965 and 1970, I found myself drawn to the work of C. G. Jung. Two things were most attractive to me:

- He recognized the reality of the inner world in the tradition of such greats as St. Augustine and Meister Eckhart.
- He recognized that the individual human psyche was only a small part of a much larger psyche that was indwelling in both the individual and larger groups of people. From the Jungian perspective, the psyche is vast and deep.

This second point seemed particularly important to me because it was clear from the profound transformations taking place among young people around the world in the 1960s that something was going on in the collective psyche that was much bigger than the change in any single individual psyche. Psychology is not just individual; it is collective. Even now as we focus on the individual psychology of Donald Trump, for instance, we often lose sight that what is going on is hardly just about Donald Trump's individual psyche but is, instead, reflective of deep shifting currents in the American psyche (Singer, 2017).

Jung himself experienced being overwhelmed by contents from the collective psyche in his harrowing visions in 1913, just after his breakup with Freud in 1912 and just prior to the beginning of World War I. He had recurring visions of Europe being flooded with blood. Fearing for his sanity, he worried that the personal crisis caused by his split from Freud was plunging him into a psychosis. Not long after these visions, Europe was indeed flooded with the blood of World War I. What Jung feared as the onset of a personal psychosis was, in fact, his porousness to forces of the collective psyche that were flowing through him and, as it turned out, through all Europeans.

For most of my professional life, my primary interest has been in the individual inner life. But sometime in my early 60s I found myself returning to my original interest in Jung's notion of the collective psyche that had caught my attention some three or four decades earlier (Singer, 2000).

I began to focus on forces in the collective or group psyche as they manifest in politics and in what I came to explore as *cultural complexes* – complexes that belong not only to the individual psyche but also to the psyche of groups of people. Actually, it was my growing disillusionment with how the Jungian tradition was using Jung's notion of archetypes to speak of collective events that drew my concern. Every time some troubling political or other social upheaval occurred, Jungians would reflexively trot out something about the "shadow" or the "hero" as an explanation – some archetypal force overtaking or seizing events. I got tired of these reductive Jungian explanations or interpretations – as if by labelling something "the shadow" or "the hero" they had explained why something was happening and the meaning of its occurrence. I found these interpretations boring, repetitive and somehow hollow. I also came to believe that turning to the deepest archetypal levels of the psyche as Jung understood it opened Jung and our tradition up to serious dangers and, in my mind, misunderstandings. The most notable example of this was in Jung's essay *Wotan*, written in 1936. In *Wotan*, Jung argues that the German psyche was being seized by an archetypal force of enormous destructive potential in the form of a possession by the ancient Northern European war god of lightning and destruction. In other words, he saw dangerous archetypal energies unleashed in the German psyche. He was right enough about that, but at times his essay is filled with too much energy. It is clear to me that Jung – even in that essay – is issuing a warning about the dangers of Wotan, but that is not what many took away from their reading of the essay. They thought that Jung himself had been seduced by the unconscious Nazi attraction to Wotan. I believe that one reason this reading occurred is that Jung did not provide enough of the social, political, economic and cultural context about the German people in the 1930s for one to understand why they might be prone to such a seizure (Jung, 1936/1968, CW 10).

Jung went straight to the archetypal level of the psyche and its seizure by Wotan, bypassing the mid-belly region of what was happening to the German psyche as a consequence of their despair following the humiliation of World War I. Jung left out the cultural level of the psyche and went straight to the archetypal as an explanatory principle. I felt the Jungians who followed Jung (from 1950–2000) were ironically making the same mistake as Jung – that is, not paying enough attention to the cultural or social level of the psyche and turning instead to archetypal explanations.

Following World War II, Jung was attacked as being a Nazi, particularly among American Freudian Jews who held Jung personally responsible for the deaths of their own family members. They saw Jung as participating in and encouraging Nazism. The small group of analysts who followed Jung – many of whom, ironically, were also Jewish – were in a permanent state of exile because of the relentless Freudian Jewish attacks on anything having to do with Jung. As a result, the post-World War II Jungians in America came to see themselves as a fringe minority and tended to turn away from the social, political and cultural affairs of the everyday world, focusing instead on the development of the individual's inner world. The so-called collective psyche that belongs to groups of people (which is simultaneously indwelling in individual members of a given collective) came to be seen as too dangerous and shadowy, too collective (like mass man or the *Man in the Gray Flannel Suit*) – something that one should "individuate out of." As a result, when it came to understanding affairs of the group psyche as expressed in politics and social dissent, Jungians too quickly turned to archetypal explanations about politics and social divisions. It was this aspect of the Jungian tradition that I became disillusioned with – archetypes were offered as explanations for everything, without any cultural context or setting being necessary to justify the archetypal perspective. It was not that I renounced the archetypal dimension of psychic reality as being true. It was the way in which it was being bandied about in an almost magical explanatory way that I became increasingly uncomfortable with. In short, innovation often begins with disillusionment with some aspect of one's tradition.

The second step of innovation: Joseph Henderson's notion of the cultural unconscious

It never occurred to me not to stay within the Jungian tradition, but I did want to give voice to the fact that our sense of being such individuals may be an illusion and that we are far more creatures of collective psychology and our cultures than we might like to believe. For all the talk that the theories of Freud, Darwin and Marx took the individual human being out of the centre of the creation, paradoxically, the psychological emphasis on the individual in the various psychoanalytic traditions seems to have placed the individual right back in the centre of everything, with the highest premium placed on separation/individuation.

Interestingly enough, the beginnings of the innovative theoretical breakthrough to my disillusioning impasse with the Jungian use of the archetype to explain everything came from one of Jung's most introverted and, in some ways, unworldly students. Joseph Henderson, a revered Jungian from San Francisco, who lived and practiced to the age of 104, introduced the layer of the so-called cultural unconscious as a midzone between the personal and collective unconscious (Henderson, 1962/1964, 1984, 1990). In this theoretical scheme of things, the realm of the personal unconscious remains the source of some of our most difficult problems. This is where the family dramas of mother, father, siblings and others play themselves out in our neurotic symptoms. The collective unconscious, the realm of the archetypes, is where the core of our more universal human themes of death/rebirth, hero, spirit and individuation reside. Henderson took the hugely innovative step in the 1960s (1962/1964) of adding a middle zone as the seat of the more social, political and cultural unconscious forces that play themselves out in the individual and collective psyche at any given time. For instance, around the world today, large numbers of immigrants and refugees are triggering dramatically powerful, reactionary forces in the cultural unconscious of many in Western Europe and the United States who feel threatened with displacement by displaced immigrants and refugees. This has resulted in all sorts of powerfully destructive emotions and behaviours that have driven political and social life in both Europe and the United States. This does not come from the personal unconscious. It comes from that level of the psyche that we can think of as the *cultural* or *social* unconscious.

Joseph Henderson's pioneering work in imagining the cultural unconscious as a middle zone of unconscious contents that were neither personal nor archetypal was a major theoretical contribution because it established the notion that there were unconscious contents in the cultural or social strata of the unconscious that were shaped by collective forces over time. Imagine, for example, that Palestinians and Israelis, based on profoundly different historical experiences and equally devastating but different traumas, have accumulated in their separate cultural or social unconscious transgenerational memories, affects and beliefs that have been transmitted from generation to generation. Or that Americans have a shared cultural unconscious with deep roots that are nursed on the notion of the American dream, with life, liberty and the pursuit of happiness at the core of our group's deepest beliefs about itself. These memories, beliefs, feelings and shared experiences of trauma and renewal are unique for different ethnic, racial, religious and geographic groups around the world. Of course, these unconscious cultural contents can get all mixed up with contents from either the personal and/or collective unconscious. Sometimes they get deeply embedded in the unconscious complexes and/or personal identity of an individual. And sometimes these unconscious cultural contents participate in more universal themes, such as the death and rebirth archetype that we imagine as coming from the collective unconscious. Henderson's innovative step opened up a vast arena for new thought and development within the Jungian tradition that allowed us to begin filling in the gaping hole that led Jung to go straight to the archetypal level to explain the rise of Nazism. We could now begin to consider what it was in the German cultural unconscious, growing out of traumatic historical experience, that led a whole population to be ripe for seizure by a demonic and destructive archetypal force.

The third step of innovation: the notion of cultural complexes

The next innovative step that Sam Kimbles and I took was to formulate the nature of the contents of the cultural unconscious (Singer & Kimbles, 2004). Just as Freud imagined an id filled with aggressive and sexual drives as the prime contents of his unconscious, so we began to imagine what the contents of the cultural unconscious might be. In our wish to renew and transform the Jungian tradition in its understanding of social or cultural forces in the psyche, our innovation had a wonderful paradoxical twist. We turned back to Jung's original theoretical and clinical work on complex theory to begin describing the contents of the cultural unconscious. Jung's complex theory – not very well known to many outside the Jungian tradition – formed the core of his thinking about the contents of the personal unconscious. We are all familiar with the idea of an inferiority complex or a power complex, but Jung also wrote at length about the contents of the personal unconscious in terms of the mother complex, the father complex and so on. Our innovative theoretical leap was quite simple really. What if the cultural unconscious also has complexes whose contents are different from those of the personal unconscious? Perhaps I should stop for a moment and describe the basic characteristics of a complex for those of you unfamiliar with this basic Jungian theory.

Basic characteristics of complexes

Through a hundred years of clinical experience, those of us working in the Jungian tradition have come to know well that complexes are powerful forces in the lives of individuals that can be profoundly disruptive of everyday ego functioning. We define a complex as follows: a complex is an emotionally charged group of ideas, emotions, memories, images and behaviours that cluster around an archetypal core. Jung wrote:

> The complex has a sort of body, a certain amount of its own physiology. It can upset the stomach. It upsets the breathing, it disturbs the heart – in short, it behaves like a partial personality. For instance, when you want to say or do something and unfortunately a complex interferes with this intention, then you say or do something different from what you intended. You are simply interrupted, and your best intention gets upset by the complex, exactly as if you had been interfered with by a human being or by circumstances from outside.
> (Jung, 1935/1976, CW 18, para. 72)

Today, we can say the same is true of a cultural complex when it possesses the psyche and soma of an individual or a group. It causes us to think and feel in ways that might be quite different from what we think we should feel or think, or, as Jung put it, "We say or do something different from what we intended" (Jung, 1935/1976, CW 18, para. 72). In other words, cultural complexes are not always "politically correct," although being "politically correct" might itself be a cultural complex. The basic premise of our work, then, is that another level of complexes exists within the psyche of the group (and within the individual at the group level of their psyche). We call these group complexes *cultural complexes*, and they, too, can be defined as emotionally charged aggregates of ideas, images, memories and behaviours that tend to cluster around an archetypal core and are shared by individuals within an identified collective.

At the heart of our innovative renovation of Jungian theory in regard to the powerful conscious and unconscious currents that are part of our living in a group or many groups, we rearranged and added the following building blocks:

(a) We adopted Henderson's notion that there is a layer of the unconscious that he called the "cultural unconscious," which sits between the personal unconscious and the collective unconscious.
(b) As personal complexes emerge out of the level of the personal unconscious in its interaction with deeper levels of the psyche, cultural complexes can be thought of as arising out of the cultural unconscious in its interaction with both the archetypal and personal realms of the psyche and with the broader outer world arena of schools, work and religious communities, media and all the other forms of group life.

It is useful to know how to recognize when one is in the presence of a complex – whether one's own or another person's or a whole culture's. Although personal complexes and cultural complexes are not the same, they can get all mixed up with one another. We suggest that personal and cultural complexes share the following characteristics:

- They express themselves in powerful moods and repetitive behaviours. Highly charged emotional or affective reactivity is their calling card.
- They resist our most heroic efforts at consciousness and remain, for the most part, unconscious.
- They accumulate experiences that validate their point of view and create a storehouse of self-affirming ancestral memories.
- Personal and cultural complexes function in an involuntary, autonomous fashion and tend to affirm a simplistic point of view that replaces more everyday ambiguity and uncertainty with fixed, often self-righteous attitudes to the world.
- In addition, personal and cultural complexes both have archetypal cores; that is, they express typically human attitudes and are rooted in primordial ideas about what is meaningful, making them very hard to resist, reflect upon and discriminate.

It is easy enough to see that much of the United States, and perhaps much of the world, is in the midst of cultural complex landmines that are firing off all the time in our fragmented social and political life. Again, we can recognize groups or individuals in the grip of cultural complexes because of their extreme emotional potency and reactivity, their highly selective memory about what is real and true, their insistence on simplistic ideas that replace the more nuanced ambiguity that is required to attend to complex problems in a complex society. Attending to the personal, cultural and archetypal levels of complexes requires respect for each of these realms without condensing or telescoping one into the other, as if one realm were more real, true or fundamental than another.

Cultural complexes are based on repetitive, historical experiences that have taken root in the collective psyche of a group and in the psyches of the individual members of a group, and they express archetypal values for the group. As such, cultural complexes can be thought of as the fundamental building blocks of an inner sociology. But this inner sociology does not claim to be objective or scientific in its description of different groups and classes of people. Rather, it is a description of groups and classes of people as filtered through the psyches of generations of ancestors. It contains an abundance of information and misinformation about the structures of societies – a truly inner sociology – and its essential components are cultural complexes.

This then is a brief summary of the innovative renovation of the Jungian theory that has been at the heart of my work for at least two decades. This reworking of our tradition grew directly out of disillusionment. Now I want to turn to two examples of how one can apply these theoretical renovations to the understanding of an individual in the grips of a cultural complex and to a society in the grips of a cultural complex.

The fourth step of innovation: applying the new theory of cultural complexes to the psyche of an individual

What follows is an example of how a cultural complex took shape in the psyche of an individual (Tom Singer & Kaplinsky, 2010).[1] This was creatively worked through in relation to the man's personal complexes and illustrates how the energies bound up within the cultural complex were freed up to contribute to a transformative experience. The individual, now deceased, was an exiled white South African and a professor in a European university. The shape of the cultural complex expressed itself in a recurrent dream that was communicated in a letter to his friend, Cathy Kaplinsky, around the time of South Africa's democratic transition from the institutionalized racism of Apartheid in 1994. He writes:

From the ages of 35 to 40 or so I had a recurrent dream. The dream experience was always pleasant. It was very simple:

> A small black boy, who I somehow knew to be Xhosa, sat on a beach. The beach was very long and very beautiful, with heavy surf. If you looked at the surf from the beach it seemed high, with big waves banked up on one another. Above the surf, the air was filled with a light haze. The boy was about 4 years old. He played with a whole lot of cowrie shells which were "cattle." He was putting these cattle into a kraal (African enclosure) made of sand. He was happy. I was not present in the dream. I could not talk to him, only observe him. . . .
>
> The little boy was a puzzle, and I took a long time to home in on him. Then at one point I had a strong set of feelings about my identity which was somehow mixed up with *being* Xhosa. At that period I realized that the little boy was – in a curiously inadmissible way – myself. This I think was why I was not present in the dream except as an observer, unable to talk to the little boy.
>
> Why was I the little boy? . . . What I found was the following: In early childhood I was with my mother and little sister in the Ciskei where my cousins and uncles were farmers. My father was "up north" in the army. In that time my "relationship" with my mother was terrible. You can say that she was jealous of my childhood because she wanted to be looked after herself and resented having to be a responsible parent. She was, to all intents and purposes, a competitive child . . . only a grown up one, with great power over me. I have no recollection of meaningful love from her.
>
> On the other hand I was loved and properly mothered by Rosie Ngwekazi who was a servant-cum-nursemaid in my aunt's house. . . . I depended on her far more than most South African children might depend on their black nursemaids, because of my mother's opting out of her role – and because my mother actually hurt and humiliated me. Rosie on the other hand loved me and was the only source of unconditional loving. . . .
>
> When I discovered this some years ago, I experienced a sort of unbounded joy and freedom. The discovery that I had been loved like

that was also my first adult recognition that, like everyone else, I was "lovable" and that it was also OK to love myself.

I came to understand that I had been denied this recognition for so many years (recall it only came to me at about 40) because after my father's return, we went to Cape Town and I was subject at home and at school to extremely strong racist conditioning. I simply could not own a Xhosa woman as my mother. . . . All the black part of me which had come into being in the Ciskei became inadmissible. I could not allow myself to own the experience with Rosie. And although by the age 25–30, I had disentangled a large amount of the racist shit that was pushed into me in the post-Ciskei years, this critical bit remained. After all, it raised very fundamental questions. At the same time, since Rosie's love was so central to my emotional survival, I held on to it in a subconscious way in the dream-sequence.

I saw Rosie at the Feni location when I visited the Ciskei region two weeks ago. It was a wonderful meeting. I was able to thank her for the love she gave me then. She knew perfectly well how important it had been and, very discreetly, made it clear that she knew a great deal about my mother's inabilities. She said that it was important that I had come back because I was Xhosa and because my "navel is buried" in the Ciskei. I know what she means.

So there's your dream. Make whatever use you can of it. I share all the usual reasons for hating Apartheid, but I have my own additional one . . . it prevented me from owning the most important experience of childhood by making it inadmissible. I could not own the central Black part of myself. I don't have the dream any more. It must be because I can own the reality.

(Kaplinsky, 2008, p. 2)

Dr. Kaplinsky comments on this dream in the following manner: "It is clear from the dream and the dreamer's "working through" how the interface between cultural and individuation processes have created conflict and stress for him. The dreamer needed both to "own" his experiences with Rosie in order to be "true" to himself, and he needed to "disown" them in order to be "true" to his family and the white racist culture into which he was born. However, he then came to resent the positive experiences he had had to "disown" with Rosie. This propelled him on his personal journey.

A kind of layering of complexes, splits and shadow formation developed. First, he described his mother as having been "terrible." His infant self therefore had to set up a defensive structure, a second skin function, to survive (terrible mother complex). But he also sought appropriate responses elsewhere – bodily and emotional – and he found them in Rosie (positive great mother complex). Later, as he "belonged" to and interacted with white reference groups, he learned to "disown" Rosie, giving rise to a sense of betrayal and guilt that resided in the cultural complex. We can see, therefore, how complexes developed out of an intricate network of affect, absorbed via mother, Rosie and intimate others who, in turn, reached out to and imbibed from this culture.

The theme of power and dependency ran through both the personal and the cultural complexes. The dreamer describes the "great power" his mother had over him – thus necessitating his defensive structure. From the cultural point of view, there was an interesting twist. Although the whites dominated and controlled the blacks economically, they also depended on them, not only for their labour but also very often for emotional care – as was the case with the dreamer. To keep the status quo, a rigid political structure was required, which fed the cultural complex. Apartheid means "separateness," thus signifying a rigidification of the us/them dynamics in terms of skin colour. As we know, all manner of negative projections were aimed by the ruling white population at those with non-white skin.

Skin colour triggered emotional reactions and was key to the cultural complex. The cattle game in the dream was the dreamer's attempt to disentangle himself from what he called the "racist shit which had been pushed into [him]" and which made up part of the cultural complex in which he lived. This, in turn, affected his personal complexes.

The cowrie shells were pretend cows. The transition from cowrie to cows is particularly inventive. The hard defensive structure of the shells, with the feminine underside, became softer creatures that interacted with one another, providing milk and nourishment. They also easily evacuated waste and they had looser skins. Within the cattle game, it was as if the cowrie/cow/complexes were being loosened and shifted about, in and out of the kraal/container, allowing for experimentation and exchange. The dreamer was finding a way to reach into his hidden, vulnerable underside.

The colouring of the cowries is particularly significant when addressing the cultural complex of the Apartheid era. Cowrie shells vary in colour, but where the dreamer played on the beach, they were generally a mixture of white with blotchy brown, black or caramel markings. Cows have similar colouring, commonly more defined – possibly addressing a firming up of the dreamer's colour consciousness as well as his struggle to loosen his complexes in relation to skin colour. He had after all written "all the black part of me . . . became inadmissible." His infant self had assumed he was black and Xhosa, one and the same as Rosie. Thus, we see the transcendent function at work, producing symbols where the multi-colouring in a single skin – of both cowrie shells and cows – helped disentangle and loosen both his personal and cultural complexes."

Commentary on Catherine Kaplinsky's example

The following is my commentary on the material presented by Catherine Kaplinsky from the perspective of the theory of cultural complexes. There are many ways to consider this extraordinary material, but I created the following schematic diagram (Figure 3.1). This schematic diagram illustrates what we have in mind concerning the structure of the psyche and how cultural complexes operate with regard to the various unconscious levels (personal, cultural and archetypal).

Complexes (personal and cultural) and archetypes (shadow, great mother and divine child) interact in the exiled professor's recurrent dream and in his subsequent "working through." The diagram was developed to help understand how a cultural complex shaped itself in the psyche and how the energy trapped within it was released, thus effecting a profound sense of renewal for this individual. This seemed to occur through processes of spontaneous active imagination – though we cannot know how much personal therapy, and the transference and countertransference experiences, played a part in this transformation.

Within the collective unconscious lie the archetypes as preconditions. The seeds for polar opposites, such as idealizing and denigrating tendencies, reside here, as do shadow energies and a potential for morality. Here lies also the potential for the extremes – the great and terrible mother, the divine child and so on.

Within the personal unconscious, we see the opposites at work when the dreamer describes his mother as "terrible" and Rosie as his "only source of unconditional loving." The "all terrible," "all powerful" mother of his

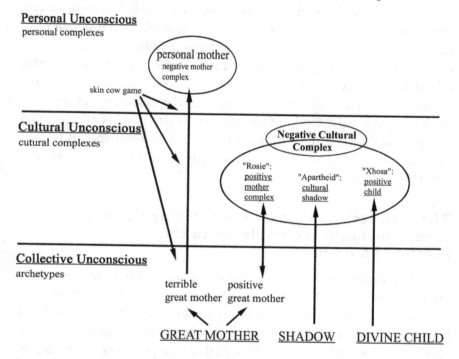

Figure 3.1 Example of a cultural complex in the psyche of an individual, by Thomas Singer (Kaplinsky & Singer, 2010)

Source: Diagram created by Thomas Singer, M.D. and is reprinted with permission by Open Court Publishers.

infancy resulted in a defensive second skin structure like the cowrie shell. This "terrible mother" complex lived on in his personal unconscious. Later the "great and positive mother" was "found" in Rosie as part of his individuation process – but this had particular cultural implications.

The cultural unconscious then came into effect when the positive experience with Rosie needed to be denied. Thus, the love of and from Rosie was embedded in the negative cultural complex, which was coupled in an unholy marriage with the shadow projections of the Apartheid era.

In the dream, the cow game – or cowrie game – is the play that facilitated and symbolized the movement of psychic energies from one level of the unconscious to another, eventually leading to a profound transformation in the psyche itself. The unconscious memory/energy of the "positive great mother" had been fused for decades in the unholy union with the "shadow" of Apartheid and was thus contained within the negative cultural complex at the level of the cultural unconscious. This fusion of positive mother and cultural shadow in the cultural complex was finally broken down and the energies contained within the negative cultural complex released. The repressed experience of Rosie's love – the positive mother complex – became available to consciousness through the dream figure of the Xhosa boy, and the grip of the personal negative mother complex on the ego was then also further released. Thus a new experience of the ego became possible, and what Jungians sometimes refer to the ego-self axis could be restored.

The fifth step of innovation: applying the new theory of cultural complexes to the psyche of a nation

Since introducing the theory of cultural complexes, I have been conducting research around the world with Jungian colleagues. We have been focused on teasing out the specificity of cultural complexes in different parts of the world, each with their own histories and geographies as well as ethnic, racial and religious heritages. Rather than go straight to the archetypal level to understand what is happening in the collective psyche of a group of people (as Jung did in his *Wotan* essay), in our cultural complex studies we emphasize the specificity of a particular country or group of people.[2] Archetypes are presumably universal potentials in the psyche of all people; cultural complexes are specific to the time, place, history, ethnicity and religions of any given group of people. While we emphasize the specificity of cultural complexes from culture to culture, we also imagine cultural complexes to have similar structural characteristics from culture to culture as they take shape in the psyche of different groups of people.

What follows is an example of a specific type of cultural complex, the structural elements of which can be observed in groups in conflict around the world. But this particular example of a cultural complex focuses on Trumpism in the United States.

I hypothesize a direct link between Trump's personal narcissism and the collective psyche of those American citizens who embrace his perception of America and who feel that he understands and speaks to them. This is not a political analysis. It is a psychological analysis of what we can think of as the *group psyche*, which contributes enormously to and fuels political processes. This analysis is based on the notion that there are certain psychological energies, even structures, at the level of the cultural or group psyche that are activated at times of heightened threats to the core identity of the group – what we might think of as the group Self. Three of these most important energies/structures are the shadow, archetypal defences of the group Self and the group Self itself. These energies/structures take shape around social, political, economic, geographic and religious themes that are alive in specific contexts and with particular contents. This same type of analysis may currently apply in the Brexit crisis in Great Britain or in the Palestinian-Israeli conflict with very different contexts and contents in which various groups can be seen as protecting their threatened or wounded Self from being further injured by pursuing a defensive, aggressive attack against imagined or real dangerous enemies.

What is it about Trump that acts as an irresistible magnet with ferocious attraction or repulsion? Is Trump the end product of our culture of narcissism? Is he what we get and deserve because he epitomizes the god or gods that we currently worship in our mindless, consumerist, hyper-indulged cult of continuous stimulation and entertainment? Here is how Christopher Hedges stated it in *Empire of Illusion: The End of Literacy and the Triumph of Spectacle:*

> An image-based culture communicates through narratives, pictures, and pseudo-drama. Scandalous affairs, hurricanes, untimely deaths, train wrecks – these events play well on computer screens and television. International diplomacy, labor union negotiations, and convoluted bailout packages do not yield exciting personal narratives or stimulating images. . . . Reality is complicated. Reality is boring. We are incapable or unwilling to handle its confusion. . . . We become trapped in the linguistic prison of incessant repetition. We are fed words and phrases like *war on terror* or *pro-life* or *change*, and within these narrow parameters, all complex thought, ambiguity, and self-criticism vanish.
>
> (Hedges, 2009, p. 49)

In addition to our collective inability to sort out illusion from reality, our culture gets further hopelessly entangled with our cult of celebrity. Hedges does not spare us the dire consequences of our intoxication with celebrity that both fuels the split between illusion and reality while simultaneously filling the gap between the two.

> Celebrity culture plunges us into a moral void. No one has any worth beyond his or her appearance, usefulness, or ability to *succeed.* The highest achievements in a celebrity culture are wealth, sexual conquest, and fame. It does not matter how these are obtained. . . . We have a right, in the cult of the self, to get whatever we desire. We can do anything, even belittle and destroy those around us, including our friends, to make money, to be happy, and to become famous. Once fame and wealth are archived, they become their own justification, their own morality.
>
> (Hedges, 2009, pp. 32–33)

It seems clear that Trump's narcissism and his attacks on political correctness dovetail with deep needs in a significant portion of the American population to enhance their dwindling sense of place in America and of America's place in the world. There is a wound at the core of the American group Self/spirit that is deeply felt by many, especially by those who have not participated in the well-being of our nation's prosperity and by others who are relatively well off but keenly aware that our system of government and our way of life are threatened at the core of our collective being. Here is a working definition of the group Self or spirit that I put forth in an earlier paper:

> The *group spirit* is the ineffable core beliefs or sense of identity that binds people together . . . that [is] known to its members through a sense of belonging, shared essential beliefs, core historical experiences of loss and revelation, deepest yearnings and ideals, . . . One can begin to circle around the nature of a group's spirit by asking questions such as:
> What is most sacred to the group?
> What binds the group's members together?
>
> (Singer, 2006, pp. 9–10)

Here is how Joseph Epstein described the injury to the group Self/spirit of those attracted to Trump:

> Something deeper, I believe, is rumbling behind the astounding support for Mr. Trump, a man who, apart from his large but less than pure

business success, appears otherwise entirely without qualification for the presidency. I had a hint of what might be behind the support for him a few weeks ago when, on one of the major network news shows, I watched a reporter ask a woman at a Trump rally why she was supporting him. A thoroughly respectable-seeming middle-class woman, she replied without hesitation: "*I want my country back*". . . .

I don't believe that this woman is a racist, or that she yearns for immigrants, gays and other minorities to be suppressed, or even that she truly expects to turn back the clock on social change in the U.S. What she wants is precisely what she says: her country back. . . . [S]he couldn't any longer bear to watch the United States on the descent, hostage to progressivist ideas that bring neither contentment nor satisfaction but instead foster a state of perpetual protest and agitation, anger and tumult. So great is the frustration of Americans who do not believe in these progressivist ideas, who see them as ultimately tearing the country apart, that they are ready to turn, in their near hopelessness, to a man of Donald Trump's patently low quality.

(Epstein, 2016)

The Self or group spirit of America is built on more than 300 years of progress, success, achievement, resourcefulness and ingenuity, accompanied by almost endless opportunity and good fortune. We love and believe in our heroic potential, our freedom and independence, our worship of height and speed, youth, newness, technology, our optimism and eternal innocence. We have enjoyed the profound resilience of the American spirit, which has shown itself repeatedly through very difficult historical trials, including our Civil War, World War I, the Great Depression, World War II, the Vietnam War, the 9/11 attacks, the Iraq War, the financial collapse in 2008 and other major crises, including the one we may be in now. As a country, we have been blessed in our capacity to transcend loss, failure and the threat of defeat in the face of crisis time and again, and this has contributed to a positive vision of ourselves that has been fundamentally solid at the core for a long time. Of course, that Self-image is subject to inflation, arrogance and a morphing into *hubris* that believes in our own exceptionalism and is blind to our causing grave injury to peoples at home and abroad. It is quite possible that Trump's personal inflation, arrogance and *hubris* represent a compensatory antidote in our group psyche that is beginning to suffer severe self-doubt about our ability to navigate a highly uncertain future – the nostalgic longing of which is perfectly articulated in the phrase, "*I want my country back.*"

A significant number of people in our society feel cut off from what they believe to be their birth right as American citizens. Although they would not use this language, they are suffering a wound and threat at the level of the group Self, even as they are also suffering individually. We can think of this as a narcissistic injury at the group level. I suggest that Trump has somehow intuited that injury and is playing to it, both as a self-proclaimed carrier of the group renewal and as a defender against those who would do further harm to it – be it terrorists, immigrants, Washington political insiders, the established Republican Party, Barack Obama, Hillary Clinton, James Comey or anyone else who gets in Trump's way.

Trump is at his best when he is at his most awful: his willingness to be politically incorrect became a sign of his "truth-telling" to many. Amid a most dangerous battle between the "alternative facts" of the Alt-right and "Fake News" came an outpouring of the paranoia and hostility embedded in the cultural complex of those who loathe "the deep state." Collective emotion is the only truth that matters. A group caught up in a cultural complex has highly selective memory – if any historical memory at all – and only chooses those historical and contemporary *facts* that validate their pre-existing opinion. Evidence of this is that no matter what Trump does or how many lies he tells, his base remains steadfast in their support of him, as the polls tell us.

This kind of shadow energy is available for exploitation if a group, such as white middle-class Americans in the Rust Belt or coal miners in West Virginia, who previously saw themselves as having a solid place in American society, finds itself marginalized and drifting downward – both socially and economically. How easy it is for them to see recent immigrants to this country as stealing the American dream from them.

Donald Trump uncovered a huge sinkhole of dark, raw emotions in the national psyche for all of us to see. Hatred, envy and fear surfaced in a forgotten, despairing, growing white underclass who had little reason to believe that the future would hold the promise of a brighter, life-affirming purpose. Trump tapped into the negative feelings that many Americans have about all the things we are supposed to be compassionate about – ethnic, racial, colour, gender and religious differences. It would be a huge mistake to underestimate how successfully Trump has mobilized the crude underbelly of long-standing American suspicions of people who are different from themselves. What makes Trump's unleashing of the shadow in the American psyche even more dangerous is that these energies become linked or even identical with what I call *archetypal defences* of the group spirit:

> When this part of the collective psyche is activated, the most primitive psychological forces come alive for the purpose of defending the group and its collective spirit or Self. I capitalize *Self* because I want to make it clear that it is not just the persona or ego identity of the group that is under attack but something at an even deeper level of the collective psyche which one might think of as the spiritual home or *god* of the group. The tribal spirit of the clan or of the nation often lies dormant or in the background, but when it is threatened, the defences mobilized to protect it are ferocious and impersonal. The mobilization of such potent, archaic defences is fuelled by raw collective emotion and rather simplistic, formulaic ideas and/or beliefs [that] dictate how the group will think, feel, react, and behave.
>
> (Singer, 2006, p. 7)

Trump's example gives permission for shadowy thoughts, feelings and actions on behalf of the Self. This underlying group dynamic explains the comparison of Trump to Hitler. Evoking an archaic image of the German Self, Hitler mobilized the most shadowy forces in modern history in the so-called service of that Self-image, which centred on the supremacy of the Aryan race – first the Brownshirts, then the Gestapo, SS and other forces of the Third Reich, including its highly efficient bureaucracy. Trump seems to be toying with the collective shadow, encouraging its acting out in the name of the Self. From a Jungian perspective, when the shadowy defences of the group spirit and the group Self closely align, there is great danger of violence, tyranny and absolutism – especially with an authoritarian leader and a citizenry responsive to authoritarianism.

The third and final component of this intertwined triad of forces in the group psyche is Trump's implicit promise of providing a cure for the wound at the level of the group Self. This is where Trump's narcissism is most prominent and most dangerous. The unconscious equation can be stated as follows: "I am the Greatness to which America may once again aspire. By identifying with how great I am, you can rekindle your wounded American dream and make yourself and America great again."

Or even more bluntly, "I have achieved the American dream; I am the American dream; I am the incarnation of the Self that the country aspires to." This, of course, is a massive inflation. Trump identification of his personal being with the Self of America is his source of demagogic appeal. He is encouraging those who have lost a foothold in the American dream to place their trust in him as a mirror of their own potential – a potential that he has already achieved.

It is almost as if Trump is saying, "My grandiosity is the greatness of America. We can make America great again by following me and then, you, too, can be like me: aggressive, successful, big, powerful." This has tremendous appeal for many. This is the narcissism of Trump joining with the injured narcissism of those Americans who have seen their chances for well-being and security rapidly slipping away. In that sense, Trump is not only speaking for the shadow; he is also speaking for the Self of America – or at least his version of it. His version is the materialistic power version of the American dream – of the big man who has made himself rich and, through his wealth and strength of personality, powerful. He is free to speak his own mind and to pursue, without limits, his own self-aggrandizing goals.

The negative aspects of Trump's narcissism strike those who have been repelled rather than attracted by him as a symbolic mirror of everything negative about America's culture of narcissism. Just as some think that Trump is the embodiment of everything that has made America great in the past and will make us great again, some see Trump as the very embodiment of everything terrible that we have become as a people. Undoubtedly, this is also what many in the rest of the world see as the worst of America.

Ultimately, I believe that the Trump phenomenon is less about Trump than it is about us – about who we are as a people: the elephant in the room turns out to be, "We the People of the United States." How terrifying to think that our politics and our lives today have gotten horribly confused with reality TV, social media, computer and cell-phone technology, and their infinite capacity to turn reality into illusion. The task of all Americans might be identified as bringing to greater consciousness those cultural complexes related to our sense of entitlement, our ferocious consumerism, our addictions to celebrity, constant entertainment and stimulation and our incessant need to dominate the environment.

Cultural complexes, whether expressing themselves in the psyches of individuals or of groups, are potent unconscious contributors to how we think, feel, behave and remember, and to the symbolic images that compel us. The more unconscious our cultural complexes remain, the more powerful they are in directing the course of our individual and collective lives. It is not an exaggeration to say that they are primary forces that will determine our future.

Notes

1 Adapted from Singer, T., & Kaplinsky, C. (2010). Cultural complexes in analysis. In M. Stein (Ed.), *Jungian psychoanalysis: Working in the spirit of C.G. Jung* (pp. 22–37). Chicago, IL: Open Court Publishing Company.
2 Books in the cultural complex series include *Placing Psyche: Cultural Complexes in Australia, Listening to Latin America*, and *Europe's Many Souls*, all published by Spring Journal Books.

References

Epstein, J. (2016). Why Trumpkins want their country back. *Wall Street Journal*. Retrieved June 2010, from www.wsj.com

Hedges, C. (2009). *Empire of illusion: The end of literacy and the triumph of spectacle*. New York, NY: Nation Books.

Henderson, J. (1962/1964). The archetype of culture. In *Der Archetyp*. In A. Guggenbühl-Craig (Ed.), *Proceedings of the 2nd international congress for analytical psychology*. Basel and New York, NY: S. Karger.

Henderson, J. (1984). *Cultural attitudes in psychological perspective*. Toronto: Inner City Books.

Henderson, J. (1990). The cultural unconscious. In *Shadow and self: Selected papers in analytical psychology* (pp. 102–113). Wilmette, IL: Chiron Publications.

Jung, C. G. (1935/1976). The Tavistock lectures. In *The symbolic life, Vol. 18*. In W. McGuire (Ed.), *The collected works of C. G. Jung*. Princeton, NJ: Princeton University Press.

Jung, C. G. (1936/1968). Wotan. In *Civilization in transition, Vol. 10*. In W. McGuire (Ed.), *The collected works of C. G. Jung*. Princeton, NJ: Princeton University Press.

Kaplinsky, C. (2008). Shifting shadows: Shaping dynamics in the cultural unconscious. *Journal of Analytical Psychology*, *53*(2), 189–207. doi:10.1111/j.1468-5922.2008.00716.x

Singer, T. (Ed.). (2000). *The vision thing: Myth, politics and psyche in the world*. London and New York, NY: Routledge.

Singer, T. (2006). Unconscious forces shaping international conflicts: Archetypal defenses of the group spirit from revolutionary America to confrontation in the middle East. *The San Francisco Jung Institute Library Journal*, *25*(4), 6–28.

Singer, T. (2017). Trump and the American collective psyche. In B. Lee (Ed.), *The dangerous case of Donald Trump* (pp. 281–287). New York, NY: Thomas Dunne Books.

Singer, T., & Kaplinsky, C. (2010). Cultural complexes in analysis. In M. Stein (Ed.), *Jungian psychoanalysis: Working in the spirit of C.G. Jung* (pp. 22–37). Chicago, IL: Open Court Publishing Company.

Singer, T., & Kimbles, S. (Eds.). (2004). *The cultural complex: Contemporary Jungian perspectives on psyche and society*. London and New York, NY: Brunner-Routledge.

Chapter 4

The subject in the age of world-formation (*mondialisation*)

Advances in Lacanian theory from the Québec Group

Jeffrey S. Librett

Psychoanalysis can never become either worldly or unworldly enough.

It is under this thesis, whose sense will gradually become clear, that I would like to inscribe the following sketch of innovations that have been developed in Québec City and Montreal in recent years by a Lacanian group called the *Freudian Interdisciplinary Group for Research and Cultural and Clinical Interventions* (*Groupe interdisciplinaire freudien de recherches et d'interventions cliniques et culturelles*), *Gifric* for short, founded in 1970, under the leadership of Willy Apollon (a Haitian philosopher and psychoanalyst), along with Danielle Bergeron (a Quebecois psychiatrist-analyst) and Lucie Cantin (a Quebecois psychologist-analyst). Because Gifric created in 1997 the *Freudian School of Québec* (*L'école freudienne du Québec*), the innovations that are my theme here can also appropriately be associated with this school. The innovations I will discuss turn specifically around the development of an ethno-psychoanalytically informed concept of *world-formation* (in French: *mondialisation*), as a concept for the broad set of changes (including but going far beyond the purely economic realm) that are currently taking place in connection with what we commonly call "globalization." I will be arguing that the introduction of this concept provides perspectives crucially useful to the practice of psychoanalysis today. In connection with the discussion of our current age of world-formation, moreover, I will in what follows circumscribe, within the description of the subject who inhabits this age, the psychoanalytic site of the production of the *new* in general. This site is marked by a certain unworldliness, as it exists outside any given cultural world-construct. So I will speak here about innovation in two ways: first of all, by speaking of new ideas about the age in which we live, insofar as these ideas help us understand the situation and tasks of psychoanalysis today; and secondly, by speaking of where the new, in general, comes from, in the sense of "the new" as a product of human creativity, and of how this site of the emergence of the new is positioned, from a psychoanalytic point of view, within (and yet outside of) the cultural and civilizational context(s) of the current age. I will begin by discussing the concept of *world-formation*, then proceed to examine the structure and place of the *subject* of the *unconscious* in culture and civilization in general.[1] I will subsequently link these two themes in application to an example by considering the more concrete phenomenon of *adolescence* in terms of this model of the psychoanalytic subject as it takes shape in the age of world-formation. Finally, I'll conclude with some remarks on the function of the *aesthetic* dimension in the consideration of adolescence and of the psychoanalytic subject more generally today.

Before beginning, three preliminary remarks are in order concerning the conditions that have enabled the innovative perspectives of Gifric on the subject in the context of contemporary global cultural interactions. First, the Québec group has had the good fortune to find itself in some respects in a marginal and heterogeneous cultural site. It represents the Lacanian orientation in North America – already a kind of contradiction in terms – at a cultural distance from the Parisian center of Lacanian thought and in the province of Québec, a Francophone island in a sea of Anglo-Saxon culture, at once at a cultural distance from the political-cultural center of Canada, and in close proximity to the US, the land of the "ego-psychology" that Lacan so insistently criticized from his earliest work on the imaginary onward (and for persuasive theoretical reasons overdetermined by cultural and ideological ones).

Second, the group has affirmed heterogeneity from the start in both cultural-civilizational and disciplinary terms. The principal analyst-theoretician of Gifric (Apollon) is of Haitian origins, and the Gifric group includes clinicians and scholars from both Europe and the US of diverse civilizational origins, which provides further heterogeneity of viewpoints and subjective experience.[2] And the group has included quite consciously from the start – while preserving its independence from the discourse of the university – scholars in anthropology, sociology, religious studies, political science, and so on, as well as artists and representatives of diverse clinical specialties.

Third, Gifric has focused since the beginning on the analytic (but also interdisciplinary and multimodal) treatment of psychosis. This work has unfolded for the past 35 years around the state-sponsored *388: Center for the Psychoanalytic Treatment of Young Adult Psychotics*, and its results have been elaborated and disseminated in numerous lectures and publications (Apollon, 1999; Apollon, Bergeron, & Cantin, 2008). Because the psychotic subject structure involves the placing in question of the foundations of culture and civilization, the development of the theory and practice of the treatment of psychotics led Apollon and Gifric to articulate a position that could accommodate and respect such a placing in question, i.e. the insights proper to the psychotic structure. This required a psychoanalysis that would situate itself outside of the specifically neurotic recognition of cultural norms and civilizational beliefs. Empirical ethno-analytic study of the kinship structures and family alliances in the families of users of "388" accompanied, moreover, the clinical and theoretical work (Apollon, 1999, pp. 97–150). The elaboration of a new ethno-psychoanalytic model of the position of the subject in general with respect to culture and civilization was the result, which in turn enabled the analysis of the effects of globalization on culture and civilization (and their subjects) that will be the theme of the following remarks.[3]

Globalization and world-formation

To begin with a point concerning at once terminology and translation: discourse in the French language on the phenomenon whose various aspects and manifestations we summarize, in English, under the term "globalization", uses not just this term in its French form – "globalisation" – but also another one, based on the French for "world" – *monde* – which is "mondialisation." The term means something like "world-becoming" or "becoming-world." I am translating it with the somewhat less awkward term, "world-formation," with the proviso or caution that "world-formation" refers here to a historical *process of becoming*, not to a result or structure.[4] The Frenchness of the terminological bifurcation does not make it better, of course, nor worse, than the English usage. But the initial difficulty of communicating between the two cultural traditions and their languages takes us to the very heart of the situation of "globalization" and its attendant "world-formation," the culturally disjointed and enriched character or "nature" of our own times, to which we'll return in a moment. The terminological problem can first be clarified sufficiently in short order. The French term "globalisation" tends to be reserved for the narrower financial, economic, industrial dimensions of the internationalization of the marketplace and scene of production, along with the increasing power of multinational corporations vis-à-vis states. In contrast, "mondialisation" tends to be applied to other aspects of the current shrinking of the world and interpenetration of cultures. In English, we have other linguistic means for the management of these distinctions. The important point here is that in the context of the clinical and scholarly research at Gifric and the Freudian School of Québec that Gifric founded, "world-formation" is understood as a broader process of internationalization that accompanies and follows "globalization," a process that entails significant difficulties but also contains elements that run counter to the neo-liberal form and consequences of the latter: there exists some tension between "globalization" and "world-formation." The Gifric group, under Apollon's leadership (he has been holding public lectures on "Psychoanalysis and World-formation" in Québec City and Montréal since 2010), approaches the question of world-formation with a view to its consequences for the psychoanalytic subject (and vice versa). It takes into account, in addition to the economic sphere, also the changing status of the natural environment, the changing forms of social and cultural structures and values, and the changing contexts and manifestations of subjective drives in our age. On this broad basis, world-formation is regarded as a process for which we are all ethically co-responsible and in which we are presented with both positive possibilities and grave problems and dangers.

Before going into details, let me point out in a preliminary and general manner a few of these possibilities and problems. First, the notion of world-formation implies both plurality of worlds and increasing unification of the world, and both of these aspects have positive and negative sides. On the one hand, there is the interaction, in conflict as well as communication, of separate worlds defined by different civilizations and – within these civilizations – different cultures. On the other hand, we are confronting the (still in many respects distant) possibility of a melding of these worlds into a single global civilization, with all the potential benefits and pitfalls that the latter might entail, both politically and for individual subjects. Secondly, world-formation also involves a certain world-*de*-formation or even world-suspension, however, insofar as the worlds that come together must to some degree come apart – fall apart internally – as they come together. Third, the productively destructive process of this interaction and melding of worlds represents a new and significant turning point in the history of humanity: not merely a particular period within modern or postmodern history but, beyond this, a crucially decisive moment in human evolution. The very existence and essence or meaning of humanity are here at stake. In the following account of some specifics of world-formation, I will draw principally on the work of Apollon, pointing in notes to some of the other contributions of the Gifric group (Savoir, 2016).

For Apollon, the concept of world-becoming or world-formation, as distinct from that of economic globalization, involves eight interacting factors, each of which continues to provoke events.[5] The factors themselves can be indicated very briefly, although some further elaboration would be necessary to explicate them more fully than can be done here. First, there is the enormous problem of *global warming and climate change*. In order to be dealt with successfully, Apollon argues, these problems will require not only technical and political solutions but also changes in the very (self) conception of humanity, namely a rethinking of national sovereignty in relation to a new articulation of human rights with the rights of citizenship within nations. This is the case because global climate change affects us all at once and cannot be solved within any given nation or nation-state. It requires the participation of all nations and states on the earth. Erosion of identification with national identity will necessarily be promoted by these developments (even as, needless to say, this erosion will be – and is being – resisted).[6] Second, partly because of global climate change, we are living in an age of unprecedented displacement of populations, *migrations* that will continue to grow and that will continue to disrupt the structures of particular forms of the social bond as well as value systems within given cultures. Third, *urbanization* of the global population proceeds apace, which further alters the structure of the social bond wherever it occurs, because the heterogeneity of city-dwellers forces them to confront the limits of their regional and national cultures, idioms, and values. This confrontation, as I'll discuss below, has profound implications for individual subjects. Fourth, in connection with these developments (and especially migration), *borders* everywhere are being transgressed and broken, placing in question nation-state sovereignty and cultural purity at the very limits of each state that finds itself incapable of determining its limits. (The fact that there is currently an international backlash against this event, notably in the US and Europe, does not imply that it can be stopped.) Fifth, through the development of digital communications technology – especially the internet, smart phones, and social networking – for media and power elites, as well as consumers, *information is becoming increasingly difficult to control*. This leads obviously not only to the happy result that more and more people have access to all kinds of knowledge, but also to the unhappy result that information can be falsified and the very possibility of true knowledge questioned. Wars of information, including cyberwarfare in increasingly complex forms, assert themselves in such a way as to undermine also from this angle the solidity of the symbolic order and to produce anxiety in new ways on a massive scale. Sixth, as a result again of all of these developments, *cultural points of reference (values, norms, ideals, and prohibitions) become disarticulated*, and our very grasp on reality, as well as our confidence in our capacity to grasp reality, are placed in question in palpable ways. Not simply the symbolic order but also aesthetic dimensions of everyday life that operate on the levels of the imaginary and of affective excess are unsettled by the collisions and collusions of civilizations and cultures. Seventh, in connection especially with the loss of control of information, but in a more hopeful sense (at least for those who support this development), *women are and will be gaining more general access to education and to power*. This unleashes an enormous creative and intellectual and political potential that has been profoundly constrained and excluded from the public institutions within the social bond, even as it questions further many aspects of traditional value systems across the globe, producing resistance and confusion but also a positive movement that is most likely unstoppable. Eighth – and here we come to the properly psychoanalytic aspect – all of these forces, by undermining traditional cultural value-systems – the symbolic and imaginary orders of cultures and civilizations – *liberate and unleash drive energies* that have no pre-given points of orientation in the social bond as hitherto constructed in the given cultures, for both good and ill. These drive energies are what psychoanalysis encounters in the clinic and what it needs to understand in terms of world-formation as circumscribed by the preceding eight factors. In order to be in a position to discuss how these drive energies are related to the natural, cultural, and political factors that are shifting on the level of the collectivity, however, we have to consider first how the structure of the subject is related to culture and civilization in general. In this regard, we need to consider in what sense and on what level the psychoanalytic subject belongs to its world, where and how it remains unworldly, and how world-formation (and its attendant world-*de*-formations) must affect the position of the subject of the unconscious with respect to its world(s).

The subject of the unconscious in the worlds of culture and civilization

As I indicated earlier, while taking as their point of departure the Lacanian oeuvre, especially Lacan's theory of psychosis and his later elaboration of the notion of the real of jouissance, Apollon and his colleagues at Gifric have always been strongly interested in anthropology and ethno-analysis. This interest has been concretized, for example, in their analyses of the kinship system in Québec and more specifically their attempts to track the family systems of the psychotics they have treated at *388: Psychoanalytic Center for the Treatment of Young Adult Psychotics* since its inception, as well as in diverse cross-cultural inquiries on psychoanalytic topics.[7] This interest in the specificity and breadth of the "human" – an anthropological interest in the broadest sense – concerns both the development and the structure of the human. Accordingly, Apollon and his colleagues have worked to develop a structural model of the subject of the unconscious that echoes the developmental history of the human, in a specific new version of the notion that ontogeny recapitulates phylogeny. Here, I will focus primarily on the ontogenetic aspect, providing only brief marginal indications of the phylogenetic aspect.[8]

According to this approach, the human is marked above all by its capacity to create what is radically new, i.e. to experience and to conceive – and subsequently in some cases to construct in reality – what initially has no relation to reality. Such a view of the human has many partial precedents and models, of course, both nonpsychoanalytic and psychoanalytic. The nonpsychoanalytic model I would recall in passing, although it is not one mentioned by Apollon or other Gifric colleagues, is that of late-nineteenth century aestheticism, for which, as Oscar Wilde put it in various texts, nature imitates art, rather than the converse. My point in recalling the generation of Wilde is not to suggest that Gifric is adherent or beholden in general to aestheticist doctrine. Rather, my point is that the hyperbolic and provocative position taken by this doctrine emphasized in its way – and this in the period of Freud's earliest writings – that the specificity of humanity consists in its construction of the radically new, which is not pre-given by nature (whereas empiricism, for example, assumes our ideas come to us from the given world). According to this point of view, the human is naturally (if not wholly) unnatural, naturally artificial. This tenet, in the absence of its other aestheticist trappings, is crucial to Apollon's thought of the subject.

The most notable psychoanalytic points of reference for this approach to the initiation of the human are the Freudian notion of the hallucination and the Lacanian notion of speech, which Apollon displaces and links together in a surprising way. More specifically, he argues that the human adventure begins with the capacity to hallucinate – to create what he calls – also recalling here Kantian vocabulary (where *Vorstellung* – a term likewise crucial to Freud – is the word for "representation") – "pure mental representations" of something not given in perception.[9] Such mental representations, insofar as they do not belong to the "perception-consciousness system" (in Freudian parlance), neither derive from perception (even if they incorporate some material and forms from perception) nor are they perceptible by others.[10] The radical interiority and singularity of these postulated representations – which manifest themselves indirectly in fantasy, symptoms, dreams, creative work, the body, and even the form of a life-trajectory – isolates the individual from the others as it also separates her/him from the immediate environment. At the same time, the production of such mental representations at once inaugurates the still-distant *possibility* of language (which among other things will allow us to share signifiers, or external representations of supposedly shared internal mental representations that remain invisible and unheard) before language appears. Because language cannot emerge – i.e. be invented – in phylogenetic or evolutionary history all at once in a complete form (assuming any language is ever a complete system), evidently it must in some sense anticipate itself. (And on the ontogenetic level, the same goes for the learning of language.) Borrowing the term "parole" (i.e. "speech") from Lacan (who opposed it to "langue" or "language," following Saussure), while connecting it with hallucination, Apollon suggests that this anticipation in mental representation, which entails an attempt to "say" itself, can be thought of as "speech."[11] Language anticipates itself, that is, in hallucinatory experience. This is the case because the experience of the mental representation structurally involves the nascent address to another. In turn, this is the case because the mental representation cannot appear in the "world" except by being addressed to another, and because private experience structurally implies or involves an impulse to be shared insofar as it contains an implicit claim to objectivity, even as it retains a fundamental dimension of the invented. It presents itself to me (before any "me") as what should be there also for the others.

However, to speak to another about an absolutely singular experience in the absence of language is to find oneself radically isolated. In this sense, speech fails until it can find a language in which to articulate itself. And yet equally, speech – at its core an impulse to communicate subjective experience – will encounter a different limit, indeed a different impossibility, even and precisely when it can avail itself of language. For language is a *general* code of reality that establishes a social link or order, whereas speech intends, according to this phenomenology, the absolutely *singular*.[12] Hence, speech remains desire: desire is the desire for speech, and speech is the evocation of desire.

But before considering language, it is crucial to note that the development of the capacity to hallucinate and the impulse to share the hallucination is not just a cognitive event in the narrow sense. Rather, the hallucination, or the creative production of an internal image, is always also, Apollon argues, a libidinal event, or rather the event and eventuality of the libidinal. There are, of course, psychoanalytic precedents on which this thought builds and which it displaces: Freud generally speaks of hallucinations as related to "wishes," which are never unrelated to libidinality, and in the Lacanian register, the libidinal energies are phrased in terms of jouissance in order to emphasize their excessive, unbound character. In the version developed by Apollon and Gifric, the nascent – always nascent – human subject hallucinates within an experience of some sort of affective and bodily excess, whether we understand the excess as leading to the hallucination or as a response to it (for it makes sense to assume it is both). In other words, with the hallucination – or as we might also say in less provocative terms, with human productive imagination – the "drives" are born, insofar as "drives" are radically distinct from "instincts," because drives exist *outside* of the natural world (or as the unnatural in the natural), and they *affect* the organic body in turn, as all kinds of symptoms and acts continually attest. We can also reformulate this by saying that there are two ways of talking about or indicating this earliest specifically human experience, which as such escapes representation in turn: the cognitive vocabulary of "mental representations" and the affective one of "jouissance," the former model operating in terms of a concept of experiences of delimited forms, while the latter operates in terms of a concept of the transgression of all limitation.

On the ontogenetic level, this birth of drives or jouissance in connection with singular mental representations is the core of infantile experience, as on the phylogenetic level it is the core of early human pre-linguistic experience. The event of "speech" in early homo sapiens or in the baby is the impulse towards the creative expression of something new and singular, a free act of inventive discovery or positing that involves a universalizing and therefore a communicative intent. Here, something within the human being diverges from nature (and its pleasure principle), casts itself out beyond nature and beyond the pleasure principle, into the realm of (non-mimetic) mental representations and their attendant jouissance, potentially unbearable impulses towards an indefinable something else.[13] Such hallucinatory jouissance constitutes what will be the unconscious core of human subjectivity once consciousness comes on the scene with the invention (or in the young child, the learning) of language.[14]

Somewhat surprisingly, if also somewhat refreshingly (to my "mind") in a time of perhaps all-too-easy and unthinking reductionistic "materialism," Apollon calls this unconscious core nothing less than "spirit": the human (as) spirit. This makes sense because the singularity of such experience is not directly perceptible as a material existent, even though its effects on the body and in the world can be observed. Terminologically, Apollon opposes this dimension of the *spirit* to the *psyche*, which one might call the animal soul of the human, or the human insofar as it is still an animal, still in a state of nature. In this connection, he argues that the *spirit* radically disrupts the *psyche*, breaking it open onto something radically alien to it, in a (henceforth ongoing) *trauma* of alteration that he calls "the effraction" – the breaking-in or breaking-out of something unnatural in the natural. In line with its traumatic dimension and its relation to the real of jouissance (of the drives), he also characterizes this event as "real castration."

At a later stage of development, both phylogenetically and ontogenetically, language intervenes. Phylogenetically: humanity had invented language by around 50,000 years ago, which enabled it to live in larger groups and to undertake ever more complex collective projects. Between two and three years of age, correspondingly, the child of today internalizes and inserts itself into the system of representations that are sanctioned by the given civilization and culture. Through language, however, the collective works to *limit* the mental representations of the subjects comprising the group and also to limit phantasy to a finite set of situations that are allowably sayable, i.e. to the already-said or to the expressible as what is the already-expressed: convention. Language serves as a kind of conventional "second nature," setting limits on the utterances and acts of the individual spirit, asserting reality (the symbolic order) against the spirit of phantasy that is marginally both within and beyond the psyche. This assertion of the substantivized reality of names is what Apollon, drawing on the Lacanian tradition, calls "symbolic castration." The symbolic order of language and the social link cuts the being off from the real of its inventive spirit. The unconscious (as a level of subjective experience that exceeds language) comes into existence as such insofar as language – which is above all the language of names for things (in some respects akin to what Heidegger calls "das vorstellende Denken" or representational thinking) – comes to determine what we are enabled and allowed to be conscious of.[15] Language determines consciousness in censoring the singular mental representations and the (henceforth) "inchoate" fantasies, which nonetheless continue to register their effects on the level of drives in the body, whose movements they mediate. The Freudian elaborations on "censorship" reappear here, slightly displaced, as the "censorship" exercised by language (which is here conceived as the determining source of the social link) on the dimensions of singular experience.

But given that language, like the social link it founds, is arbitrary (and here the structuralist legacy makes itself felt), language (or the social link) always requires a supplementary guarantee of its meaningfulness and credibility. Belief – or faith – becomes crucial to the world of society in general, because we deal there with social representations, or semblances, which are not only always unfounded (society could always be constructed differently) but also alien and inadequate to the unsayable singularity of experience. More particularly, and with particular importance, belief becomes a necessity in society because society centrally concerns the establishment of exogamous kinship systems that link women from one group to men from another. Paternity, especially, becomes a question of belief. The beliefs of the given civilization (in its cultural concretization) define the frame, Apollon writes, within which pure mental representations are receivable by the collective. Representations or experiences outside that framework are censored but remain at work through the dispersed drives that constitute their wandering habitations in the erotogenic body.

With this question of belief, then, is where cultural – and beyond that, on a higher and later level of organization, broad civilizational – developments of a mythical, political-ideological, and religious character become structurally necessary or useful.[16] Language and the process of the self-reproducing social link build, and henceforth call upon, narrative and symbolic attempts to shore up the authority of some transcendent Other who serves as guarantor of the substantiality of the social order. This Other – chief, god, king, father, leader, etc. – serves, further, not only as the guarantor of the socio-cultural coherence and legitimacy but also as the potential Other of an address (e.g. in prayer, complaint, or poetry). It thereby provides a place – even if an illusory and compensatory one – for the address of "speech" that has been censored through the establishment of the social order. This Other that language establishes as the absolute addressee – who is furthermore concretely mirrored in miniature by each social other who is thought to be created in the Other's image or otherwise to share in his substance – guarantees the limits imposed by language as legitimate and dependable, and vouches for the wholeness and completeness of this language of names that, within the given culture, links the subject to the world. Which helps us to understand what subjective and libidinal chaos is produced when cultural and civilizational coherence begins to unravel, as in world-formation, a point to which we'll return in a moment.

But before coming to the subject in world-formation, it is necessary to consider briefly two further dimensions of cultures, in the narrower and more concretely localized sense, and of the civilizations that operate on a broader, more abstract or general level. First, these collective forms do not institute just mythico-religious narratives (sometimes in a more secularized form – e.g. Enlightenment narratives of progressive emancipation through the advance of rationality and scientifico-technical mastery) of their origins, character, and justifications. They also institute and inculcate the determinations of the guiding limits of thought and behavior through socio-cultural norms, ideals, and prohibitions, as well as of the guiding limits of affect through aesthetic traditions in the broadest sense (comprising forms of beauty and sublimity, arts and crafts of all sorts, and modalities of pleasurable social interaction).[17] The beliefs, behavioral conventions, and aesthetic habituations and contexts of a cultural-civilizational context are mutually interlinked but also mutually relatively autonomous. The result of this relative autonomy is that one dimension can persist for some time even if the others change (for example, a given culture's aesthetic sensibilities can outlive belief in its founding myths), but it will not persist unaltered in its previous form. Indeed, the anxious and even panicky resistances to cultural and civilizational interactions and communication on all levels make it clear that we all know this even when we don't articulate it, ready as we are to defend, at times with our lives, the very structures that sustain repression in the forms that constitute our always alienated group identities.

Second, before coming to some clinical implications of the situation of the subject of culture in the age of world-formation, a word should be said on the position of sex and gender in this ethno-psychoanalytic thinking of Apollon and Gifric. For – needless to say – cultures and civilizations have traditionally applied particular attention to the control of the feminine, and specifically of (the) feminine (as) jouissance, and the forms of this attention are shifting today. According to the approach I am sketching out here, they do this for the precise reason that the effraction of the spirit – which appears from the standpoint of language and consciousness as an "inchoate" flow of unconscious representations and drives – arises in the psyche, since the inception of homo sapiens, initially during the state of dependence of the baby on its mother. Because the state prior to inscription in language is that of in-fancy, because babies seem (to men) to emerge (like pure representations?) out of nowhere, as it were, and yet from within the (consequently "mysterious" or uncanny) bodies of women, and because women (until very recently, in some places) were those who were responsible for the care of babies and indeed for their initial inscription into the language of the "mother tongue," from the standpoint of the languages of culture hitherto, the woman has been strongly associated with this dangerous (but also socially precious and hence religiously "sacred") eruption of the creative potential of humanity that exceeds language, culture, and civilization. The control of women, and by extension of the "feminine," on the part of cultures and civilizations, including all of the manifold aesthetic as well as moral and political elaborations of this control, which extend to what Apollon calls "the cultural montage of sex" (the theories, practices, and images a culture develops to contain the sexual dimension) – all of this works in subordination to the goal of a given culture (and its englobing civilization) to defend itself against the unconscious core of humanity, i.e. the dangerously limitless inventive spirit of the always singular subject. The confinement of the feminine to the maternal and/or to the sexual or the bodily thus functions as a symbolic-imaginary bulwark or border-wall of culture and civilization against the new, i.e. against the creative power of the unnamable that remains threateningly within its own foundation.[18]

The subject in world-formation and the psychoanalytic clinic: listening to the voices of adolescence

If the subject of the unconscious is always situated within a given cultural concretization of a civilization in something like the manner just described, then what happens for such a subject when, in our age of world-formation, the edges of cultures and civilizations start interfering with and disrupting each other to a relatively sudden, extreme, and ever increasing degree? Clearly, it's not just a matter of "not knowing who one is" or "to what culture one belongs," although this ego-uncertainty also broadly exists (if often under the sign of disavowal, especially with the populist right wing). To be sure, innumerable phenomena attest to such an uncertainty, from identitarian self-affirmations (which in the case of oppressed and marginalized minorities obviously have their own validity and pressing importance in terms of justice pure and simple) to the current passion for determining one's genetic "ancestry." But from a psychoanalytic point of view, with the disruption and intermingling of given cultural languages, what is more fundamentally important is that the entire libidinal economy of subjects "world-wide" is unsettled. The containing social forms of sanctioned jouissance, fantasy, and thought are breaking down (and re-forming in new ways), traditional forms of the receivability of pure mental representations can no longer maintain their credibility, and the new generations especially find themselves faced with a personal disarray and lack of faith in traditions that are matched only by their elders' bafflement, extending affectively from consternation to despair, over the unsuspected and incomprehensible rift between the generations. The "disappearance of civility," for example, understandably and broadly bemoaned (if mostly by those above the age of 35 or 40), because it presents an actual obstacle to dialogical negotiation, would be one symptom of these developments, to illustrate the point in a preliminary manner. But it is merely a symptom. In the following, I will restrict myself to a brief discussion of the relevance of the theoretical and historical considerations discussed earlier for the way in which we might listen analytically, in the West but also elsewhere, to the "problems" related to "adolescence." In so doing, I will suggest that the range of extension of adolescence might be, indeed will have to be, unsuspectedly large in the current conjuncture. Here again, I will draw on recent work by the Gifric group, as informed by and informing my own clinical work with adolescents and adults in both agency and private practice settings.[19] I'll consider briefly the subordinate questions of: listening to adolescents per se, listening to adults in their relation to their own experiences of adolescence, the repetition of adolescence in an analytic treatment. I'll close with a few remarks on the aesthetic dimension with respect to adolescence, the analytic trajectory, and the question of humanity in general – anthropology in the broadest sense – in the age of world-formation.

Concerning adolescence in general: Freud spoke in a profoundly insightful manner of this phase as the repetition of infantile sexual experience under the force of the maturation of the body and the maturation of the mental and social development of the individual during puberty. The approach of Gifric adheres to yet also reformulates and extends this thinking in relation to language and culture by stressing that the adolescent re-experiences the upsurge of the unnamable as s/he realizes that the absolute Other – concretely embodied in parental and social-institutional formations of the given culture and civilization – is not just inconsistent (e.g. "hypocritical") but lacking in consistency, porous, fragile, crumbling. At the limit, s/he realizes that the Other is absent and that language is inadequate to the singularity of desire even as it is the vehicle of desire's articulation. The resurgence in adolescence of the quasi-unknowable real in the body, in its conflict with a fragmenting symbolic reality, remobilizes (and alters) the phantasies whose initial constitution proposed or adopted certain forms to account for, and so overcome or manage, the rift between singularity and collectivity. In different ways, male and female youth (and those who find themselves somewhere in between) attempt to negotiate the contradiction between singular jouissance and the available cultural languages in commerce with their peers, friend-groups, gangs, and so on.

But in the contemporary situation, adolescence is complicated and exacerbated by the fact that the very age in which we live is an age of adolescence, because for everyone, i.e. in historical objectivity, the languages of given cultures are coming undone through ineluctable operations of infinite translation. (Not to mention that the apocalypticism of adolescence is supported in us all by the prospect of climate disaster.) The contradiction of singular subjectivity with a given concrete cultural universality – and with repressive and ideological state apparatuses, for example, to use the language of Louis Althusser – is doubled and contradicted in turn by the contradiction between any given social, cultural, and civilizational order, on the one hand, and its virtual absence or suspension, its immediate relativization, on the other hand. Repression is uncannily present and absent, and the adolescent finds himself or herself under the necessity to rebel, for example, against an authority-figure who, by virtue of the process of world-formation, seems at once not only the representative of superannuated values but also himself or herself an adolescent in turn. This creates confusing situations and symptomatic manifestations for all involved, which it is incumbent on analysts to listen for and be able to track and unravel.

Beyond this, however, the advance of multicultural coupling means that it is increasingly normative for analysands to be of mixed culture, in part from civilizations beyond the limits of the "West," meaning first of all that analysts will need increasingly to divorce themselves in their analytic work from presuppositions and values that are culturally bound (as they are in principle required to do in any case). Beyond this, however, with regard to the treatment of adolescents, one would have to listen for the clash of different systems of norms, ideals, prohibitions, beliefs, and aesthetic sensibilities within a given subject. One would do so not primarily with a view to "identity"-integration but in order to discern there the concomitant clash of fantasies, modalities of feeling, and manifestations of the experience of overwhelming excess. To be composed of two systems of censorship is to be composed of two different forms of the unconscious: to be able to say or realize from one side what is silently forbidden to one from the other, and so on. And given world-formation, it is also to wrestle with the at least partial failure or disintegration of two systems of censorship at once, as well as the suspended animation of two sets of incompatible or at any rate divergent ideals and norms. Finally, it is to be at odds with one's feelings in every case. Or rather, and ultimately, it is to be confronted with the task of mediating between and exceeding these models in terms of one's experience, on the level of the jouissance at work in the body, and the fantasies that enact this in particular ways. The Oedipal overdeterminations of such cultural differences within the individual adolescent will always constitute an attempt (by the parents, by the ego, and by the society) to articulate these differences together into a seamless narrative – some individual myth – but it is beyond the limits of the narrative (or in its hidden interior) that one must look for the singular jouissance that is at stake there, which needs to invent (paradoxically) a "language" of its own within the social languages, such as they are.

Concerning the analytic treatment of adults in the age of world-formation, the reconsideration of the analysand's traversal of adolescence gains new importance, if only because the current conjuncture is structurally different from what it was 20 or 30 years ago, never mind 40 or 50 years ago, even if world-formation does not emerge all at once on the historical scene. Thus the solutions to the problem of the articulation of singularity with cultural generality that the analysand constructed in her or his own previous *Bildungsroman* are no longer adequate or functional to the degree that they may have been earlier. After all, some crisis has brought the person in for treatment, indicating that the seduction-narrative re-fashioned by the ego in the adolescent repetition of the pre-Oedipal and Oedipal years is no longer functioning to the person's satisfaction. The crisis, whatever it was, has brought the analysand face to face again with the question of how they can articulate some singular desire and vision or sensibility with a socio-cultural surround that feels both as if, because it is so solid and opaque, it closes them out, and as if, because it is so hard to grasp, it gives them nothing with which to connect, or no foundation on which to stand. In this situation, revisitation of the adolescence becomes particularly pressing, and productive, even if it tends to be magnetized by the ego's narrative of self-justification, to the degree that it can also give way to the subject's renewed search for the original forms of its desire and for the possible forms of its (always paradoxical) articulation with the social link in the present and future.

But beyond the revivification of the ghost of adolescence past (and so also of infancy) through narrative reconstruction and both voluntary and involuntary memory, there is a specific phase in an analysis, as conceived by the Gifric group and the Freudian School of Québec, where it re-enacts or re-experiences something closely akin to the adolescent situation more radically in the present. Without detailing the trajectory of an analysis as conceived by this group, one can say that, beyond a certain exhaustion of the ego-narrative and its will to self-justification, and beyond even the exploitation of the resources of dreams for the (re)constitution of the signifiers that structure the analysand's unconscious, the private language of symbols through which it situates its jouissance and holds it at an internal distance, the analysand will begin to come to terms more radically with its solitude and with the lack of the Other, i.e. the inadequacy of the social order as such to what it has to say. Apollon and the Gifric group have called this phase in analysis the "traversal of castration" (a trope on the more orthodox Lacanian notion of the "traversal of the fantasy"), because in this phase one is assuming, processing, and seeking new ways of dealing with the double trauma of both real and symbolic castration, i.e. the unsettlement of the homeostasis of the organism by the drives and the (always partially failed) capture of the drives in the networks of language, and reckoning in new ways with the fantasies through which one has attempted to come to terms with this double trauma.[20] This phase – which requires of the analysand the development of a new ethics and a new aesthetics beyond those received from the Other of the surrounding culture (because the received morals and aesthetic strictures have fallen into a state of inner desubstantialization and desuetude) – replays and replaces the never fully completed adolescence from the past. In the age of world-formation, where adolescence is becoming ever more complex – think, for one small example, of all the difficulties of "launching" in the US family today – this phase of an analysis becomes more important than ever before, if no more assured of success in advance.

(Un)worldliness and the aesthetic dimension

Finally, concerning the dimension of the aesthetic – which includes but is not exhausted by the production or reception of works of art – from a psychoanalytic point of view, one can perhaps begin to see at this point its importance especially for the later phases of analysis, as also for the stakes of adolescence in the age of world-formation. Whether in adolescence or in the later stages of an analysis, the renewed experience of the incompatibility of the absolute singularity of the unconscious (turning around jouissance in the body and mental representations that have nothing to do with reality or pleasure), on the one hand, and the given cultural-civilizational languages (which always imply a certain universality, a specific but universalized view of the position of the human in its "world"), on the other hand, raises the question of how the one is to be articulated with the other. This question is displaced and complicated in the age of world-formation to the degree that the repressive force of any given social link is at once maintained and diminished – dispersed – leaving the ego both less exiled from jouissance and less protected against its ecstatic ravages, more disoriented than before amidst the storms, for example, of potentially senseless, deceptive, or useless information. How does the aesthetic realm relate to this question?

Even if the aesthetic sphere is partially absorbed into (or determined by) cultural-civilizational languages, in modernity (at least according to aesthetic theory since the eighteenth century), it has been most generally conceived as the space of mediation between feeling and thought, imagination and understanding, concrete singularity and abstract universality, or subject and culture.[21] Moreover, modern notions of the aesthetic involve innovation and distance from the social status quo, not just in *l'art pour l'art* but even in engaged art (above all in Marxist aesthetics), which claims to intervene in and alter the societies it critically depicts. Thus the aesthetic would be a dimension of civilization-culture where the latter (in the sense developed earlier) opens to its outside and where the outside presses in on it. The aesthetic realm exists marginally outside meaning, indeed at the intersection of "sense" as "meaning" and "sense" as "sensuality" or "the body," and so always escapes to some extent the constructions of the meaning of beliefs and the belief in meanings to the sustaining of which a given civilization applies itself. The vaunted universality of music and art, even if perhaps open to criticism, evidently has some plausibility by contrast with the stark cultural and civilizational divisions that are induced by beliefs, norms, ideals, and prohibitions. If we cannot argue over taste, as the saying goes, then evidently taste is not that easy to nail down in terms of specific civilizational-cultural norms, even though these norms continue to be developed and applied.

Drawing on these determinations, we can see how the aesthetic sphere is well-suited as the evocative realm of the mediation between the subject and cultural convention, and all the more so in a world that is in the process of becoming "one" world beyond the civilizational and cultural divisions we still inherit. In this spirit, Apollon and the Gifric group have emphasized in recent years the importance of aesthesis both to the crisis of adolescence and to the analytic process, both of which increasingly need to culminate in a wider access to the realm of the human as such. Again in accord with the thinking of modern philosophical aesthetics, while inflecting this thinking in an analytic direction, the Gifric group has associated beauty with the feminine, sublimity with the masculine, but they have invoked these gender categories in a nonessentialist manner and under the heading of something like an androgynous conception of the human (as indeed was already the case in Friedrich Schiller's "On Grace and Dignity," for example), a displaced version of Freud's constitutional bisexuality. How do these two dimensions of the aesthetic sensibility differ and interrelate?

Departing in "letter" but not, I think, overmuch from the "spirit" of the other writings of the Gifric group (nor from that of the modern Western tradition of philosophical aesthetics, which – let us note in passing – is itself also exposed to the effects of world-formation), I would suggest briefly the following construal. The logic of the beautiful and the sublime is in each case the logic of a paradoxical (and partial) synthesis of the contradiction. In the case of the beautiful, one says, in effect: *the singular is the universal*. This means – and one should think here of the aesthetics of the "symbol" specifically – that the singular contains the whole in the mode of a concrete universal.[22] The beautiful is the subjective experience that the singular contains all other singularities within itself, and it emphasizes the felt experience that we share in a commonality, the affective experience of the harmony that stands out against the dissonance. In the case of the sublime, one says, conversely, *the universal is the singular*. This means here: the singular – the unsayable, or what cannot be directly shared, is what we share. That is, we share that we cannot share directly what we have to say, each one's singular experience of (and as) something nonrepresentable.[23] Such an experience emphasizes the dissonance of harmony or dissonance against the background of harmony. It emphasizes "allegory," as opposed to "symbol," because it stresses that the representation is always distinct from the represented.[24] And in a certain sense, as the Gifric group suggests, the sublime experience aims at the human as such because the human appears for such a sensibility ultimately as the experience of the rift between speech and language. The human is the shared distance from being able to share the truth of subjectivity as such.[25] On such a conception, to invoke an image that was dear to Lacan, the aesthetic space as comprised of the beautiful and sublime would be like a Moebius strip. Since the two sensibilities constitute two aspects of the same (impossible) mediation, the one always leads into the other, even as they remain opposed.

To return in conclusion to the clinic, and to the world(s) of our (also worldless) lives, these sensibilities are not reserved to artists per se, nor to those who have the opportunity to do a long analysis, nor to adolescents.

They structure the creative endeavors of people in the widest possible range of specific activities and undertakings, great and small. We find them in work at a social services agency (where in fact many clients are direct economic victims of economic globalization) every bit as much as in the work with a more well-healed and post-secondary-educated clientele. From the retired roofer, disabled through injury, a self-professed "redneck" who struggles to do right by his transgendered son and looks back nostalgically upon the days when he worked with loving intensity to make the tiles sit right, and who is in search of new ways to signify a singular exposure to the lack of protection; to the conservative Christian, regionally displaced from his home and in physical ill-health, who wants nothing so much as to have his own place to live precisely so he can set up his sewing machine and get going again; to the intellectually sophisticated artist and poet who, having in a crisis lost his bearings and become homeless and alone, is struggling to get back to that work, but only in case it would somehow serve humanity; to the middle-aged woman who numbs reverberations of trauma with alcohol while splendidly and over-generously serving others but finds a place and rhythm for herself in doing crafts projects for her children and grandchildren; to the young man of mixed French and American descent who struggles to make sense of that dual heritage and finds his most ecstatic solace in making music: we find these beautiful and sublime sensibilities everywhere in our practices and everyday lives, and can see the importance of the aesthetic realm to the survival of humans as subjects amongst objects in the age of world-formation. Aesthesis is here the space for the unworldly work of the unconscious in the world(s) of the becoming of the human. In attending to this dimension, as to the others discussed earlier, psychoanalysis can never be too (un)worldly.

Notes

1 It would be importantly useful in a more detailed textual and historical study to mark the distance from Freud's conception of the "world," which he experienced in the phase of international modernism, to the "world" of globalization and world-formation and to consider the distance between the social link and its repressive functioning in Vienna of the early twentieth century and the social link today (in diverse regions), but such examinations far exceed the scope of the current essay.
2 For his writings on Haitian cultural-political topics, see especially Apollon, 1976, 1997.

3 On ethno-psychoanalysis from the standpoint of Gifric, see Apollon, 2018. For examples of earlier, non-Lacanian sources, see Devereux, 1978; Róheim, 1950. For a recent Lacanian sketch of a possible articulation of psychoanalysis with anthropology not associated with the Gifric group, see Kodre, 2011.
4 In Nancy, 2007, the translators use "world-forming" for the most part to translate "mondialisation," and I attach myself to them metonymically here, replacing "forming" with "formation" because the gerundive form of "forming" fits with the Heideggerian idiom Nancy in many respects appropriates, whereas the awkwardness of the gerund has no justification in the Lacanian context of the work I am presenting and disseminating here.
5 I draw here on Apollon's article, "Citoyen du monde, . . . mais de quelle nationalité?" in Savoir, 2016, pp. 205–274.
6 The situation is rendered more complex by the fact that defenses of national sovereignty appear currently to be possible only in right-wing terms, whereas left-wing concerns about national popular sovereignty remain largely silent. See Savoir, 2016, pp. 251–265.
7 See Lacan, 1966; Apollon, 1997, 1999.
8 I draw in this section on Apollon, 2017, 2018.
9 Drawing on current anthropological studies, Apollon assumes the beginning of human radical interiority occurs approximately 300,000 years ago.
10 In addition to aestheticism, the background of rationalism (as opposed to empiricism) so important to the French tradition, and to Lacan, is palpable here.
11 Apollon refers explicitly here to the human being as the "parlêtre," the "being-who-speaks," alluding to Lacan's later development of this term. For a discussion of this term in its specifically Lacanian implications, see Miller, 2014.
12 Cf. the striking analysis of the incompatibility of singular speech with (the universalizing tendencies of) language in *The Phenomenology of Spirit* (Hegel, 1970, pp. 82–92).
13 Cf. Kleinian articulations of the appearance of the death-drive in the infant. Apollon, 2017, p. 54, describes this infantile experience of what will not be available to language, for example, as follows: "A set of lived experiences that will have marked the being since its early infancy, even before its entrance into language, will inscribe itself in it, definitively affecting its body, such as danger, apprehension, immense joy, terror, disappointed expectations, forbidden ecstasies [*jouissances*], maddening surprises, etc., . . . there are no words for such experiences in the culture in which the being evolves."
14 Language is thought to emerge approximately 50,000 years ago.
15 This determination of the unconscious as what is radically outside of language follows Freud in "The Ego and the Id" and elsewhere.
16 Cf. Raymond Lemieux, "Dans l'œil du cyclone: religion et politique dans la mondialisation," in Savoir, 2016, pp. 19–44.
17 In elaborations that I will not detail here, Apollon understands the control of the aesthetic dimension by a given civilization as an "affective formatting" that delimits the space in which the individual spirit can operate, linking that space to the system of sanctioned beliefs. (For example, aesthetic traditions in a Christian civilization are different from those in a given Muslim

civilization, etc.) In each case, however, the action of the singular spirit, which disrupts the organism, remains to some degree at odds with the cultural and civilizational "formatting" of the affective-aesthetic domain, operating "beyond the pleasure principle" in the sense that it functions without concern for the adaptation of the organism to the cultural-civilizational environment. The subject of the unconscious (as distinct from the ego) is never quite at home within a culturally-civilizationally given aesthetic space. Because the spirit of the hallucination is at odds with the cultural and civilizational "formatting" of the aesthetic, in turn, the aesthetic sphere is a privileged site for the creative articulation of the subject with its social surround, and thence with humanity in general.

18 See the interview-dialogue between representatives of Gifric and Lise Payette and Martine Desjardins, feminist activists, political actors, and political commentators in the province of Québec, titled "Féministes, à l'heure de la mondialisation" in Savoir, 2016, pp. 275–320. See also the essays by diverse authors in Cantin, 1995.

19 See in Morin & Cantin, 2017: W. Apollon, "Adolescence, Masculine and Feminine," pp. 47–56; D. Bergeron, "Adolescence, the Moment to Center Everything on Humanity Despite the Siren-Song Lure of the Sexual Montage," pp. 57–64; and L. Cantin, "The Hold of Cultural Constructs: a Mortgage on the Future of Desire," pp. 65–74.

20 For essays on this phase of an analysis, see in Morin & Cantin, 2017: N. Jean, "Il n'est jamais trop tard pour arrêter d'étouffer," 5–10; L. Rouleau, " 'Je parle à un fauteuil vide," pp. 11–16; D. Bergeron, "Castration: un futur pour les énergies de la deuxième mort et le passage au troisième temps," pp. 17–22; L. Cantin, "L'absence de l'Autre, le sujet de la pulsion et sa quête intraitable," pp. 23–30; and W. Apollon, "Castration et transfert," pp. 31–42. See also Apollon, 2006.

21 The central tradition to which I am referring extends from Kant's *Critique of Judgment* through Schiller's aesthetic writings, and thence through German Idealism in Schelling and Hegel into post-Hegelian modernity.

22 Cf. the interview with Robert Lepage, an internationally recognized multidisciplinary artist (in Savoir, 2016, pp. 321–359), who seems to adopt such an aesthetic approach, following Michel Tremblay, when he asserts, "plus on est local, plus on est universel" [the more local one is, the more universal] (323). Such an attitude reflects what Kant called, in the *Critique of Judgment*, the "subjective necessity" of the experience of the beautiful.

23 Jean-Luc Nancy, a philosopher who has also devoted much attention to the aesthetics of the sublime, articulates such a position in his development of the concept of "community" as "the community of those who have no community," in Nancy, 1991.

24 For the important distinction between symbol and allegory from romanticism to modernism, see de Man, 1983.

25 In an insightfully nuanced essay, "La rupture du sujet et l'institution dans la mondialisation" (in Savoir, 2016, pp. 131–156), Yvan Simonis captures something of this spirit of the sublime in his emphasis on figures of negativity (the "no" and the "void") as figures of the site of the birth of the subject insofar as

that birth requires an interruption of any relation to the Other (in the sense of the latter as transcendent guarantor of the substantiality of the social link).

References

Apollon, W. (1976). *Le vaudou: Un espace pour les "voix"*. Paris: Éditions galilée.

Apollon, W. (1997). *L'universel, perspectives psychanalytiques: Conférences et écrits*. Québec: GIFRIC.

Apollon, W. (1999). *Psychoses: L'offre de l'analyste: Conférences et écrits*. Québec: GIFRIC.

Apollon, W. (2006). The untreatable (S. Miller, Trans.). *Umbr(a): Incurable, 1,* 23–39.

Apollon, W. (2017). *Le sujet de la quête*. Unpublished manuscript of lecture given in 2017 in Toronto.

Apollon, W. (2018). L'ethnopsychiatrie entre civilisations et mondialisation. Hier encore . . . c'était l'ethnopsychiatrie. In J-J. Ronald & Y. Lecomte (Eds.), *Ethnopsychiatrie en Haïti* (pp. 45–64). Port-au-Prince: Collection revue haïtienne de santé mentale.

Apollon, W., Bergeron, D., & Cantin, L. (2008). *La cure psychanalytique du psychotique. Enjeux et stratégies*. Québec: GIFRIC.

Cantin, L. (1995). La féminité [Special issue]. *Savoir: Psychanalyse et analyse culturelle, 2*(1–2).

De Man, P. (1983). The rhetoric of temporality. In P. de Man (Ed.), *Blindness and insight: Essays in the rhetoric of contemporary criticism* (pp. 187–228). Minneapolis: University of Minnesota Press.

Devereux, G. (1978). *Ethnopsychoanalysis: Psychoanalysis and anthropology as complementary frames of reference*. Berkeley, CA: University of California Press.

Hegel, G. W. F. (1970). *Phänomenologie des Geistes*. Frankfurt am Main: Suhrkamp.

Kodre, L. (2011). Psychoanalysis for anthropology: An introduction to Lacanian anthropology. *Anthropological Notebooks, 17*(1), 53–72.

Lacan, J. (1966). On a question prior to any possible treatment of psychosis. In J. Lacan (Ed.), B. Fink (Trans.), *Écrits* (pp. 445–488). New York, NY: W. W. Norton & Co.

Miller, J-A. (2014). *The unconscious and the speaking body (L'inconscient et le corps parlant)*. Retrieved from www.lacan.com/actuality/2014/07/lecture-by-jacques-alain-miller-paris-41514/.

Morin, D., & Cantin, L. (Eds.). (2017). Enseignements des analystes de l'école [Special issue]. *Correspondences, courrier de l'École freudienne du Québec, 17*(2).

Nancy, J-L. (1991). *The inoperative community* (P. Connor, L. Garbus, M. Holland, & S. Sawhney, Trans.). Minneapolis: University of Minnesota Press.

Nancy, J-L. (2007). *The creation of the world, or globalization* (F. Raffoul & D. Pettigrew, Trans.). Albany: SUNY Press.

Róheim, G. (1950). *Psychoanalysis and anthropology: Culture, personality and the unconscious*. New York, NY: International Universities Press.

Savoir: Psychanalyse et Analyse Culturelle. (2016). *Mondialisation, défis pour l'humain*. Québec: GIFRIC.

Chapter 5

Existential psychoanalysis
The role of freedom in the clinical encounter

M. Guy Thompson

My goal in this chapter is to explore the existential dimension to psychoanalysis and to show how this has been latent in psychoanalysis since Freud, yet never incorporated into psychoanalytic theory and practice explicitly. Indeed, many of the elements of contemporary relational psychoanalysis owe a considerable degree of its so-called innovations to the existential tradition, though these are frequently deemed "postmodern," a philosophical movement that is generally hostile to the existential perspective. The result of this convoluted state of affairs is that what is and is not innovative in contemporary psychoanalysis is both old and new: old in the sense that it has been around for a long time, and new in the sense that it is rearing its head again after having been suppressed in the 1980s, the same decade that the relational and postmodern perspectives flowered.

There is no question that the postmodern turn in contemporary culture has changed the way we look at the relationship between psychoanalytic practitioners and their patients. The so-called classical method of conducting analysis, epitomized by Melanie Klein and ego psychology, occasions an authoritative approach that effectively indoctrinates patients into another way of seeing the world. Success is measured by the degree to which the patient adopts the analyst's perspective. Failure is typically placed at the doorstep of the patient's resistance to this process. Alternately, the postmodern turn is epitomized by a radical deconstruction of the analyst's authority and views the analytic process as a dialogue between two equals, neither of whom is presumed to know the truth. Instead of indoctrinating patients into the analyst's worldview, the analyst's task is seen as one of helping patients to determine *their* worldview and, having acquainted themselves with it, to help make it work.

Yet this is no easy matter to accomplish. Try as we may, it is only human nature to wed ourselves to a judgment on the matter: what, for example, is the matter with my patient, and how can I best get this patient to change his or her current manner of being into the one I deem preferable? Even relational psychoanalysts are prone to indoctrinating their patients into a manner of behaving that the analyst is convinced is more healthy, more engaged, more "relational." We are often left wondering, what happened to the patient's freedom and their right to simply be – by becoming – themselves?

Despite the often hostile relationship between the existential and postmodern traditions, I believe there is considerable overlap between them. I have explored this issue previously in a study on postmodernism and psychoanalysis (Thompson, 2004) where I compared and contrasted the existential and postmodern elements in Nietzsche, so I won't repeat them here. What I want to show in the following is how the existential approach to the problem of freedom, most explicitly delineated in the philosophy of Jean-Paul Sartre, has been both implicit and repressed in the psychoanalytic lexicon since Freud, and that once we take note of its efficacy, we cannot help but recognize that this is where the postmodern turn was always trying to take us. The turn to postmodernism has finally made it possible to realize that all our patients ever wanted was to become the person they already are by finally abandoning the notion that we can better ourselves by becoming someone else. This task, I argue, is best effected by placing freedom front and center, thereby rendering the analytic enterprise into a truly *existential* psychoanalysis.

What, then, is "existential psychoanalysis," and how should one go about distinguishing it from other conceptualizations of psychoanalysis that are not blatantly existential? Moreover, myriad approaches to existential therapy are not expressly psychoanalytic and may even be opposed to the psychodynamic perspective. The existential sensibility is an inherently personal one, which is to say, its point of departure is the *person* of the practitioner administering the treatment. In order to illustrate this point, I will draw from my own journey of becoming an existentialist as well as a psychoanalytic practitioner.

It is perhaps ironic that relational psychoanalysis, which draws so many of its ideas from the existential perspective – including the concept of intersubjectivity, the emphasis on the personal dimension of the analytic dyad, and privileging authenticity – singularly ignores its roots in existential philosophy. It has, as it were, slipped in through the bathroom window, keeping its philosophical sources closeted. That isn't to say that relational psychoanalysis is existential psychoanalysis by another term. Yet what I characterize as existential psychoanalysis has, if only indirectly, exercised a profound impact on contemporary American psychoanalysis.

Because existential psychoanalysis is a hybrid of two independent disciplines – existential philosophy and psychoanalysis – its conceptualization and especially its application are not so easy to articulate. First and foremost, I regard Sigmund Freud an existentialist. I know this sounds absurd. After all, existential practitioners as well as relational analysts typically rail against Freud, that Cartesian simpleton that initiated a clever idea hopelessly housed in a convoluted theory that was ever-changing and obscure, yet too scientific and authoritarian to plumb the depths of the human condition. I won't get into all the crimes against humanity that Freud allegedly committed, but it is difficult to deny that he has become the prototypical straw man against whom many analysts feel free to enunciate their position. To go against Freud is a badge of honor, suggesting one has wrested free of orthodoxy and blazed one's own singular path. I don't see Freud that way. I see him instead as a radical, a genius whose take on the human condition was so deep yet unpalatable that the culture he so wanted to enlighten perceived in him the devil incarnate, a sexually obsessed Jew who had obviously lost his mind, a danger to society.[1] That sentiment is still with us today. I actually agree with that assessment, the part that sees Freud as a danger. He was, and still is, a danger to conventional mores and likely always will be. Isn't this psychoanalysis at its best, to get us to look at our own prejudices with fresh eyes, that should unsettle us to the core?

So why such hostility to Freud? I would argue for the same reason there is similar hostility to the existentialists, especially Sartre, Heidegger, and Nietzsche, the three existentialists closest to Freud in temperament. Freud was an existentialist because he came out of the same stew as his existential brethren, with the same agenda: to get people to look at their hypocrisy and to free themselves of their repressions. Freud's take on the human condition was born from the same European, post-World War I existential perspective that is anathema to the typical American mind-set. Whereas in the United States psychoanalysis was enthusiastically embraced as a tool of psychiatry in its never-ending war on "mental illness," in Vienna and other European capitals such as Berlin, Paris, and London, psychoanalysis was marginalized by psychiatry and became a refuge for artists, writers, and intellectuals – and anyone wealthy enough to pay for a six-times-a-week analysis. Many of Freud's patients came to see analysis as a means of facing the harsh realities of living instead of a device for the relief of their symptoms. Of all the existential philosophers, Sartre got this. He recognized that Freud, like himself, was a trouble-maker and that his original method was destined to change the world, and it has. Because the term "existential psychoanalysis" was coined by Sartre, it would be irresponsible of me to explore what it means without reference to Sartre himself and his ideas. This is why my critique of existential psychoanalysis, a hybrid of Freud and Sartre, is essentially an homage to Sartre's take on Freud and his efforts to radicalize it even further than Freud himself was able to.

My relationship with existential philosophy and psychoanalysis is both complex and idiosyncratic. It begins with Sartre, who I discovered in my teens, the perfect age, looking back, to make his acquaintance. As it happens, I grew up in Cuba in the 1950s, where my father, an American entrepreneur and chemical engineer, became friends with Ernest Hemingway, among the few American expatriates living on the island. I was fond of Hemingway, and remember his mentioning his friend, Sartre, who was about to visit Cuba with Simone de Beauvoir after Castro seized power (this was in early 1960). Hemingway thought that Sartre was a shit, the epitome of the French intellectual that Hemingway got to know when living in Paris during the 1920s. But he admired Sartre's writing, as well as his celebrity, and most of all he admired his success. Though Sartre was not awarded the Nobel Prize for literature until after Hemingway's death, which Hemingway won in 1954, they were bonded by Hemingway's impact on French writing, especially Sartre's, and their mutual admiration. They were both non-conformists, and they each insisted that the only way to live is authentically, no matter the cost. One of the things I admired most about Hemingway was that he knew how to live! He loved the life he was living and treated it as an adventure. Hemingway and Sartre were, as my Irish grandmother once told me, a pair to draw to.

I was too young to read Sartre then, but a few years later, after my family had abandoned Cuba for their native Tennessee, I checked him out. Sartre introduced me to existential philosophy, and it became a sort of religion for me. This was also around the time I discovered Sigmund Freud, and I soon arrived at the novel conclusion that Sartre and Freud were saying the same thing but in different languages. In the years that followed, I managed to get through Sartre's early philosophical works, but it was the section devoted to existential psychoanalysis in *Being and Nothingness*

(1943[1954]) that riveted my attention. By the time I graduated from high school, I had decided I was going to become an existential psychoanalyst – whatever that was.

Life has a funny way of throwing us a curve now and then. Without warning, Tennessee drafted me into the Army and sent me to Vietnam in the summer of 1966. Like many of my compatriots there, I was convinced I was sent there to die. I was lucky, however, to be assigned to an intelligence unit in Saigon, and this afforded me the luxury to read in my off time. I dove into Sartre and Nietzsche. They taught me that we are always dying, that the closer we get to death, the more precious life becomes. I think Sartre in particular helped me live my death and survive it, and for that I will always be in his debt.

After I separated from the Army in 1970, I moved to San Francisco to study psychology. That was when I discovered R. D. Laing, the Scottish psychiatrist and existential psychoanalyst. By this time, Laing was the most famous psychiatrist in the world due to his bestselling books (1960[1969], 1967) and his groundbreaking work with schizophrenia. I was soon on my way to London, having abandoned my graduate studies, in order to work with this charismatic figure.

Like me, Laing was passionate about Sartre. One may even read Laing's classic, *The Divided Self* (1960[1969]), as an integration of Sartre's philosophy and object relations theory. This was unusual. Nearly all the psychiatrists who were drawn to existential philosophy after World War II embraced Heidegger (1962), not Sartre. Perhaps this was because so many of them were German-speaking psychiatrists or because they were captivated by Heidegger's impenetrable prose. Or they may have been put off by Sartre, the bad boy of existential philosophy. Perhaps worst of all, Sartre was a Frenchman!

I think what bonded me to Laing was that we had both discovered Sartre in our youth, in the throes of rebelliousness, and were each drawn to his contempt for everything *bourgeois* and conventional. This attitude is not typical of people who choose to enter the so-called mental health professions. As a class, I would characterize my colleagues as unremittingly conventional, uncommonly anxious, and too preoccupied with their status. This may sound harsh, perhaps petty, yet some of my best friends are psychoanalysts. Really. Yet this is the kind of observation that Sartre inspired, perhaps the reason why few of my colleagues gravitated to him.

Freud, too, was a bad boy, a trouble-maker, obsessed with sex. This was probably what drew me to him as a teenager. Sartre and Freud: *another* pair to draw to. So here I am, in the company of the three bad boys of the twentieth-century *avant-garde*: Sartre, Laing, and Freud. I was in heaven.

So what is the relation between Sartre and psychoanalysis? In order to address this question, I focus on how Sartre's philosophy provided the tools to transform psychoanalysis into a truly human, which is to say, inherently personal way of conceptualizing clinical practice. In order to do this, I explore three topics that are basic to understanding the analytic process. The first concerns Freud's conception of the unconscious. The second is Sartre's critique of the emotions and their role in psychopathology. And third, what do we understand by the notion of freedom, and how does it inform the nature of psychic change?

Freud's conception of psychic reality

Let us begin with Freud's concept of the unconscious and the problems this concept continues to engender. Freud's (1910) first topography for demarcating a distinction between conscious and unconscious aspects of the mind concerned the nature of fantasy and the role it plays in neurosis. After he experimented with hypnotism, Freud surmised that each person is preoccupied with two kinds of fantasies: one I am aware of and the other I am not. Freud opted to label those that I am not aware of "unconscious," because we have no reflective experience of them. These so-called unconscious fantasies have been repressed, but because they still reside "in" the unconscious, they engender psychic conflict, which results in our dream life as well as our psychopathology.

Freud's first, topographical, model of the unconscious was simple: one portion of the mind is conscious and the thoughts it contains are in the forefront of awareness (or *reflective experience*), whereas another portion of the mind is unconscious and composed of fantasies that are inaccessible to conscious awareness. Freud also included a third element in this topography, the "preconscious," which contains unconscious thoughts and memories that can be recollected at will. Freud's topographical model served as a map of what he terms "psychic reality." Freud's notion of psychic reality is contrasted with *factual* reality, which is investigated by the empirical sciences and readily available for study.

Yet, in what sense can one treat fantasies as "realities" when, after all, they are not *real*? Freud recognized that fantasies can be *experienced* as real in a similar way that objective reality is experienced. In other words, fantasies, though not literal depictions of the past, nevertheless convey meaning, and such meanings are capable of telling us more about our patients than the so-called facts of their history. By *interpreting* both fantasies and their consequent symptoms as meaningful, Freud was able to obtain truths about his patients that were otherwise hidden. His opposition between "psychic" and "external" realities served to juxtapose an inherently *personal* reality with a more *concrete* one. This isn't to say that concrete, or objective, reality is necessarily false, but it was Freud's genius to see that the truth about one's history can be derived from the communication of otherwise innocuous reflections, by interpreting a patient's fantasies as disguised messages. The recognition that fantasies could be conceived as messages suggested there was something concealed in them that the patient neither recognized nor understood.

This means that fantasies serve a purpose: they disclose the intentional structure of the individual's deepest longings and aspirations. They tell us what we desire. But Freud lacked a conception of intentionality that could explain how his patients were able to convey truths they didn't "know" in a disguised and indirect manner. In other words, his patients *unconsciously intended* their symptoms and the attendant fantasies that explained them – they weren't "caused" by their unconscious. Yet, Freud seemed conflicted as to the origin of such symptoms. He never entirely abandoned the idea that they must be *caused* by some "traumatic" something or other. If not external reality, then perhaps the vicissitudes of our unconscious fantasy life?[2]

Despite the recent development of relational analysis, which claims to approach the treatment situation from a more interpersonal perspective, contemporary psychoanalysts, with few exceptions, find it agreeable to use terms in which the *impersonal* aspect of the unconscious predominates. Analysts remain wedded to the notion that non-personal aspects of the mind account for the unconscious motives that guide us in our daily affairs, which in turn produce our psychopathology.

Sartre's critique of the unconscious

Whereas Freud depicted psychoanalysis as essentially a science of the *unconscious*, it is impossible to deny that it is also a science – if we can call it that – which is preoccupied with *consciousness*, if only implicitly. Terms like truth, epistemology, knowledge, understanding, and comprehension pervade every psychoanalytic paper that is devoted to the unconscious as a concept. This is also the subject matter that Sartre (1957, 1962, 1981), Merleau-Ponty (1962), Heidegger (1962), and Ricoeur (1970) devoted a considerable amount of their philosophical writings to: what is the nature of knowledge and what role does it serve in our everyday lives? Of all the phenomenologists, it was Sartre who took psychoanalysis the most seriously, devoting a considerable amount of time to coming to grips with Freud's conception of the unconscious.

In Sartre's critique of psychoanalysis (1962, pp. 48–55, 1981, pp. 153–171), he rejected Freud's topographical model for similar reasons that Freud eventually did (Thompson, 2001). In the topographical model, the only thing separating the system-conscious from the system-unconscious is the so-called "censor," which, according to Freud, regulates what is permitted into consciousness and, contrariwise, what is repressed into the unconscious. This means that the censor is aware of everything, that which is conscious and unconscious alike. Yet because the ego is *unaware* of the censor, this model posits a "second consciousness" (the censor) that is both unknown and unknowable to the ego. Sartre's problem with this model is obvious: the so-called censor is the de facto "person" who is being analyzed and disclaims knowledge of all the shenanigans he employs in order to disguise what he is up to, an edition of what Sartre terms "bad faith." Freud (1923) also had problems with the implications of a "second thinking subject" and decided to discard this model for one that contained only one subject that *knows* anything – the conscious portion of the ego – and not one, but *three* subjects that do not know anything: the id, the superego, and the unconscious portion of the ego that employs defense mechanisms.

Freud's subsequent revision of his earlier model, however, fares little better in Sartre's opinion. The topographical model is replaced with one that is less concerned with demarcating conscious and unconscious portions of the psyche than with determining the complex nature of psychic "agency" or subjectivity. Sartre's complaint with the new model is that it still fails to resolve the problem of *bad faith*, the problem of a "lie without a liar." If anything, the new model gets even further away from Sartre's efforts to *personalize* the unconscious by instituting three psychic agencies that protect the conscious ego from any responsibility for its actions. How would Sartre propose to remedy this situation, to account for those actions that Freud claimed the "conscious" patient is "unconscious" of devising, while holding the conscious patient responsible for performing them?

Sartre (1957) accomplishes this by introducing two sets of critical distinctions into the prevailing psychoanalytic vocabulary. The first is a distinction between *pre-reflective* consciousness and *reflective* consciousness, and the second is between *consciousness* and *knowledge*. Sartre summarizes the basic dilemma in Freud's conception of the unconscious with the following questions: how can the subject not know that he is possessed of a feeling or sentiment that he is in possession of? And if the unconscious is just another word for *consciousness* (Sartre's position), how can the subject not know what he is "conscious" of? Sartre's thesis of "pre-reflective" consciousness is his effort to solve this riddle. Following Husserl, Sartre saw consciousness as *intentional*, which means it is always conscious *of something*. This means there is no such thing as "empty" consciousness; nor is there such a thing as a "container" or "receptacle" that houses consciousness. Instead, consciousness is always "outside" itself and "in" the things that constitute it as *consciousness-of* something. In Sartre's (1957) words:

> Intentionality is not the way in which a subject tries to make "contact" with an object that exists beside it. *Intentionality is what makes up the very subjectivity of subjects.*
>
> (pp. 48–49, emphasis in original)

In other words, the concept of intentionality renders subjectivity as already a *theory of intersubjectivity*, since to *be* a subject is to be engaged with something "other" than one's self – even if this other something is merely an idea. Sartre elaborates how this thesis would be applied to the social world in this famous passage:

> When I run after a streetcar, when I look at the time, when I am absorbed in contemplating a portrait, there is no *I* (or "ego"). There is [only] consciousness *of the streetcar-having-to-be-overtaken*, etc. . . . In fact, I am then plunged into the world of objects; it is *they* which constitute the unity of my consciousness; it is *they* which present themselves with values, with attractive and repellent qualities – but

me – I have disappeared; I have annihilated myself [in the moment of conscious apprehension].

(pp. 48–49)

This means that when I experience a rock, a tree, a feeling of sadness, or the object of my desire in the bedroom, I experience them just where they are: beside a hill, on the meadow, in my heart, in relation to myself and my beloved. Consciousness and the object-of-consciousness are given at one stroke. These things constitute my consciousness of them just as I constitute their existence *as* things through the act by which I perceive them and give them a name. And because naming things is a purely human activity, these things do not exist as rocks, trees, or emotions in the absence of a human consciousness that can apprehend them through the constitutive power of language.

Yet such acts of apprehension don't necessarily imply "knowledge" of what I am conscious of. This is because Sartre distinguishes between the *pre-reflective* apprehension of an object and our *reflective* "witnessing" of the act. Ordinarily when I am pre-reflectively conscious of a feeling, for example, I intuit the feeling of sadness and, in turn, reflectively acknowledge this feeling *as* sadness: I feel sad and experience myself as a sad person simultaneously. But I am also capable of feeling sadness, or anger, or envy without *knowing* I am sad, or angry, or envious. When this is suggested to me by my analyst, I am surprised by this observation. Initially, I may resist my analyst's interpretation and reject it. But I may eventually admit it because, when bringing this to my attention, I am also capable, after reflection, of recognizing this feeling *is mine*. Sartre argues that I would be incapable of recognizing thoughts or ideas that I claim no awareness of *unless I had been conscious of these feelings in the first place, on a pre-reflective level*. Though conscious, the pre-reflective isn't known; according to Sartre, it is *lived*.

In other words, what Freud labels consciousness, Sartre designates "reflective consciousness" (i.e., knowing *that* I am conscious of this or that), and what Freud labels the unconscious, Sartre designates as that moment of pre-reflective consciousness that, due to *bad faith*, has not yielded to reflective awareness and, with that awareness, "knowledge" of it. This is why I can be conscious of something that I have no immediate knowledge of, and why I can become knowledgeable about something that

I am, so to speak, "unconscious" of, but am subsequently able to recognize and acknowledge. This implies that I can only experience something I have knowledge of but not what I am pre-reflectively "conscious" of.

The difference between Sartre's and Freud's respective formulations isn't that it merely substitutes Freud's terminology with Sartre's. On a more radical level, it eliminates a need for the notion of a "second thinking subject" *behind* or beneath consciousness and offers a way to personalize the unconscious in a manner that eluded Freud.

Sartre and emotions

I now want to review Sartre's (1962) critique of the emotions and his transformation of a psychoanalysis rooted in psychology to one rooted in phenomenology. First I want to ask, what *are* emotions? There is no shortage of theories that try to tackle this problem, yet no consensus on a definition. For some, emotions are distinct from cognition and judgment, while for others, our feelings are central to decision making and even determine our judgments. It's undeniable that emotions tell us things that our cognitions often miss. Moreover, emotions are often the driving force behind our motivations, whether positive or negative. And what about the relationship between emotion and desire? Are emotions derived from desires, or are they determinant? Whatever they are, we cannot deny that we would not be human without them.

The term emotion dates back to 1579, when it was adapted from the French *émouvoir*, meaning "to stir up." It was first introduced to academic circles to replace a similar term, passion. Though the two terms have often been used interchangeably, passion is typically employed when referring to sexual feelings. There is also the problem with their respective etymology. Passion derives from the Latin *pati*, meaning to suffer or endure. One can see why the term passion began to take on different connotations than when simply feeling this or that. The French *émouvoir* appeared to solve the problem. Like the term feeling, with which emotion is used synonymously, an emotion is of brief duration, whereas moods last longer. The more recent "affect," adopted by psychoanalysts, encompasses all three.

Psychoanalysis went a long way in explaining how human behavior is not orchestrated by random events, because actions always have a motive, an intention, a specific end, even if we are ignorant of what the end is. Psychoanalysts were the first to emphasize the *significance* of psychic phenomena, that this seemingly innocent thought or emotion usually stands for something else. The child who steals from his mother's purse is only trying to reclaim the mother's love. A girl who faints at the sight of parsley can't bring herself to recall a painful childhood incident when she was forced to eat vegetables. Yet often as not, the psychoanalytic interpretation, if only surreptitiously, tends to privilege causal antecedents masquerading as interpretations in order to explain pathogenic behavior. History plays a crucial role in our lives, and this is just as true for people suffering from emotional disturbance. This is why I can project onto all women the quality of withholding because my mother was too depressed to comfort my needs. Each time I feel attracted to a woman, I find myself consumed with ambivalence, fear, consternation. The feelings I experience in these situations not only color my understanding of reality. To a significant degree, they determine *who I am*.

Freud's term for that traumatic moment every child is supposed to experience is the *Oedipus* complex. What makes this complex so compelling is the sense of betrayal that occasions it, feelings that every boy and girl must eventually come to terms with. I can't say whether Sartre was influenced by Freud's dark assessment of the role that love plays in our lives. Yet their respective views on the matter are remarkably similar and form the basis of Sartre's many plays and novels.

Emotions may be pleasing or painful. The pleasurable kind we don't question until they are self-destructive, but even then we rarely oppose them. The emotion introduces us to pleasure. Painful emotions are more invasive. Because they elicit distress, we can bear them for only so long. Like Jason clutching the Medusa, we divert our eyes and blind our experience of them with magic, what Freud termed "defense mechanisms." Our emotional life, always a mystery to us, inhabits a spectrum between desire and anxiety, each feeding the other. If we are creatures of desires, and anxiety is the price we pay for them, then emotions must be entangled inside those desires in principle. Emotions are not merely barometers that tell me when my desires are satisfied or thwarted. They also possess an intelligence that aims to make my life as agreeable as possible. That's not all. My emotions shelter me from realities that are too painful to bear. Sartre suggested that emotions are our way of magically transforming a situation we get stuck in, like a fly on a sticky-mat, that we can neither accommodate or escape. In other words, emotions provide a way of escaping situations that would otherwise drive us crazy. According to Sartre (1962):

> When the paths before us become too difficult, or when we cannot see our way, we can no longer put up with such an exacting and difficult world. All ways are barred and nevertheless we must act. So then we try to change the world; that is, to live it as though the relation between things and their potentialities were not governed by deterministic processes, but by magic.
>
> (p. 63)

The woman who faints at the sight of her attacker does so not because it reminds her of some previous event, but because it removes her, albeit magically, from the present situation. She no longer has to face the immediate danger she is in. But this isn't to say she willfully faints with deliberation. She is seized by the situation, a situation that makes demands on her and with which she is unable to cope. Or rather, her manner of coping is so ingenious that it is unrecognizable as such to the unwary observer. The unlikelihood of finding a solution to the problem she faces demands that she invent a solution instead. If she can't take flight in reality, she can do so emotionally, which is to say, magically. Yet an emotional response isn't just a substitute for other kinds of action, other ways of coping, because it isn't effectual. It doesn't act on the world but merely changes my perception of it. This is why emotion is closely related to madness, the loss of reality.

On a more basic level, the emotion is a structure of desire. It may be a way of enhancing a desire I enjoy or a way of coping with a desire that becomes risky. The person in danger wants to be somewhere else, so the fainting magically fulfills the wish to disappear. Similarly, if I want something I cannot have, my emotions can help remove the desire itself, allowing me to escape a bitter disappointment. Sartre invokes the sour grapes analogy as a common rationalization for this strategy.

> I lift my hand to pluck a bunch of grapes. I cannot do so; they are beyond my reach; so I shrug my shoulders, muttering: "they are too green" and go on my way. . . . [T]his little comedy that I play under the grapes, thereby conferring this quality of being "too green" upon

them, serves as a substitute for the action I cannot complete.... I confer the required quality upon the grapes magically.

(pp. 65–66)[3]

Sartre's purpose in his early phenomenological study, *Sketch For A Theory Of The Emotions* (1962), was to show why behaviorism is incapable of explaining the phenomenon of emotions, because behaviorism is stuck in a cause-and-effect universe that cannot account for the *intentional structure* of our motives, our folly, or our emotions. Psychoanalysis goes further because it is sensitive to human agency but then ascribes our motivations to unconscious responses to trauma that, if we aren't careful, may be just as causal as behaviorism. At its best, what is often lacking in the psychoanalytic explanation is the personal dimension to motives, because unconscious motives are not, strictly speaking, personal, so we cannot assume responsible for them.

Freedom and choice

So what are therapy patients supposed to make of this? How are they supposed to effect change in their lives? Isn't this the purpose of psychoanalysis: to change our manner of being in the world and *improve* it? How can this happen without turning the therapeutic situation into a technology, a disembodied set of techniques designed to manipulate and even mystify the patient this way or that? The essential task of existential psychoanalysis as envisioned by Sartre is hermeneutic, that is, deciphering the meaning of acts in relation to a synthetic totality underpinned by an original project of being, manifested in a *fundamental choice*. But what is choice, exactly? We ordinarily speak of choice as a volitional, deliberate act that is transparent to itself. This suggests that we are always behind our choices, that we weigh them in our minds and, having decided upon this or that option, execute them. Sartre is even sometimes accused of adopting this model, but it isn't that simple.

Say I want to go to the cinema. Which movie do I choose to go see? I look at the options and pick this one over the other. There! I have deliberated, weighed my options, and chosen the one most desirable. Or have I? One of the things that both Freud and Sartre share in common is that neither buys this explanation. Though separated by an enormous gulf in theory, temperament, and vocation, each concluded, as did Heidegger, that choices are free but not willful. Instead, they are *predetermined*. Something or other predisposed me into making that choice. Freud would say I did so unconsciously, whereas Sartre would argue that the choice occurred on a pre-reflective level. In both cases, it wasn't my ego or "I" that chose the action. The choice executed was rendered before the fact, beneath awareness, in my engagement with the world. The so-called *conscious* choice merely makes it official, after the fact.

In other words, I cannot get *behind* my choices, they are always one step ahead, guiding me this way or that, so the choices themselves, and the reasons I make them, are a puzzle. This is why psychoanalysis, as envisioned by Freud, is always retrospective, not prophylactic. Only in behavioral psychology do we play the fiction of deliberating what we intend to do and then execute the act. In psychoanalysis, the idea is to review previous actions and to learn something about ourselves from them. The actions reviewed may be buried in our childhoods, or they may have occurred moments earlier, in the analytic session. In either case, we are not talking about an executive function but a *reflective* one.

This has led some commentators to conclude that Freud's conception of the unconscious was deterministic. If we don't make our choices "consciously," which is to say, *volunteeristically*, then our choices must be made *for* us – *by* our unconscious. This implies there is no free choice in the matter, if the choice isn't willfully executed. Psychoanalysts make this assumption because the unconscious is supposed to be *impersonal*, not personal. In Freud's tri-partite structure, it isn't "me" guiding my decisions, but the *id*, Latin for "it." This is the crux of Sartre's problem with the psychoanalytic conception of the unconscious, the problem of a lie without a liar, a thought without a thinker, an action without an actor.

What is at stake here is our notion of the self, what comprises the self, and how free the self is. For Sartre, there is no self, so to speak, no "I," not even a subject, if by subject we mean some sort of entity that, like the censor, or a god, orchestrates our lives *via* executive decision making.

Unlike Freud, Sartre roots the person not in psychology but in *situation*, in the world to which we belong, the world where we live and die. All of my choices derive from my engagement with that world, not in my psychology. That doesn't mean that I'm determined by that engagement. I *am* that engagement. I have choices in the matter, and those choices are free, but that doesn't mean I am in control of the situation. The fact that my choices are free doesn't mean I am Superman. Freedom doesn't make me omnipotent. It isn't a freedom to rule but a freedom to be me and ultimately to embrace the me that I am.

This means that my choices are ontological rather than deliberative. Sartre suggests our neuroses go all the way back to a fundamental choice, in childhood, when we chose what our neurosis would be on a pre-reflective level. In other words, we *intend* our psychopathology, we are not the "consequence" of this or that trauma. Contrary to psychoanalysis, nothing *caused* my condition. Rather, I *chose* to experience this or that incident *as* "traumatic." Like the magical choice, there is always something to be gained by every neurotic turn, though we don't realize it at the time. After all, if we didn't "choose" to be this way or that, how would change be possible?

Given this thesis, how is therapy even possible? If I cannot will myself to health, then how does it come about? As Kierkegaard (2004) would say, through indirection. In this context, all my conscious, knowing mind is good for is to acquaint myself with the mystery of my existence and plummet its depths over an unpredictable amount of time. I cannot *will* myself to overcome my fear of intimacy. I cannot compel myself to love more fully, behave more compassionately, or feel more alive. Yet, all of these transitions may and often do result from the analytic endeavor. How? We don't know, exactly. All we do know is that knowing oneself has the potential to change our lives in this way, to become who we are, authentically. If we are intrepid, over time, this process of self-reflection may result in a change of perspective, and with it, a change in our selves, which is to say, our lives.

This can only happen *indirectly*, over time, *without ever knowing that we have made these changes until after having made them* – and without ever knowing why. This is where authenticity comes into the picture. When I tell myself I hate the person I am, that I cannot give up my addictions, that I wish I could be more this or less of that, I am lying to myself. Because every choice I make is a free choice, and because everything that I am is a consequence of the choices I have rendered, I am always the person I wish to be. To be in conflict with myself is to pretend that something or other has "caused" me to be this way – something other than my free choice to be me. Even this form of ambivalence is a choice. Nothing I think or do is inflicted on me. To pretend otherwise is our favored method of escape. This is bad faith in its essence.

This also means that the goal of existential psychoanalysis is to *become* the person I am already, not ambivalently, but unreservedly, wholeheartedly, passionately. This is not an ethical endeavor to make me a "better person." I don't know if Sartre would agree with this, but it seems to me this form of radical self-acceptance that it aspires to is an act of love. It entails falling in love with the person I am and always have been, the same person who lived this life, who suffered its folly, up to this very moment. I hope Sartre will forgive me for this, but at the end of the day, existential psychoanalysis is precisely what Freud said it was, a cure through love.

Conclusion

In conclusion, how has this perspective affected my way of working with psychoanalytic patients? I think, like perhaps all analytic practitioners, I assumed early in my career, going back some 40 years or so, that the therapeutic enterprise was all about change. This word has always haunted me. I remember thinking that I wanted to tackle this problem head-on and to write a book about change, what it is, how it is effected, and so on. I abandoned this project once I realized that the very concept of change is problematic. We don't even know what it is. It was only later, when I had absorbed some insights from the existential philosophical tradition, that I finally came to realize that psychoanalysis isn't about change but rather becoming. Change implies that something that was should be discarded and replaced with something else. This works fine in the physical universe, where we readily change one flat tire for a new one, a house we no longer cherish for one more desirable, and so on. But you don't discard the person you are for a new, improved model. You are stuck with who you are, for better or worse, for life. This is when it came to me that we are always becoming but not, strictly speaking, changing. In becoming, we are always what and who we are, but we are never finally that person until the end, until the day we die. Meantime, we are constantly, ceaselessly, becoming more and more ourselves. But this becoming isn't a panacea.

Without reflection, without care, and without concerted effort to reflect on our situation, we very well may simply become more and more miserable instead, more and more alienated from ourselves in order to escape the anguish of living. Existential psychoanalysis provides an opportunity to become something different than that. It offers the opportunity, with no guarantees, to become more and more the magnificent creature that we already are. Once on the road to becoming and embracing ourselves, we have a chance to be at peace with ourselves. When we are finally at peace with ourselves, we are at peace with the world.

Notes

1 The same fate, we know, fell to Socrates before him, who was actually executed for advocating views similar to Freud's that were a danger to orthodoxy.
2 See my paper, "The Demise of the Person in the Psychoanalytic Situation" (2010), for a detailed study of Freud's problem with retaining the personal dimension in the unconscious.
3 See Chapter Three of my recent book, *The Death of Desire*, 2nd edition, 2016, for a more in-depth exploration of emotion in our psychopathology.

References

Freud, S. (1910). Five lectures on psycho-analysis. *Standard Edition, 11*, 3–56, 1957.
Freud, S. (1923). *The ego and the id. Standard Edition, 19*, 3–66, 1961.
Heidegger, M. (1962). *Being and time* (J. Macquarrie & E. Robinson, Trans.). New York, NY: Harper & Row.
Kierkegaard, S. (2004). *Training in Christianity* (W. Lowrie, Trans.). New York, NY: Vintage.
Laing, R. D. (1960[1969]). *The divided self.* New York, NY and London: Penguin Books.
Laing, R. D. (1967). *The politics of experience.* New York, NY: Pantheon Books.
Merleau-Ponty, M. (1962). *Phenomenology of perception* (C. Smith, Trans.). London: Routledge and Kegan Paul.
Ricoeur, P. (1970). *Freud and philosophy: An essay on interpretation* (D. Savage, Trans.). New Haven, CT and London: Yale University Press.
Sartre, J-P. (1943[1954]). *Being and nothingness* (H. Barnes, Trans.). New York, NY: Philosophical Library.
Sartre, J-P. (1957). *The transcendence of the ego* (F. Williams & R. Kirkpatrick, Trans.). New York, NY: Noonday Press.
Sartre, J-P. (1962). *Sketch for a theory of the emotions* (P. Mairet, Trans.). London: Methuen and Co.
Sartre, J-P. (1981). *Existential psychoanalysis* (H. Barnes, Trans.). Washington, DC: Regnary Gateway.
Thompson, M. G. (2001). Is the unconscious really all that unconscious? The role of being and experience in the psychoanalytic encounter. *Contemporary Psychoanalysis, 37*, 571–612.
Thompson, M. G. (2004). Nietzsche and psychoanalysis. *Existential Analysis, 15*(2), 203–217.

Thompson, M. G. (2010). The demise of the person in the psychoanalytic situation. *Psychotherapy in Australia, 17*(1), 26–34.

Thompson, M. G. (2016). *The death of desire: An existential study in sanity and madness* (2nd ed.). London and New York, NY: Routledge.

Chapter 6

Moving forward
New findings on the right brain and their implications for psychoanalysis

Allan N. Schore

In 1997, celebrating the 100th anniversary of the primordial origins of psychoanalysis, I published "A century after Freud's *Project*: Is a rapprochement between psychoanalysis and neurobiology at hand?" in the *Journal of the American Psychoanalytic Association*. Referring to Freud's early career in neurology, the *Project* represented his attempt "to furnish . . . a psychology which shall be a natural science" (Schore, 1997, p. 295), and towards that end he introduced the concepts that to this day serve as the theoretical foundation and scaffolding of psychoanalysis: primary and secondary processes; principles of pleasure-unpleasure, constancy, and reality testing; cathexis and identification; wish-fulfillment theory of dreams; psychical regression and hallucination; systems of perception, memory, unconscious and preconscious psychic activity; and the concept of regulation. Freud also offered his earliest thoughts about two problems he struggled with for the rest of his career, affect and motivation. He later repudiated the *Project*, and over the rest of the 20th century, connections between psychoanalysis and science were weakened and strained. Due to the loss of its moorings to the rest of science, it became an easy target to criticism that it was untestable, and that therefore it was not a proper science (Grunbaum, 1984). Yet in 1913, Freud asserted that in the future, "we shall have to find a contact point with biology; and we may rightly feel glad if that contact is already assured at one important point or another" (pp. 181–182).

In 1994, in *Affect Regulation and the Origin of the Self*, I asserted that right brain social-emotional and regulatory structures and functions represented such a contact point, and the time was right for a rapprochement between psychoanalysis and neuroscience. Over the ensuing three decades, I continued to elaborate the interpersonal neurobiological perspective of regulation theory to describe how beneath levels of conscious awareness, brains align and synchronize their neural activities with other brains, especially in emotional interactions. The theory also describes how the development of the right brain-mind are shaped continuously by social experiences, especially those involving emotional relationships, including therapeutic relationships. Indeed, over the last three decades I have built upon Freud's *Project* in order to elaborate modern neuropsychoanalysis, the study of the brain systems that process information at a nonconscious level, specifically suggesting that the right brain represents the psychobiological substrate of the human unconscious. This rapidly expanding research on the right brain acts as a source of the essential origins, adaptive functions, rapid dynamics, and pathogenesis of the human unconscious. These experimental, theoretical, and clinical studies can elucidate the deeper mechanism of the invisible, omnipresent unconscious in everyday life.

Furthermore, recent discoveries in neuroscience of the right brain and neuropsychoanalysis of the unconscious mind can act as an integrating force in psychoanalytic theory and clinical practice. Neuropsychoanalytic structure, located in the right brain, integrates various psychoanalytic theories of different functions of the mind, all of which are centered in the fundamental construct of psychoanalysis, the unconscious, the central organizing principle of the field. The construct of the unconscious has thus shifted from an intangible, immaterial, metapsychological abstraction of the mind to a psychoneurobiological heuristic function of a tangible brain that has material form. Thus we now have a rejoinder to previous critics of psychoanalysis: scientifically informed psychoanalytic theory can generate hypotheses that can be experimentally tested as well as able to formulate more complex clinical approaches. Brain research thus offers valuable data to psychoanalysis, "the science of unconscious processes" (Brenner, 1980). On both fronts, the theory is now genuinely "heuristic," defined by the *Oxford Dictionary* as "serving to find out or discover something."

In this contribution, I will begin with changes within the consulting room and re-formulations of theoretical psychoanalysis and then advances and new directions in clinical psychoanalysis and psychoanalytic psychotherapy. Finally, I will conclude with thoughts on how the interface of neuroscience and psychoanalysis challenges us to think about how the field needs to change as we move forward. Everything that follows is an expansion of regulation theory, a theory of the development, psychopathogenesis, and treatment of the right brain unconscious subjective self. What I continue to offer is a broad ranging theory, a systematic exposition of the general principles of a science. The internal consistency, coherence, scope, pragmatic usefulness, and power of the theory is expressed in its ability to formulate testable hypotheses and generate research, as well as to generate evidence-based clinical interventions.

Right brain, laterality research, and changes within the consulting room: psychoanalytic theory

Brain laterality (hemispheric asymmetry), originally discovered in the 19th century, is now experiencing a resurgence in neuroscience. This rapidly expanding research is describing the functional and structural differences between the left and right brains and thereby between a conscious "left mind" and an unconscious "right mind." A large body of studies are converging to support the idea of a left brain surface, verbal, conscious, analytical explicit self versus a right brain deeper nonverbal, nonconscious, holistic, emotional, corporeal, subjective implicit self. The right brain is thus the psychobiological source of the rapid spontaneous information processing of the psychoanalytic unconscious mind.

Overviewing human studies, Iain McGilchrist (2009) concludes, "The right hemisphere . . . has the most sophisticated and extensive, and quite possibly most lately evolved, representation in the prefrontal cortex, the most highly evolved part of the brain" (p. 437). In more recent work (2015), he offers characterizations that bear directly upon clinical psychoanalysis: "The right hemisphere both grounds our experience of the world at the bottom end, so to speak, and makes sense of it, at the top end" (p. 100), that this hemisphere is more in touch with both affect and the body, and that "neurological evidence supports what is called the primacy of affect and the primacy of unconscious over conscious will" (p. 100). Further support for the construct of a right brain unconscious mind comes from neuropsychology. According to Tucker and Moller (2007), "The right hemisphere's specialization for emotional communication through nonverbal channels seems to suggest a domain of the mind that is close to the motivationally charged psychoanalytic unconscious" (p. 91).

Writing in the journal *Neuropsychoanalysis*, Guido Gainotti (2005) asserts,

> The right hemisphere subserves the lower 'schematic' level (where emotions are automatically generated and experienced as 'true emotions') whereas the left hemisphere the higher 'conceptual' level (where emotions are consciously analyzed and submitted to intentional control).
>
> (p. 71)

In another contribution (2012), he cites neurological data indicating that the unconscious processing of emotional information is subsumed by a right hemispheric subcortical route. These data confirm Freud's hierarchical structural theory. They are also consonant with my own model of hemispheric asymmetry, first articulated in 1994, that the right brain is centrally involved in not only the *intrapsychic* implicit processing and self-regulation of emotions and social information but also in the *interpersonal* communication and interactive regulation of emotion by a right brain *relational* unconscious, via right brain-to-right brain communications, of face, voice, and gesture. Current neurobiological models of Freud's unconscious are now shifting from focusing on unconscious mental contents to adaptive, essential unconscious psychobiological processes.

Indeed, psychoanalysis is currently undergoing significant changes in its central construct, the dynamic unconscious, which for its first century was defined as conscious material that has been repressed by an active force that removes certain elements unacceptable to censorship from consciousness. Yet by 1915, Freud stated, "the repressed does not cover everything that is unconscious. The unconscious has the wider compass: the repressed is a part of the unconscious" (1915, p. 166). This reformulation is the central theme of a recent book, *Unrepressed Unconscious, Implicit Memory, and Clinical Work* by Craparo and Mucci (2017). Within these chapters, a number of authors link *implicit* right brain functions with the "*unrepressed unconscious*," that is, other essential functional contents of the wider domain of the unconscious. This equivalence of the constructs of implicit and unconscious has been stressed by, for example, Mancia's work on implicit memory and early unrepressed unconscious (2006) and myself ("The right brain implicit self lies at the core of psychoanalysis,"

2011). In the latter, I concluded that the unconscious contains much more than what is repressed by the conscious mind, highlighting the essential role of not only implicit cognition but implicit affect, communication, and regulation in current relational psychoanalytic models. I then discussed recent developmental and neurobiological studies of implicit processes in early development and psychopathogenesis of the implicit subjective self, as well as implicit affective processes in psychotherapeutic change processes.

In my own ongoing work, I continue to offer a large body of research implicating right brain structural systems in implicit, rapid, and spontaneous anticipation, recognition, expression, communication, and regulation of bodily-based emotional states beneath levels of awareness (see Schore, 2012). In very recent neuroscience, authors are reporting studies on "Right hemisphere dominance in nonconscious processing" (Chen & Hsiao, 2014), concluding that the right hemisphere has an advantage in shaping behavior with implicit information, whereas the left hemisphere plays a greater role in expressing explicit knowledge. Another on "the unconscious guidance of attention" documents that the right hemisphere temporo-parietal junction plays an essential role in implicit attentional functions that operate outside conscious awareness (Chelazzi, Bisley, & Bartolomeo, 2018). In terms of voice and face processing, Schepman, Rodway, and Pritchard (2016) offer a study titled "Right-Lateralized Unconscious, but Not Conscious, Processing of Affective Environmental Sounds," and Crouzet, Kirchner, and Thorpe (2010) another on "Fast Saccades toward Faces: Face Detection in Just 100 ms," documenting efficient "ultrarapid" processing of unconscious information. Hassin (2013) cites a large body of research documenting the adaptive functions performed by the human unconscious:

> The function of extracting patterns from our environment, also known as implicit learning, has been repeatedly demonstrated; maintaining evidence from past experience, also known as memory, can happen outside of conscious awareness; people can extract information about emotion and gender from subliminally presented facial expressions; comparing oneself with others, a central social function, occurs nonconsciously and even with subliminally presented others; and physical sensations affect perception and social perception. . . . A review of the literature through functional glasses quickly reveals that many

functions that were historically associated with conscious awareness can occur nonconsciously.

(p. 200)

In an earlier study, Hassin and his colleagues showed that in contrast to (left hemispheric) explicit working memory, implicit working memory operates unintentionally and outside of conscious awareness (Hassin, Bargh, Engell, & McCulloch, 2009). Note that each hemisphere has its own working memory system, one verbal, the other nonverbal.

Furthermore, due to the incorporation of neuroscience and neurophysiology, psychoanalytic theory is now being transformed from a theory of the unconscious mind into a theory of mind/brain/body: unconscious systems operating beneath levels of conscious awareness are inextricably linked into the body. Spontaneous release of "bottom-up" bodily-based autonomic and hormonal systems, including stress steroids such as cortisol, sex steroids such as androgens and estrogens, neuroendocrines such as oxytocin and vasopressin are now understood to operate at levels beneath conscious awareness. These neurochemical products of what were previously known as id processes are thus also part of the domain of the right brain unconscious system.

The unconscious system also contains imprints of early relational trauma, as well as the defense against this dysregulation. Clinically, current therapeutic models are experiencing a shift from left brain repression to right brain dissociation, especially in pre-Oedipal psychopathologies. In 2003, I cited extant neurobiological research suggesting that repression is a developmentally more advanced left brain defense against affects that are represented at the cortical level of the right brain, while the earlier appearing and more primitive dissociation is a right brain defense against traumatic affects like terror, rage, and shame that are stored subcortically in the right brain (Schore, 2003b). In *Awakening the Dreamer*, Bromberg (2006) asserts that repression defines a process that is designed to avoid disavowed content that may lead to *unpleasant* intrapsychic conflict, whereas dissociation blots out *unbearable* experience from consciousness. The right brain unconscious system thus contains not just repressed but also dissociated ("not me") states of self (see Schore, 2012, 2019a for a discussion of clinical differences in working with the early-forming defense of dissociation and the later-maturing defense of repression).

Moreover, neuropsychoanalysis reveals essential information about the deeper levels of the topography of the mind, Freud's iceberg model of conscious, preconscious, and unconscious. Recall, only 10% of Freud's iceberg is visible (conscious), whereas the other 90% lies beneath water (preconscious and unconscious). Within the subconscious mind, the preconscious is allotted 10%-15%, while the unconscious an overwhelming 75%-80%. Recall Jung's (1963) dictum, "Man's task . . . is to become conscious of the contents that process upward from the unconscious." In my own work, I have offered a modern neuropsychoanalytic update of Freud's topographic model of stratified conscious, preconscious, and unconscious systems (Schore, 2003b). In line with developmental neurobiological research, the brain matures in a caudal to rostral progression, with subcortical areas maturing before cortical areas. Similarly, the "lower" core of the unconscious develops before higher levels of the preconscious, which in turn evolve before the highest levels of the conscious mind. This progression also mirrors the fact that the right hemisphere matures before the left (Schore, 1994, 2003a, 2003b, 2012, 2019b).

Thus I have proposed that the limbic and emotion processing areas of the right brain unconscious represent a hierarchical system with an outer, later-developing cortical, orbitofrontal-limbic regulated core, an inner, earlier developing cingulate-limbic regulating core, and an earliest evolving subcortical amygdala-limbic regulated core that lies deepest within, like nested Russian dolls. The three levels of organization of the right brain represent, respectively, three levels of the system unconscious: preconscious, unconscious, and deep unconscious. The unconscious systems of the hierarchical three-tiered cortical-subcortical limbic core thus reflect the early developmental history of the subjective self (Schore, 2012).

Right brain, laterality research, and changes within the consulting room: psychotherapy

These data fit well with my interpersonal neurobiological model of right brain-to-right brain unconscious communication and regulation across a co-created intersubjective field, that is, an interbrain synchronization of two right hemispheres in an emotion transacting psychotherapeutic context. In a recent contribution in the American Psychological Association Division 29 journal *Psychotherapy*, I offer neurobiological and clinical data to argue that "the right brain is dominant in psychotherapy" (Schore,

2014). Right brain-to-right brain unconscious affective communications "beneath the words" are expressed in the therapist-patient transference-countertransference relationship. This mechanism is essential to working in preverbal-onset developmental disorders, whereby the optimal clinical approach is to "follow the Ariadne's thread of transference affects" (Brierley, 1937).

In therapy, this right lateralized system is used to access deeper unconscious systems beneath the surface of the left hemisphere conscious mind. In his most recent psychoanalytic writings, Philip Bromberg (2017) asserts,

> The foundational perspective that shapes my thinking is enriched by, and, in an ever-expanding way, intertwined with Allan Schore's groundbreaking contributions to the fields of both psychotherapy and neuroscience . . . in addition to the key importance of affect regulation and dysregulation, both Allan and I place special emphasis on the phenomenon and concept of '*state-sharing*' (Schore, 2003b, 2011, 2012) – that is, the right-brain to *right-brain communication process through which each person's states of mind are known to the other implicitly.*
> (p. 7, my italics)

Bromberg states that this organized dialogue of dynamically fluctuating moment-to-moment state sharing underlies "a good psychoanalytic match."

In my own work, I arrive at a similar conclusion. Within the session, moment-to-moment right brain-to-right brain "state-sharing" represents an organized dialogue occurring within milliseconds. In this interactive matrix, both partners match states and simultaneously adjust their social attention, stimulation, and accelerating arousal in response to their partner's signals. In applying neurophysiology to psychotherapy, Geller and Porges (2014, p. 183) propose,

> [The] bidirectional influence between our brain and visceral organs explains how the therapist's social and emotional responses to the client can potentially, by influencing the physiological state of the client, mediate either an expansion or restriction of the client's range and valence of socioemotional responding. . . . Bidirectional communication between areas in the right hemisphere promote adaptive interpersonal functioning between therapist and client (Allison & Rossouw, 2013; Schore, 2012; Siegel, 2012)

Furthermore, this communication system is a central mechanism of therapeutic presence, which "involves therapists using their whole self to *be both fully* engaged and receptively attuned in the moment *with and for the client* to promote effective therapy" (p. 178, my italics).

Echoing these ideas in psychiatric writings, Meares (2012) refers to "a form of therapeutic conversation that can be conceived . . . as a dynamic interplay between two right hemispheres" (p. 315). In his words,

> [A]n interplay between two right brains provides a structure for the therapeutic engagement . . . right hemispheric language . . . is abbreviated, with the utterance often incomplete, and lacking formal syntactical structure. In particular, the subject of a sentence tends to be left out, including pronouns. . . . Furthermore, the language is emotionally expressive. As a consequence, the phonology is salient, the toning and inflections of the voice have a powerful communicative effect that is combined with facial expressions and the movements of the body. This kind of language creates the feeling of *'being with'* in a way that is greater than a logical, completely syntactical left-hemisphere utterance, which sets up a different kind of relatedness.
>
> (pp. 312–313, my italics)

Similarly, in the clinical psychology literature, Greenberg (2014) notes:

> implicit affect regulation that results from a good therapeutic relationship occurs through right hemispheric processes, is not verbally mediated, is highly relational, and is most directly affected by such things as emotional communication, facial expression, vocal quality, and eye contact (Schore, 2003a, 2003b).
>
> (p. 351)

These communications underlie the clinician's state of "therapeutic presence," which involves:

> (a) being in contact with one's integrated and healthy self, while (b) being open and receptive, to what is poignant in the moment and immersed in it, (c) with a larger sense of spaciousness and expansion of awareness and perception. This grounded, immersed, and expanded awareness occurs with the intention of *being with and for the client*, in service of his or her healing process.
>
> (p. 353, my italics)

Note a common theme in these descriptions: at the most essential level, the intersubjective work of psychotherapy is not defined by what the therapist does for the patient or says to the patient (left brain focus). Rather, the key mechanism is *how to be with the patient*, especially during affectively stressful moments (right brain focus). The therapist's regulated receptive state allows for participation in the intersubjective communication and interactive regulation of the patient's conscious and unconscious emotional states via an interbrain synchronization between two right hemispheres. In this manner, interpersonal resonance allows for a "specifically fitted interaction" (see Schore, 2012).

In this right brain-to-right brain context, the creative therapist in turn enhances the patient's "integrative self." In the social and personality psychology literature, Kuhl and his colleagues (2015) offer an article, "Being someone: The integrated self as a neuropsychological system," in which they distinguish a right hemisphere unconscious "integrative self" from a left hemisphere conscious "conceptual self." The functions of this right lateralized self include unconscious processing, emotional connectedness, broad vigilance, utilization of felt feedback, extended trust, resilience, and integration of negative experiences. There is currently agreement on the critical role of "integration" as a goal of psychotherapy. Research now clearly demonstrates that integration is not a function of the left brain conscious mind, but of the right brain unconscious subjective self. This change in the right brain unconscious integrated self in successful psychotherapy is beyond left brain cognitive insight. Relational, affectively focused treatment promotes *changes in the patient's right brain* interpersonal competence, social intelligence, and affiliated motivational systems.

Within the perspective of the relational interpersonal neurobiological context of psychotherapy, *changes also occur in the therapist's right brain*. Discussing the right brain neuroplasticity of clinical expertise, I have suggested that the professional growth of the clinician reflects progressions in right brain relational processes that underlie clinical skills, including affective empathy, the ability to tolerate and interactively regulate a broader array of negative and positive affective self-states, implicit openness to experience, clinical intuition, and creativity (Schore, 2014). I am now exploring the right brain origins of creativity, including interpersonal creativity in the therapeutic context (Schore, 2019a).

Of course, psychoanalysis has long been interested in the problem of creativity, especially in the earliest stages of the process which occur beneath levels of conscious awareness. In 1953, Ernst Kris proposed that "regression in the service of the ego" acts as a source of creativity, and that all manifestations of creative imagination are expressed in subjective experience. Three characteristics of this experience are outstanding. First, the individual is aware of the limitation of conscious effort. Second, there is awareness of a specific feeling and frequently a very high, emotional charge. Third, even if excitement rises, the mind tends to work with high precision, and problems are easily solved. A further common element involves the reaction of others to the creator. Note the link between creativity and emotion, and the impact of the creator's mind on the other via what he termed "creative communication."

At the same time, another psychoanalytic pioneer in the study of creativity, Theodor Reik (1948), suggested that creative individuals are more capable of shifting between secondary and primary modes of thinking and thereby to "regress" to primary process cognition, which is necessary for producing novel, original ideas. Reik argued that if the clinician "surrenders" to the regression required to access an uncanny insight, a conscious intuition into the patient's dynamics emerges. If insight originates in the unconscious, then the only way to reach it is through some degree of regression to the primary process. He observed, "As rational consciousness gives way to the primary process, it may feel as if 'the ground' is threatening 'to slip away'" (Reik, 1956, p. 492). Thus it is important that transient regressions are tolerated, as a rigidly rational consciousness will stifle nonrational hunches. Accordingly, "you have to mistrust sweet reason and to abandon yourself to the promptings and suggestions emerging from the unconscious" (Reik, 1956, p. 481). Indeed, he warned that in therapy creative insight can be displaced by technical machinations.

This proposal is supported by current neuroscience. In groundbreaking studies on split brain patients, Bogen and Bogen (1969) proposed that the right hemisphere is the seat of creativity and that the major obstacle to high creativity is left hemispheric inhibition of right hemispheric functions. Huang et al. (2013) offer data showing that the left frontal lobe is negatively related to creativity, and that the right hemisphere's predominance in creative thinking may be inhibited by the left part of the brain in normal people. Shamay-Tsoory, Adler, Aharon-Peretz, Perry, and Mayseless (2011) observe that the right medial prefrontal cortex mediates creativity, while the left hemisphere language areas may compete or interfere with creative cognition. A release of right prefrontal cortex from this competition facilitates the expression of an original creative response. Note the similarity of this disinhibition to "surrender." In more recent work, Mayseless and Shamay-Tsoory (2015) show that in enhancing verbal creativity, altering the balance between the right and the left frontal lobes can be used to modulate creative production. Reducing left frontal activity and enhancing right frontal activity reduces cognitive control, thus allowing for more creative idea production. McGilchrist (2009) observes that in order to allow for a left to right hemisphere shift, "We must inhibit one in order to inhabit the other."

Adaptive, transient, creative regression thus represents a left to right callosal shift in dominance, a temporary uncoupling of hemispheres, and a disinhibition of Freud's secondary to primary process cognition. "Regression" is defined by the *Oxford Dictionary* as "The process of returning or a tendency to return to an earlier stage of development" and "the act of going back; a return to the place of origin." Synchronized "mutual regressions" represent a shift of dominance in both members of the therapeutic dyad from the later maturing left hemispheric to the earlier developing foundational right hemispheric "origin of the self" (Schore, 1994), allowing for new learning and developmental advances in the unconscious system. A modern neuropsychoanalytic perspective suggests two types of adaptive regressions: interhemispheric (topographical, conscious left cortical to unconscious right cortical) and intrahemispheric (structural, downward cortical to subcortical deeper unconscious in lower levels of right brain). These mutually synchronized regressions are prominent in dyadic (re)enactments, expressions of complex, though largely unconscious self-states, and early relational patterns (see Schore, 2012). Adaptive regulated mutual regressions can increase interpersonal creativity, new ways of being with others, in both the patient and therapist.

Over treatment, increased access to right brain interpersonal creativity allows for an expanded ability to flexibly cope with the successive social and emotional challenges to the right brain integrated self over different life stages, within changing cultural and social contexts. This therapeutic advance represents a fundamental interpersonal neurobiological mechanism that facilitates the growth and development of the right brain subjective self, the psychobiological substrate of the human unconscious, throughout life. Right brain functions, operating beneath awareness, can thus evolve to more complexity over the stages of human development. Neuroscience is now describing progressions in not only "lower" right brain survival functions of the deep unconscious but also in the high right brain, the source of the most complex human functions beyond left brain language. A large body of studies now demonstrate that the "emotional," "social" right brain is centrally involved in not only affects and stress regulation, but also in empathy, intuition, creativity, imagery, symbolic thought, insight, play, humor, music, compassion, morality, and love (Schore, 2012). Indeed, psychoanalysis, like psychology, has overvalued the functions of the surface left hemispheric conscious mind. These higher functions of the unconscious mind allow for a reformulation and expansion of the essential role of the unconscious in everyday life.

Implications for innovations and new directions

Psychodynamic theory and practice are now facing the challenges of both a period of significant cultural and political change as well as a time of rapid advances in knowledge in the mental health field. Indeed, over the last three decades there has been an explosion of knowledge across disciplines as well as an expansion of an integrative perspective within and across fields. All disciplines must move beyond their intrinsic isolation and forge deeper clinical theoretical and research connections into disciplines with which they intersect. Psychoanalysis needs to make an active commitment to this integration and connection. This is especially so in the current political environment that is anti-mental health, anti-science, anti-psychotherapy, and pro-big pharma.

Returning to the beginning of this chapter, in my article on the 100th anniversary of Freud's *Project* (1895) I asked, is the time right for a "psychology which shall be a natural science?" At the time I speculated,

> [T]he response of psychoanalysis will have to involve a reintegration of its own internal theoretical divisions, a reassessment of its educational priorities, a reevaluation of its current predominant emphasis on cognition, especially verbal mechanisms, as well as a reworking of its Cartesian mind-body dichotomies. This redefinition involves the identity of psychoanalysis itself, in terms of both its self-reference and its relations with the other sciences. In principle, whether or not a rapprochement takes place between two parties depends not only on the

information they share in common, but on their individual willingness to enter into a communicative system.

(Schore, 1997, p. 833)

Exactly 20 years on, the field has made significant movement towards these goals. But psychoanalysis, "the science of unconscious processes," needs to significantly increase its efforts to continue to incorporate advances in science in order to fuel its growth and relevance. Ernest Jones (1953, p. 384) called the *Project* "something vital in Freud that was soon to become his scientific imagination." We need a return of scientific imagination in 21st century psychoanalysis.

The unique knowledge psychoanalysis contributes to science and the humanities is its century of studies of the fundamental role of the unconscious in the human experience, the deeper realms of the human psyche. The field must update its self-definition from the frozen image of Freud's 1920s couch in order to increase its standing and status in the eyes of other fields. Psychoanalysis also needs to shift from its too narrow focus on the cognitive unconscious mind to an unconscious right brain/mind/body system.

Annual conferences need more inclusion of science from within and outside the field and more commitment to heuristic psychoanalytic research on therapy change processes and underlying mechanisms. The field must make deeper connections with disciplines not only within but beyond psychology and psychiatry. As opposed to a denial of the unconscious at the end of the last century, many disciplines are now studying "implicit" processes beneath levels of awareness. Yet many fields are still centered in a model of a left hemispheric mind, including clinical and developmental psychology. These connections need to be strengthened into not only science and psychiatry but also different fields of medicine. This could allow for a deeper understanding of the relationships between physical and mental disease and more complex models of psychosomatic disorders. In order to do this, psychoanalytic authors should publish in journals outside of the field.

Changes in education and training: There is a timely need for a critical re-evaluation of Freud's theoretical and clinical models, of what to retain, what to leave behind. Courses in developmental and affective neuroscience and interpersonal neurobiology need to be included in academic curricula.

An example is the volume *Core Competencies of Relational Psychoanalysis* (Barsness, 2018). There also needs to be an expanded alliance not only within various schools of psychoanalysis but also with the much larger population of psychodynamic psychotherapists.

Changes in clinical psychoanalysis: Right brain neuroscience can act as a generator of "evidence-based" clinical models. The field needs to continue its shift in emphasis from solely classical psychoanalysis to face-to-face psychoanalytic psychotherapy. A distinction needs to be made between short-term, symptom reduction/remission and long-term, growth-promoting treatment. More writings are needed on reducing infant, child, adolescent, and adult patients' distressing affect dysregulating symptomatology and re-establishing interpersonal functioning of a broad range of disorders, including depression and anxiety disorders, personality disorders, bipolar disorders, schizophrenia, and autistic spectrum disorders. Indeed, neurobiologically informed psychodynamic models need to be incorporated into short-term symptom-reducing psychotherapeutic interventions in such disorders. In all disorders, psychoanalysis brings an expertise in unconscious implicit right brain relational communicating and affect regulating systems within the therapeutic alliance and focuses on the bodily based internal world of the patient.

I also urge a call for a commitment to early intervention in order for the field to make a larger impact on not only the individual but also on cultural emotional and physical health, and thereby a broader improvement of the human condition. Though first forged in maternal-fetal and attachment interactions, right brain evolutionary mechanisms continue to evolve over the life span. This trajectory of right brain development can be altered by attachment trauma. Neurobiologically informed psychodynamic models of early intervention during critical periods of the human brain growth spurt (what pediatricians call "the first thousand days") can alter the intergenerational transmission and prevention of psychopathologies.

Changes in theoretical psychoanalysis: Variations in the organization of right brain circuits implicitly processing emotion and stress are relevant to individual, personality, gender, ethnic group, and socioeconomic differences. Yet the invariant properties of right lateralized limbic-autonomic circuits represent the common expressions of humanness, of fundamentally what it means to be human. As discussed, advances in knowledge of the right brain may act as an integrative and energizing force that can catalyze movement of the field out of the consulting room into the larger social and political culture. As this chapter demonstrates, this change involves replacing metapsychological abstractions with right brain neurobiological data. Neuropsychoanalysis needs to be integrated into the central constructs of its theory of *the unconscious, the foundation of psychoanalysis*. The expanding connections between psychoanalysis and neuroscience can generate innovative future directions for the field.

References

Allison, K. L., & Rossouw, P. J. (2013). The therapeutic alliance: Exploring the concept of "safety" from a neuropsychotherapeutic perspective. *International Journal of Neuropsychotherapy, 1*, 21–29.

Barsness, R. (Ed.). (2018). *Core competencies of relational psychoanalysis*. New York, NY: Routledge.

Bogen, J. E., & Bogen, G. M. (1969). The other side of the brain. 3: The corpus callosum and creativity. *Bulletin of the Los Angeles Neurological Society, 34*, 199–220.

Brenner, C. (1980). A psychoanalytic theory of affects. In R. Plutchik & H. Kellerman (Eds.), *Emotion: Theory, research, and experience* (Vol. 1). New York, NY: Academic Press.

Brierley, M. (1937). Affects in theory and practice. *International Journal of Psychoanalysis, 18*, 256–274.

Bromberg, P. M. (2006). *Awakening the dreamer: Clinical journeys*. Mahwah, NJ: Analytic Press.

Bromberg, P. M. (2017). Psychotherapy as the growth of wholeness: The negotiation of individuality and otherness. In M. Solomon & D. S. Siegel (Eds.), *How people change: Relationships and neuroplasticity in psychotherapy* (pp. 1–36). New York, NY: W. W. Norton.

Chelazzi, L., Bisley, J. W., & Bartolomeo, P. (2018). The unconscious guidance of attention. *Cortex, 102*, 1–5.

Chen, L., & Hsiao, J. (2014). Right hemisphere dominance in nonconscious processing. *Journal of Vision, 14*, 1313. doi:10.1167/14.10.1313

Craparo, G., & Mucci, C. (2017). *Unrepressed unconscious, implicit memory, and clinical work*. London: Karnac.

Crouzet, S. M., Kirchner, H., & Thorpe, S. J. (2010). Fast saccades toward faces: Face detection in just 100 Ms. *Journal of Vision, 10*(16). doi:10.1167/10.4.16

Freud, S. (1895). Project for a scientific psychology. In J. Strachey (Ed. and Trans.), *The standard edition of the complete psychological works of Sigmund Freud*. London: Hogarth Press.

Freud, S. (1913). The claims of psycho-analysis to scientific interest. In J. Strachey (Ed. and Trans.), *The standard edition of the complete psychological works of Sigmund Freud*. London: Hogarth Press.

Freud, S. (1915). The unconscious. In J. Strachey (Ed. and Trans.), *The standard edition of the complete psychological works of Sigmund Freud*. London: Hogarth Press.

Gainotti, G. (2005). Emotions, unconscious processes, and the right hemisphere. *Neuropsychoanalysis, 7*, 71–81.

Gainotti, G. (2012). Unconscious processing of emotions and the right hemisphere. *Neuropsychologia, 50*, 205–218.

Geller, S. M., & Porges, S. W. (2014). Therapeutic presence: Neurophysiological mechanisms mediating feeling safe in therapeutic relationships. *Journal of Psychotherapy Integration, 24*, 178–192.

Greenberg, L. (2014). The therapeutic relationship in emotion-focused psychotherapy. *Psychotherapy, 51*, 350–357.

Grunbaum, A. (1984). *The foundations of psychoanalysis: A philosophical critique*. Berkeley, CA: University of California Press.

Hassin, R. R. (2013). Yes it can: On the functional abilities of the human unconscious. *Perspectives in Psychological Science, 8*, 195–207.

Hassin, R. R., Bargh, J. A., Engell, A. D., & McCulloch, K. C. (2009). Implicit working memory. *Consciousness and Cognition, 18*, 665–678.

Huang, P., Qui, L., Shen, L., Zhang, Y., Song, Z., Qi, Z., Gong, Q., & Xie, P. (2013). Evidence for a left-over-right inhibitory mechanism during figural creative thinking in healthy nonartists. *Human Brain Mapping, 34*, 2724–2732.

Jones, E. (1953). *The life and work of Sigmund Freud: Volume I. The formative years and great discoveries, 1856–1900*. New York, NY: Basic Books.

Jung, C. (1963). *Memories, dreams and reflections*. New York, NY: Pantheon Books.

Kris, E. (1953). Psychoanalysis and the study of creative imagination. *Bulletin of the New York Academy of Medicine, 29*, 334–351.

Kuhl, J., Quirin, M., & Koole, S. L. (2015). Being someone: The integrated self as a neuropsychological system. *Social and Personality Psychology Compass, 9*, 115–132.

Mancia, M. (2006). Implicit memory and early unrepressed unconscious: Their role in the therapeutic process (How the neurosciences can contribute to psychoanalysis). *International Journal of Psychoanalysis, 87*, 83–103.

Mayseless, N., & Shamay-Tsoory, S. G. (2015). Enhancing verbal creativity: Modulating creativity by altering the balance between right and left inferior frontal gyrus with tDCS. *Neuroscience, 291*, 167–176.

McGilchrist, I. (2009). *The master and his emissary*. New Haven, CT: Yale University Press.

McGilchrist, I. (2015). Divine understanding and the divided brain. In J. Clausen & N. Levy (eds.), *Handbook of neuroethics*. Dordrecht: Springer Science. doi:10.1007/978-94-007-4707-4_99

Meares, R. (2012). *A dissociation model of borderline personality disorder*. New York, NY: W. W. Norton.

Reik, T. (1948). *Listening with the third ear: The inner experience of a psychoanalyst*. New York, NY: Grove Press.

Reik, T. (1956). Adventures in psychoanalytic discovery. In M. Sherman (Ed.), *The search within* (pp. 473–626). New York, NY: Jason Aronson.

Schepman, A., Rodway, P., & Pritchard, H. (2016). Right-lateralized unconscious, but not conscious, processing of affective environmental sounds. *Laterality: Asymmetries of Body, Brain and Cognition, 21*, 606–632. doi:10.1080/1357650X.2015.1105245

Schore, A. N. (1994). *Affect regulation the origin of the self: The neurobiology of emotional development.* Mahweh, NJ: Erlbaum.

Schore, A. N. (1997). A century after Freud's project: Is a rapprochement between psychoanalysis and neurobiology at hand? *Journal of the American Psychoanalytic Association, 45*, 807–840.

Schore, A. N. (2003a). *Affect dysregulation and disorders of the self.* New York, NY: W. W. Norton.

Schore, A. N. (2003b). *Affect regulation and the repair of the self.* New York, NY: W. W. Norton.

Schore, A. N. (2011). The right brain implicit self lies at the core of psychoanalysis. *Psychoanalytic Dialogues, 21*, 75–100.

Schore, A. N. (2012). *The science and art of psychotherapy.* New York, NY: W. W. Norton.

Schore, A. N. (2014). The right brain is dominant in psychotherapy. *Psychotherapy, 51*, 388–397. http://dx.doi.org/10.1037/a0037083

Schore, A. N. (2019a). *Right brain psychotherapy.* New York, NY: W. W. Norton.

Schore, A. N. (2019b). *The development of the unconscious mind.* New York, NY: W. W. Norton.

Shamay-Tsoory, S. G., Adler, N., Aharon-Peretz, J., Perry, D., & Mayseless, N. (2011). The neural bases of creative thinking and originality. *Neuropsychologia, 49*, 178–185.

Siegel, D. J. (2012). *The developing mind: How relationships and the brain interact to shape who we are* (2nd ed.). New York, NY: Guilford Press.

Tucker, D. M., & Moller, L. (2007). The metamorphosis: Individuation of the adolescent brain. In D. Romer & E. F. Walker (Eds.), *Adolescent psychopathology and the developing brain: Integrating brain and prevention science* (pp. 85–102). Oxford, England: Oxford University Press.

Chapter 7

The impact of the interpersonal innovations on contemporary psychoanalysis

Irwin Hirsch

Prominent leading psychoanalytic thinkers once associated with the classical Freudian hegemony of the American Psychoanalytic Association (e.g., Gabbard, 1995; Wallerstein, 1995), shortly prior to entering the 21st century, write of an emerging common ground with respect to theories of therapeutic action. This common ground crosses the boundaries of theoretical traditions that once were in considerable opposition to one another in this dimension. Both Gabbard and Wallerstein refer to the profoundly increased attention across much of the spectrum of the psychoanalytic literature to the concept of countertransference in particular, and more generally to the emphasis on the interacting and mutually influencing psyches of both participants in the psychoanalytic dyad. Once upon a time, the mind of the specimen patient only was the object of study, and the analyst was conceptualized as a scientist, who, when sufficiently analyzed himself, was able to view the other with a pristine objectivity. Though this latter view may persist today among a minority of orthodox Freudian, Lacanian and Kleinian analysts, it endured surprisingly long after alternate and innovative visions of analytic subjectivity were introduced initially by Ferenczi and Rank (1924), and then more systematically elaborated by Sullivan, Fromm and Thompson in the 1940s and 1950s into what became the interpersonal school or tradition (Hirsch, 2015).

This originally interpersonal conception of the analyst as a co-participant (albeit in an asymmetrical relational matrix) in a relationship between two subjectivities has in recent years been supported by a new dimension of infant research. Enhanced by contemporary technology, researchers like Stern (1985) and Beebe (2000) have been able to capture on film the micro interactions between mothers and infants, documenting the degree to which, from the earliest moments in life, the two parties invariably both engage and profoundly exert influence over one another. This provides a ready extrapolation to the psychoanalytic situation, that is, no two people can be together without having an impact on one another. Were the technology employed by infant observation researchers applied to patient-therapist interaction, it would no doubt be demonstrated that even the most subtle vocal and non-verbal actions between the two co-participants exert considerable reciprocal influence. It has become difficult to still argue that the psychoanalytic process is in any way a study of a subjective participant, the patient, through the eyes of a scientifically objective and non-participating or influencing psychoanalyst.

Early interpersonal writing, initially presenting as an innovative alternative to developmental theories emphasizing the primacy of endogenous drive states and defenses against these drives, served as a corrective to a psychoanalysis that did not fully recognize exogenous experience – the unique significance of each subtle interaction between infant and caregiver from the moment of birth (or, perhaps, intrauterine) and through the entire life cycle. Indeed, a purely interactional theory of human development, so effectively documented by this generation of infant research, has reinforced the early and continued interpersonal emphasis on the mutually constructed configurations in the dyadic psychoanalytic situation, or for that matter, in any dyadic interaction. What remains unique about this perspective is the focal emphasis on the examination of both parties in the analytic interaction – countertransference awareness on equal footing to patients' transferences. That is, the unwitting personal input of the analyst is seen as having more power in the evolution of treatment than any prescribed technique, e.g., interpretation, detailed inquiry, holding, empathy, etc. This point of view, central to early and current interpersonal thinking, has become one of the essences of relational theory and views about therapeutic action. Indeed, many key contemporary analysts identified as relational could just as well be called interpersonal. Stephen Mitchell, for instance, in personal communication had claimed that he was both interpersonal and relational, as has both Philip Bromberg and Donnel Stern. It should be noted that many of the founders of the relational perspective and its innovations were trained at the William Alanson White Institute, the home of the interpersonal tradition.

The concept of analyst as objective observer has evolved to analyst as subjective participant-observer, to analyst as observing-participant or co-participant, and more recently, to analyst as mutual enactor (Hirsch,

1996, 2015). Each step in this evolution, initiated by interpersonal thinkers, places increased stress on analysts' subjective and idiosyncratic presence. The changing conception of the analyst, and of the reciprocal nature of any analytic encounter, indeed reflects the developmental perspective that parent-child dyads, like analysts and patients, have mutual impact in every moment of interaction. Analysts' attention to countertransference now parallels attention to transference – the two are considered part of what Mitchell (1988) referred to as an inseparable matrix. The analyst can no longer purport to be an even relatively objective observer of patients' inner and outer worlds, nor free of an inevitable unwitting influence on the patient (Hirsch, 2008). As both Hoffman (1983) and Aron (1996) have illuminated, patients must be respected as capable observers of their analysts' experience, just as analysts were always thought to be exclusively sensitive observers of their patients. That the contemporary psychoanalyst must now attempt to be aware of more than the patient per se, that attention to the psyche of the analyst and to the mutual influences in treatment now carry equivalent weight, is due in largest part to the early and ongoing interpersonal contributions to our literature. This literature, first introduced over 65 years ago and continuing to the present day, has, as noted earlier, ushered in what has been called the relational or the postmodern turn in our field. Interpersonal innovation, as both Gabbard and Wallerstein have implied, has become woven into the fabric of a wide range of contemporary schools of thought or psychoanalytic identifications.

It is worth noting that though Sullivan's (e.g., 1940) introduction of the term "participant-observation" signaled the beginning of the end of the one-person psychology illusion of objective observation in psychoanalysis, he and his colleagues' contributions to the mutually subjective nature of contemporary psychoanalytic interaction are often not given their due. For example, terms like "intersubjectivity", as elaborated most thoroughly by Stolorow and his colleagues (e.g., Stolorow & Atwood, 1979), seem to me essentially synonymous to much earlier interpersonal conceptions of subjectivity and mutual influence, though are discussed as an entirely new recognition about the nature of psychoanalytic interaction – a new "school of thought", if you will. Classical Freudian analysts (see Hirsch, 1996, for a detailed discussion of this) since the middle 1980s have been writing about mutual enactments between analyst and patient, thoroughly mirroring and embracing bi-directional interpersonal conceptions of the analytic dyad. The conception of mutual enactment in particular had been introduced and addressed years earlier by Levenson (1972), though he had used a different term ("transformation") to describe this phenomenon.[1]

Unfortunately, because of the almost total absence of cross-fertilization between classical Freudian and interpersonal literature until the 1980s, few of these scholarly analysts were at all familiar with conceptions that they had essentially and innocently rediscovered. And most ironically, though relational psychoanalysis emerges directly from the interpersonal tradition – Greenberg and Mitchell (1983) were themselves trained in this tradition – many other relational writers have not sufficiently referenced and credited the earlier interpersonal forbears with whom they are so often thoroughly compatible. I do not suggest that interpersonal and relational are synonymous – I fully recognize that the latter is an umbrella term encompassing a range of theoretical traditions. I do believe, as noted earlier, that the interpersonal contribution to what has evolved as relational theorizing is by far its single most significant influence and that one would too often not know this when examining the reference sections of a fair percentage of contemporary writing identified as relational.[2]

Analysts associated with this interpersonal perspective originally viewed themselves in opposition to the hegemonic Freudians in the USA and did little to try to become integrated into the broader American or international psychoanalysis of the middle part of the 20th century. There seemed to be a certain pleasure in being considered as rebellious and radical outsiders, reading the literature of the conservative majority, if at all, with a highly critical eye. Innovative interpersonal teaching and writing was focused initially in the Washington, D.C area, where it began with Sullivan, then largely in migration to New York City. The William Alanson White Institute was its primary home, though the interpersonal voice also became very strongly represented at the NYU Postdoctoral Program, founded by White Institute graduates, to some extent at Adelphi University's Postdoctoral Program, and later at The Manhattan Institute for Psychoanalysis. Until the middle 1980s, when the interpersonal perspective was **re**introduced to the broader psychoanalytic audience, especially by Greenberg and Mitchell (1983), with the exception of the too often marginalized voice of Searles (e.g., 1965, 1979), and then reflected in Gill's (e.g., 1982, 1983) theoretical shift, this was the extent to which interpersonal ideas were acknowledged as incorporated into the larger culture of psychoanalysis. Up to this point, interpersonally identified analysts published their own journal, *Contemporary Psychoanalysis*, and interpersonal writers were virtually never invited to publish in, nor rarely read the more internationally popular, *International Journal of Psychoanalysis*, *Psychoanalytic Quarterly*, and the *Journal of the American Psychoanalytic Association*. There existed only the most minimal cross-fertilization of ideas between interpersonalists and Freudians, or as well, with the various object-relations theories (see, Slochower, 1996) that had been developing largely in England and South America.

In what follows, I will try to summarize some of the key elements of interpersonal innovations that remained largely beneath the radar to broader audiences until the 1980s. I will attempt to illustrate that interpersonal ideas, far more than any other, have been responsible, albeit very belatedly, for the relational and the postmodern turn in the broader realm of psychoanalysis, the fundamental shift from a one-person objectivist psychology to a two-person intersubjective one. In considerable summary, Sullivan's two sea-changing contributions refer to his view of human development as most exclusively a function of internalized relations with key others from birth through the life cycle, and his depiction of the analytic situation as an interaction between, as Renik (1993) described, two irreducibly subjective co-participants (see Fiscalini, 2004).

Sullivan posited an entirely interpersonal picture of human development: identifications with significant others; internalization of important self-other experience; and as both Bromberg (1998) and Stern (1997) have elaborated so well, dissociation of experiences that were potentially disruptive to creating harmonious equilibrium among various internalized self-other configurations and, as well, were disruptive to real external familial others. Real relations with real people, not the theretofore dominant psychoanalytic concept of instinctual drive states and defenses and compromise formations in relation to these, were viewed as the key building blocks of human character structure. Exogenous experience was emphasized and the endogenous minimized – aggression is learned and not instinctual, and although sexual desire is a drive state, the way any individual expresses sexuality is also learned in the context of relations with key others. In this context, universal theoretical formulations like Oedipal, castration, primal scene, guilt over masturbation and envy were rejected as truly universal in favor of the effort to inquire into the idiosyncratic developmental life of each unique individual. Wolstein (e.g., 1977) later made this anti-metapsychological argument the centerpiece of his large body of work. From the beginning, interpersonalists were skeptical of strong theory and were highly critical of a prevailing psychoanalytic literature where formulaic and universal conceptions seemed to dictate how everyone was understood.

Sullivan's second monumental contribution emerged from the German scientist Heisenberg and his principle of uncertainty and from Lewin's field theory in American social psychology. Heisenberg argued that the subjective presence of the experimenter invariably influences the outcome of any experiment, that is, the outcome of any research cannot be legitimately viewed as pristine objective truth. If the person of experimenter in the hard sciences invariably influences the outcome of his research, it is impossible for the all too human psychoanalyst to view patients with anything but a profoundly subjective eye. Sullivan's best known quote, "We are all more simply human than otherwise" (Sullivan, 1940, p. 16), leads to the portrayal of the analyst as a flawed participant-observer, a most dramatic and innovative shift from the prevailing psychoanalytic model of his time – the well analyzed analyst as an objective observer, the model of the classical blank screen (Hirsch, 2008). Social psychology's field theory presents a parallel perspective, that is, an individual cannot be studied in vaccuo – in isolation from the field within which he exists and inevitably interacts (see Stern, 2013, for a thorough explication of the notion of invariable mutual impact between participants in any field).[3]

While circa 2019, it is difficult to imagine that such a hierarchy existed – patient as sick and subjective, analyst as healthy and objective (see, Racker, 1968; Hirsch, 2008), such dichotomous thinking prevailed in the wider international psychoanalysis until the 1980s and can still be seen in some of our literature. Though it was Ferenczi and Rank, back in the 1920s, who first wrote of the person of the analyst as a factor in therapeutic outcome, with a few noteworthy exceptions (e.g., Loewald, 1960), the vast majority of the non-interpersonal literature in this country maintained that accurate interpretation of genetic material as it appeared in the context of the transference neurosis was the sole mutative factor in analysis. Though contemporary ideas like the analyst as invariably participating at least unwittingly, the study of countertransference and the interaction between transference and countertransference, mutual influence between analyst and patient and the inevitable perspectivism and co-construction of narrative that follows all existed as developing ideas within the interpersonal school between the 1940s through the 1970s, only the unusual American or international analyst would subscribe to these notions. There was some awareness that such thinking found some compatible partnership in some of England's object-relations theorists in particular, and within the developing work of Kohut (1974), though the extent of some of these largely unknown parallels came to clear light only with the publication of Greenberg and Mitchell's (1983) classic volume.

There are six other first and second generation[4] contributors (post Sullivan) identified with the interpersonal tradition whose innovative contributions to 21st century psychoanalysis are particularly pivotal and without whom we might still be close to the middle of the 20th century – I refer to Erich Fromm, Clara Thompson, Benjamin Wolstein, Edgar Levenson, Erwin Singer and Harold Searles. I believe that their contributions to psychoanalysis as we now know it are still insufficiently recognized and appreciated, though like with Ferenczi, Rank and Sullivan, their work is thoroughly incorporated into the very fabric of contemporary theory and practice.

Fromm, most known for his widely popular social psychoanalytic writing – the impact of cultural factors on the psyche (e.g., economics, race, oppression, non-traditional sexuality) – was originally trained in Berlin as a classical analyst and, along with the classically trained Thompson, helped translate the autodidact Sullivan from the realm of psychiatry and psychotherapy into psychoanalysis more proper.[5] It should be noted that his recognition of the importance of cultural factors on personality was uniformly dismissed by the hegemonic mainstream as "superficial social psychology". Anyone aware of current psychoanalytic thinking can appreciate the importance of endogenous cultural factors on all of our psyches. Fromm also made key contributions to understanding the adhesive nature of character development and the difficulty inherent in trying to help people change. He described a core conflict between unconscious personal loyalty to known and to loved others and the relative comfort remaining within these familiar self-states despite any dysfunctional elements to such a life versus the risk of individuation and an ensuing sense of aloneness. In his best-known book, *Escape from Freedom* (1941), Fromm underscores how known and familiar misery usually trumps risking the potentially liberating unknown. In a sense, as Harold Searles (1979) has said, we love our pathology, and we choose both consciously and unconsciously to remain rigidly adhered to the all too comfortable familiar. Fromm's most significant and innovative contribution to analytic praxis was his emphasis on using himself as a subjective observer of his patients' way of being within the therapeutic interaction, i.e., using his countertransference experience to try to clarify patients' transferences. This use of analysts' subjective otherness to convey to patients how they may be perceived by others in the world reflected a dramatic departure from what was generally seen as analysts' exclusive interactive purview – ambiguous questions (e.g., "tell me more about this") and interpretations. Fromm opened-up a whole new dimension of respectable participation, one now totally woven into the fabric of contemporary psychoanalysis.

Clara Thompson, Sullivan's closest colleague and friend, was trained as part of the American Psychoanalytic Association and was also dispatched by Sullivan to undergo a brief analysis with Ferenczi in Europe and then familiarize Sullivan with Ferenczi's ideas. Thompson's writing (e.g., 1950) about the concept of countertransference and the inevitable role that the person of the analyst plays in every analytic encounter set the stage for subsequent thinking about the now central and innovative concept of mutual enactment. Her analytic work focused on the here and now of the transference-countertransference matrix, viewing this interaction as an illustration of how patients construct their current life to conform to the internalized past. One can see how Thompson's thinking was a forerunner to conceptions of mutual enactment, that is, her sensitivity to how the nature of patient-therapist interaction closely paralleled the quality of patients' relationships outside of psychoanalysis. Indeed, there exists a strong existential bent in Thompson's thinking – she argued that problems in living are less a function of past troubled experience than the unconscious motivation to recreate this internalized interactional experience in the present. The transference-countertransference matrix was seen by her as a vivid and immediate forum to examine how patients shape their current interactional life. Existential ideas were central to both Thompson and Fromm – patients were seen less as simply wounded victims of bad early experience than as agents, conscious and unconscious, in repeating old and bad experience. Actually, this corresponds closely to Freud's depiction of psychoanalysis as a vehicle to address not normal and inevitable tragedy and sadness but those life problems that all humans unconsciously create and recreate for themselves. In writing about Thompson's contributions, one cannot fail to note that she was a pioneer in challenging male dominated sexist conceptions in our field, emerging as one of the very early feminists in the psychoanalytic universe. A profound illustration of this is reflected in what had been a widely accepted view that "penis envy" in women is a biological imperative to compensate for the vagina, then viewed as an inferior organ that had suffered from castration. Thompson removed this from the biological to the social register – men have more power in most societies, and women desire the freedom to exert the powers within themselves.

Benjamin Wolstein (e.g., 1954), influenced by his analyst, Thompson, was years ahead of his time in his published work on countertransference (see, Wilner, 2000; Bonovitz, 2009). He comes closest post Ferenczi to a view of the analytic process as mutual, the conscious and unconscious of both parties creating reciprocal influence on one another. Indeed, in his placing interpretive formulations far in the background, he argued that the thoroughly subjective engagement between two fairly symmetrical co-participants was the heart of mutative action (Hirsch, 2008). He described this interaction as an effort to create an atmosphere wherein both analytic participants speak optimally openly about their subjective experience of one another, the ultimate goal defined as a freeing of patients' theretofore inhibited creative unconscious. In his innovative freedom to use his subjectivity, he considerably expanded the parameters of what has been traditionally considered analytic reserve and caution. Contemporary writing about analysts' use of spontaneity and self-disclosure owes a usually unpaid debt to Wolstein.

Harold Searles (1965, 1979), writing at about the same time as Wolstein (1950s, 1960s) is as much responsible for our contemporary sensitivity to analysts' subjectivity (countertransference) as anyone in the psychoanalytic literature. Nobody more than Searles wrote so openly and bravely about their private affective experience with patients and the degree to which patients influenced analysts' emotional reactions and reciprocally, how analysts' emotional states influenced patients (Hirsch, 2008, 2015). Searles, specializing in working analytically with the most severely disturbed patients, illustrated clearly that analysts too are dominated by their emotional states and in many respects are as deeply flawed in their interactions with patients as are the patients themselves. The decline in authoritarian hierarchy between analysts and patients that is currently so emblematic had its strongest advocate in the work of Searles. And, along with Thompson, Fromm, Wolstein and Singer, Searles was a pioneer with regard to analysts' productive use of countertransference and, as well, disinhibition of the analyst in the analytic interaction. Searles was also possibly the first to argue that in order for patients to change, the analyst too must himself change in his interaction with each patient (see, Mendelsohn, 2002).

Erwin Singer, a devoted student of Erich Fromm, was a significant teacher for a generation of students at the William Alanson White Institute and the NYU Postdoctoral Program in Psychoanalysis and Psychotherapy. More than anyone else, he emphasized and expanded Fromm's clinical writing, often over-shadowed by Fromm's far better known socio-cultural thinking. Singer emphasized the value of analysts' use of countertransference experience as perhaps the primary way of getting to know patients. Like both Wolstein and Searles, he advocated analysts' optimal freedom to share countertransference-based observations with patients, holding the view that these candid observations reflected the very best that we have to give patients. That is, in spite of whatever anxiety an analyst's pointed observations might create, patients by and large benefited from the honesty and the authenticity involved in analysts' willingness to be open and frank with them. In this context, Singer had no illusions about the objectivity of analysts' observations, encouraging patients to be reciprocally candid in sharing with analysts their very often acutely sensitive perceptions about the person of the analyst and the quality of the analysts' interactions (see, Singer, 1977).

I have written elsewhere (Hirsch, 1992), in a review essay of Edgar Levenson's last book (Levenson, 1991), that he, Levenson, may be more responsible than any other contemporary writer for the postmodern, relational turn in psychoanalysis (see also, Foehl, 2008). I refer you to this paper for a more detailed explication of his contributions, for here I will focus only on his discovery, if you will, of what has become the hallmark concept of mutative action shared among analysts of many identifications (e.g., interpersonal, relational, post self-psychology, contemporary Kleinian and liberal Freudian), the concept of mutual enactment. Much of Levenson's writing from his first book (*The Fallacy of Understanding*, 1972) through the early 1990s reflects an effort to describe analysts' perception and understanding of patients as profoundly influenced by the person and the theory of the subjective analyst. He pre-dated Spence (1982) and Schafer (1983) in describing all analytic understanding as personally derived narrative based on the irreducible subjectivity of the narrator/analyst. There is no objective interpretive understanding to be derived from being in analysis – only sensible narratives that are inherently perspectival. These perspectives are derived largely from a mutually lived-out analytic interaction – what is talked about becomes mutually lived-out. The mutual engagement seen in analytic interaction appears to line up with patients' descriptions of both early experience with key caretakers and adult experience in the extra-transference. The relatively reserved analyst becomes unwittingly enmeshed in each patient's way of being with others, and all too soon the analytic interaction becomes a playground reflecting a representation of patients' internalized self-other configurations. When one or another party becomes aware of this interaction, it becomes spoken and then lined up isomorphically with both past and current configurations. The explication of this in the here and now is, in and of itself, a new experience and, as well, opens up opportunity for new ways of being in the analytic interaction and in the interpersonal world at large. As noted earlier, Levenson referred to this as "transformation" in 1972, and Sandler (1976) begat this same concept, calling it "role responsiveness", and still later, Jacobs (1986) introduced the now widely used term – "mutual enactment". Both of the latter two distinguished authors' writing was a reflection of what I earlier described as an absence of cross-fertilization, before the 1980s, between interpersonal publications and those of most others.

That the prevailing concept of mutual enactment and the irreducible subjectivity of all analytic engagement is still not widely known to stem from the work of Levenson and other interpersonally identified writers well illustrates my thesis regarding both the centrality of interpersonal innovations to contemporary thinking and the insufficient acknowledgment of these contributions. Interpersonal contributions did not begin to enter the mainstream of American and international psychoanalysis until endorsed and supported by a select few classical analysts, especially Searles (e.g., 1979) and Gill (1982, 1983), and then exposed to the psychoanalytic world further by the enormous popularity of Greenberg and Mitchell's (1983) book, later very ably reinforced by some writers identified as relational (e.g., Hoffman, 1983; Aron, 1996).

In conclusion, the prevailing developmental writing of Beebe (2000), Stern (1985), Fonagy (2001) and others identified as attachment or relational theorists all now support Sullivan's far less detailed or researched ideas. Simply said, when examined closely, interpersonal interaction, from at least birth onward, is fundamentally what makes us who we are. The current literature on therapeutic action, shared by those referring to themselves as relational, liberal Freudian, contemporary Kleinian, object-relational, post self-psychology, intersubjective, chaos theorists and process of change students, all emphasize the perspectival and co-constructed nature of knowledge, the irreducible subjectivity of the unwittingly subjective psychoanalyst and the inevitability of mutual enactment in the psychoanalytic situation. For many, the verbal exploration of the latter lies at the heart of mutative action. It took thinkers like Searles, Gill, Greenberg and Mitchell to introduce the theretofore isolated interpersonal thinking into the awareness of the wider psychoanalytic culture and to illustrate some similarities between this and other psychoanalytic traditions. However, the extent to which the interpersonal tradition has been the forerunner to so many contemporary ideas, all based on the joint pillars of a purely interpersonal theory of human development, and analysts' inherent subjective co-participation in all aspects of analytic work still remains under-recognized. This tradition has been integrated and absorbed by a range of old and new theoretical identifications under different names.

Much of my own writing, beginning in the early 1980s has, been an effort to convey the degree to which the interpersonal tradition reflects the very essence and heart of psychoanalysis as we now know it. Drive theory, not too long ago the center of psychoanalytic developmental thinking, is now deeply in the background of innovative theorizing. The conception of the analyst as a reasonably objective interpreter of the mind of the patient (Sullivan's internally contradictory notion of analyst as potential expert not withstanding) has for the most part been debunked. A purely interpersonal theory of human psychological development, though it took some time to be integrated into the wider body of psychoanalysis, marked the beginning of the challenge to Freud's drive theory of human development. As well, it is now widely recognized that the extrinsic factor of one's cultural environment invariably plays a role in human development. As already noted, at one point, this was viewed by the prevailing psychoanalytic culture as superficial social psychology and an avoidance of the power of endogenous drive states and the ego's defenses against these. This is now an anachronistic language. The introduction of the view of the analyst as participant-observer, no longer an alleged objective observer, initiated a view of the mutually subjective nature of the psychoanalytic relationship as it is now perceived by most in our field. Interpretation and the creation of optimal self-awareness are still integral to our field, though mutative action is now more likely seen to lie primarily in the evolution of the relationship between each unique analyst and each unique patient, a notion that dates way back to Ferenczi and Rank. Finally, the view of the analyst as a flawed and subjective other – anything but an authoritarian and objective scientific observer – has created an atmosphere of reduced hierarchy between analyst and patient, indeed an affirmation that we are all more simply human than otherwise.

Notes

1 It should also be noted that the South American Kleinian analyst, Heinrich Racker (1968), also elaborated the mutual influence between patient and analyst that later has been described and accepted as analogous to the concept of mutual enactment.
2 I should note that writers self-identified as relational (some have referred to themselves as "interpersonal-relational") have since the middle 1980s been far more prolific than those authors self-identified as interpersonal. So much of this excellent writing in my eyes reflects a carrying forward and expansion of earlier interpersonal contributions and had the newer designation "relational" not been introduced, much of this writing could as just well be labeled "contemporary interpersonal".
3 Sullivan's theorizing was not without contradictions, and these are well known to interpersonal scholars and beyond. The strongest contradiction in his thinking is reflected in his view of the analyst as an *expert in interpersonal relations*. It is obvious to contemporary interpersonal analysts that one cannot be both a subjective co-participant and at the same time an "expert". In a similar vein, Sullivan's embrace of detailed inquiry into the life and life history of each patient implies that something approximating *truth* can be uncovered with such inquiry. Though these elements of objectivist thinking clearly existed in Sullivan and still do among a minority of contemporary interpersonal analysts, such irreconcilable conflicts do not erase the fact that Sullivan's portrayal of the analyst as participant-observer indeed introduced analysts' subjectivity as central to all analytic processes. Some contemporary analysts who have thoroughly embraced analytic intersubjectivity theory have used Sullivan's contradictions to discredit these game-changing initiatives.
4 See the two edited volumes by Stern and Hirsch (2017, 2018) to get a more detailed picture of the contributions of second and third generation interpersonally identified writers.
5 Sullivan paid scant attention to the concept of transference, focusing almost exclusively on what Gill (1982) referred to as extra-transference relations. Fromm and Thompson, unlike Sullivan, both officially trained as psychoanalysts, were well aware of Sullivan's important omission and provided a corrective, incorporating analysis of transference into the early interpersonal literature. This addition is what morphed what was originally called by Sullivan "interpersonal psychiatry" into "interpersonal psychoanalysis" proper.

References

Aron, L. (1996). *A meeting of minds*. Hillsdale, NJ: The Analytic Press.

Beebe, B. (2000). Cocunstructing mother – Infant distress: The microsynchrony of maternal impingement and infant avoidance in the face-to-face encounter. *Psychoanalytic Inquiry, 20*, 441–440.

Bonovitz, C. (2009). Looking back, looking forward: A reexamination of Benjamin Wolstein's interlock and the emergence of intersubjectivity. *International Journal of Psychoanalysis, 90*, 463–485.

Bromberg, P. (1998). *Standing in the spaces*. Hillsdale, NJ: The Analytic Press.

Ferenczi, S., & Rank, O. (1924). *The development of psychoanalysis*. New York, NY: Dover, 1956.

Fiscalini, J. (2004). *Coparticipant psychoanalysis*. New York, NY: Columbia University Press.

Foehl, J. (2008). Follow the fox: Edgar A. Levenson's pursuit of psychoanalytic process. *Psychoanalytic Quarterly, 77*, 1231–1268.

Fonagy, P. (2001). *Attachment theory and psychoanalysis*. New York, NY: Other Press.

Fromm, E. (1941). *Escape from freedom*. New York, NY: Holt, Rinehart & Winston.

Gabbard, G. O. (1995). Countertransference: The emerging common ground. *International Journal of Psychoanalysis, 76*, 475–485.

Gill, M. (1982). *The analysis of transference, Volume 1*. New York, NY: International Universities Press.

Gill, M. (1983). The interpersonal paradigm and the degree of the therapist's involvement. *Contemporary Psychoanalysis, 19*, 200–237.

Greenberg, J., & Mitchell, S. (1983). *Object relations in psychoanalytic theory*. Cambridge, MA: Harvard University Press.

Hirsch, I. (1992). Extending Sullivan's interpersonalism. *Contemporary Psychoanalysis, 28*, 732–747.

Hirsch, I. (1996). Observing-participation, mutual enactment, and the new classical models. *Contemporary Psychoanalysis, 32*, 359–383.

Hirsch, I. (2008). *Coasting in the countertransference: Conflicts of self-interest between analyst and patient*. London and New York, NY: Routledge.

Hirsch, I. (2015). *The interpersonal tradition: The origins of psychoanalytic subjectivity*. London and New York, NY: Routledge.

Hoffman, I. Z. (1983). The patient as interpreter of the analyst's experience. *Contemporary Psychoanalysis, 19*, 389–422.

Jacobs, T. J. (1986). On countertransference enactments. *Journal of the American Psychoanalytic Association, 34*, 289–307.

Kohut, H. (1974). Psychoanalysis in a troubled world. *The Annual of Psychoanalysis, 1*, 3–25.

Levenson, E. A. (1972). *The fallacy of understanding*. New York, NY: Basic Books.

Levenson, E. A. (1991). *The purloined self*. New York, NY: Contemporary Psychoanalysis Press.

Loewald, H. W. (1960). On the therapeutic action of psycho-analysis. *The International Journal of Psychoanalysis, 41*, 16–33.

Mendelsohn, E. (2002). The analyst's bad enough participation. *Psychoanalytic Dialogues, 12*, 331–358.

Mitchell, S. (1988). *Relational concepts in psychoanalysis*. Cambridge, MA: Harvard University Press.

Racker, H. (1968). *Transference and countertransference*. New York, NY: International Universities Press.

Renik, O. (1993). Analytic interaction: Conceptualizing technique in the light of the analyst's irreducible subjectivity. *Psychoanalytic Quarterly, 62*, 553–571.

Sandler, J. (1976). Countertransference and role-responsiveness. *International Review of Psychoanalysis, 3*, 43–48.

Schafer, R. (1983). *The analytic attitude*. New York, NY: Basic Books.

Searles, H. F. (1965). *Collected papers on schizophrenia and related subjects*. New York, NY: International Universities Press.

Searles, H. F. (1979). *Countertransference and related subjects*. New York, NY: International Universities Press.

Singer, E. (1977). The fiction of analytic anonymity. In K. Frank, (Ed.), *The human dimension in psychoanalytic practice* (pp. 181–192). New York, NY: Grune & Stratton.

Slochower, J. (1996). *Holding and psychoanalysis: A relational perspective*. Hillsdale, NJ: The Analytic Press.

Spence, D. (1982). *Narrative truth and historical truth*. New York, NY: W. W. Norton.

Stern, D. B. (1997). *Unformulated experience*. Hillsdale, NJ: The Analytic Press.

Stern, D. B. (2013). Field theory in psychoanalysis, Part 1: Harry Stack Sullivan and Madeline and Willy Baranger. *Psychoanalytic Dialogues, 23*, 487–501.

Stern, D. B., & Hirsch, I. (2017). *The interpersonal perspective in psychoanalysis, 1960s-1990s: Rethinking transference and countertransference*. London and New York, NY: Routledge.

Stern, D. B., & Hirsch, I. (2018). *Further developments in interpersonal psychoanalysis, 1980s-2010s: Evolving interest in the analyst's subjectivity*. London and New York, NY: Routledge.

Stern, D. N. (1985). *The interpersonal world of the infant: A view from psychoanalysis and developmental psychology*. New York, NY: Basic Books.

Stolorow, R., & Atwood, G. (1979). *Faces in a cloud: Subjectivity in personality theory*. Northvale, NJ: Jason Aronson.

Sullivan, H. (1940). *Conceptions of modern psychiatry*. New York, NY: W. W. Norton.

Thompson, C. (1950). *Psychoanalysis: Evolution and development*. New York, NY: Hermitage.

Wallerstein, R. (1995). The relation of theory to technique. *Journal of Clinical Psychoanalysis*, 4, 527–542.
Wilner, W. (2000). A legacy of self: The unique psychoanalytic perspective of Benjamin Wolstein. *Contemporary Psychoanalysis*, *36*, 267–279.
Wolstein, B. (1954). *Transference*. New York, NY: Grune & Stratton.
Wolstein, B. (1977). From mirror to participant-observation to coparticipant inquiry and experience. *Contemporary Psychoanalysis*, *13*, 381–386.

Chapter 8

Relational self-psychology
A contemporary self-psychological approach to the practice of psychoanalysis

Estelle Shane

I'm pleased to join this conversation among the contributors to this book who come from a diversity of contemporary psychoanalytic perspectives. I will present my own integrative approach to the theory and practice of psychoanalysis: relational self-psychology. I'll begin by discussing contemporary relational theory, which, joined with assumptions drawn from Kohut's self-psychology that I will consider later, forms the significant epistemological groundwork for my thinking.

My vision of contemporary relational theory encompasses a number of different approaches, including, in addition to relational and interpersonal theories, Stolorow and his co-authors' intersubjective systems theory (Stolorow, Atwood, & Brandchaft, 1994), Coburn's (2014) complexity theory, and Beebe and Lachmann's (1994) dyadic systems theory. Additionally, my own approach, relational self-psychology, integrates a global brain-based understanding of psychoanalysis, based on Gerald M. Edelman's (2004) study of the emergence of consciousness. I believe that what all contemporary psychoanalytic theories hold in common is their diversity of inspirational sources stemming from disciplines outside of psychoanalysis that are related to, or externally coherent with, psychoanalytic theory, such as attachment theory, infant research, existential epistemological philosophy, systems theory, evolutionary biology, and such neurobiological studies as those of Allan Shore, who contributes here, and Gerald Edelman's global brain theory of consciousness that I integrate into relational self-psychology.

Further, influenced greatly by, and indeed borrowing from, Greenberg and Mitchell's (1963) work, along with my own understanding (e.g., Carlton & Shane, 2014), I appreciate that contemporary theory, unlike more traditional frameworks, does not purport to offer a *singular* approach to understanding the human being, his development, his emotional suffering, or his psychological cure; rather, contemporary analysis rejects the possibility that human experience might be understood through any single, complete, closed, explanatory system, such as offered, for example, in Freudian theory, object relations theory, Kleinian theory, or the classical Kohutian theory from which I have partially derived my own model. At the same time, contemporary analysis rejects an *eclectic* embrace of theory, as if all theories were equally useful, with no way to choose from among them. Rather, contemporary psychoanalysis recognizes and welcomes the theoretical *pluralism* that pervades our field today, emphasizing *diversity* rather than *homogeneity*, *multiplicity* rather than *unity*, and *difference* rather than *sameness*. It is unified by what Greenberg and Mitchell characterized as a postmodern view of knowledge and human existence: one that rejects knowledge as *accurate representation*, truth as *correspondence to reality*, and man as an *autonomous rational subject*. The analyst's certainty or lack thereof about his/her foreknowledge of the patient, based on a priori reasoning and theoretical argument, would seem to establish a fundamental difference between contemporary and more traditional models. Furthermore, contemporary psychoanalytic thought is sensitive to the uniqueness of each human life so that nonlinearity in growth and development replaces the idea of normal stages and phases in the life cycle. Finally, contemporary psychoanalysis acknowledges that analytic meaning is always indeterminate, co-constructed, interactive, intersubjective, and contextual, displacing the notion of the analyst as the *one-who-knows*.

In all of this diversity of thought, I believe that what *does* unify a contemporary perspective is the *attitude* that informs the analyst's work (Coburn, 2014): an attitude that was initiated with the paradigm shift (Greenberg & Mitchell, 1963) from an objective world that exists *out there* and is known through rational thought and the scientific method to a world that is organized subjectively, nonlinearly, and unpredictably.

What is paramount for me in this contemporary psychoanalytic attitude is the concept of uncertainty, of the analyst's accepting the necessity to rest in the uncertainty that ordinarily pervades the contemporary analytic situation. This seems to contrast with the traditional, classical idea of the analyst's unquestioning certainty: the notion that the analyst knows better and sees more clearly into the patient's difficulties and into life in general than does the patient, an attitude explained by Greenberg and Mitchell

Relational self-psychology 155

(1963) as the certainty derived from the position psychoanalysis had held in the world of science and then extended to the field of mental health.

I experienced for myself the disturbing effects of this unquestioning certainty very early in my own analytic training when I first attended a case conference at the American Psychoanalytic Association. A young woman who had just begun treatment was presented by her analyst to the group of 20 or so practitioners, all male, attending the seminar. The presenter opened with the patient's contention that her father had sexually abused her when she was a child and then wondered just when the patient should be confronted with *the truth*: the truth that her belief that she had been abused was really an unconscious fantasy based on her own forbidden Oedipal desires and not an experience she had actually had at all. In response, the seminar group debated whether she should be told the truth immediately, not wasting valuable treatment time, or whether the analyst should wait until the therapeutic alliance was more firmly established. At this point, the conversation moved to the value, or lack thereof, of the concept of a therapeutic alliance, with the question of abuse left behind. I was confused. "Wait," I thought, "hadn't they skipped over entirely what the patient had said?" I sat in mystified silence but finally mustered the courage to ask, "Doesn't *anyone* here believe her story? Doesn't anyone imagine that she might *really* have been molested by her father, and that her experience of abuse was a real lived experience, and something that mattered to her in her life?" My question was ignored, dismissed, perhaps, as too naive to be considered by the tableful of experienced analysts, and I felt ashamed for questioning their interpretation of the patient. The lesson I learned reluctantly in that case conference (which was, sadly, to be reinforced in my own psychoanalytic training) was that *real analysts knew better than their patients could about what had actually happened to them.* When I later read in contemporary analytic work that the patient's experience should be heard and believed, or, at the very least, accepted at face value unless and until there was evidence to question it, I felt enormous relief; some of what I had learned in my psychoanalytic studies had seemed inhumane, cynical, and suspicious. I wondered how such a stance could be helpful to the patient who imagined and trusted she was being fully heard, accepted, and believed.

In this context, it is no small wonder that I was so relieved to read Greenberg and Mitchell (1963) referenced earlier, then Mitchell's (1995) *Hope and Dread in Psychoanalysis*, both of which have so profoundly influenced my thinking. The paradigm shift in psychoanalysis they described seemed to move the field from a search for a *universal, external* reality to a search for an *individual, constructed* reality, a reality based in the patient's personal meaning and, as well, a shared reality that emerges in the dyad. So we have gone a long way from an imposition of the analyst's metapsychological truth to be imparted to and accepted by the patient, to a process of co-creating a subjective, narrative truth that is positioned in the patient's experience. Thus contemporary relational analysis not only represents a radical epistemological shift but also encompasses a wholly different way of being with and relating to the patient. In contemporary relational theory, the hermeneutics of suspicion and skepticism implicit in classical psychoanalytic theories have been supplanted by an attitude of acceptance and affirmation of individuality. This transition reflects a strong movement *against* generalization or bias of any kind, including notions of normative development or sexual or gender behavior, and *towards* the adoption of a critical and self-reflective stance. Clinically, this shift has made a world of difference.

However, as I stated earlier, it has also meant that contemporary analysts must relinquish the comfortable certainty afforded by the Freudian understanding of human development and pathology. In contemporary perspectives, the certainty found in earlier psychoanalytic theories must give way to an attitude that is simultaneously more hopeful and more humble. Our vision of human mental life as a creative expression of an embodied, embedded, ever-changing brain (Edelman, 2004) gives rise to the *hope* that people *can* change, but this vision requires the *humility* to understand that we cannot know exactly *what* that change will be, what might *evoke* that change, *who* it is in the system that is changing, which member of the system is the *agent* of that change, or even whether change will *really* come about at all (Coburn, 2014). Contemporary theory presents the paradox that our *not knowing* nevertheless engenders *hope*, and that this paradox of hopeful not-knowing is what the contemporary psychoanalyst must live with, even celebrate, and transcend; to live in uncertainty and to tolerate that uncertainty is paramount for psychoanalysis in our day.

Now I will turn to our own model, relational self-psychology (see Magid & Shane, 2017), a contemporary perspective. You will note that many of Kohut's original contributions are retained as central to that theory, but we have modernized them in accordance with current knowledge and clinical use. I will identify and discuss these basic Kohutian assumptions, showing how they have been modified in relational self-psychology, and then move to other influences on that theory.

First, I honor Kohut's focus on the centrality of subjective self-experience, assuming its vital importance, but I also re-conceptualize Kohut's concept of self, defining it in systems terms as a fluid, ever changing set of capacities for affect, awareness, and attachment, rather than, as in Kohut's original model, defining self as inherent design (Magid & Shane, 2017). Thus I integrate a systems sensibility to inform this concept of self, with mind, brain, and body conceived as elements in this nonlinear self-system, an embedded mind. The construct of self can be described using the composite term *mind/brain/body*, which illustrates the complex interdigitation of brain with body (Damasio, 1994; Edelman, 1992) as well as the interconnections of brain/body with the concomitant abstraction of thought, ordinarily designated as mind. Such a mindbrainbody concept of self facilitates a clinical understanding of multiple self-states or multiple selves, essential to working with traumatized patients who express non-conscious, non-subjective phenomena through the body. However, these fluid, ever-changing self-states are not conceptualized as inner structure, that is, not viewed as located inside the patient. Rather, they should be understood as always formed from within the patient-analyst (or child-caregiver) system. Further, self-states in the patient are revitalized through the connection and interconnection with the analyst in the analytic process.

Returning to Kohut's theory of self and its clinical applications, Kohut conceptualized the self in the newborn as neither theoretically nor clinically divided at birth; rather, Kohut's baby enters the world as a whole being, in a consolidated state, capable of receiving and organizing the ministrations of the caregiving surround. It is only in pathology, Kohut wrote, that a person's coherent self-structure shatters into drive-like, dysphoric fragments of lust and rage. However, the findings of cognitive developmental researchers – for example, Wilma Bucci (1998, 2001) and Karlen Lyons-Ruth (1999) – converge with findings of neuroscientists, for example, Gerald Edelman (1987, 1989, 1992) and Antonio Damasio (1994, 1999). These cognitive science and neuroscience researchers propose a mind (and I am reading *self*) that, in normal development, is naturally fragmented, with meaning systems not integrated with one another and with mental processing occurring at several levels in parallel. I pose a further consideration; developmental research contributors have found that implicit relational knowing (Stern, 2004, 2010, 2015; Tronick & Weinberg, 1997) – the only domain of knowing available to the infant, which remains important throughout life – is particularly vulnerable to fractionation and lack of integration when the infant lacks sufficient empathic relationships within which to integrate relational understanding and ways of being with others. Does current developmental research support Mitchell's (2000) argument for multiple selves as an inevitable, inherent feature in normal development, the existence of the aggressive self serving as one prominent example of such separate selves, as I will discuss shortly? Or does the mind's vulnerability to fractionation in the absence of empathic, collaborative relationships support Kohut's (1984) ideas about coherence being the natural property of the infant within an empathic surround? These questions are certainly of interest both theoretically and especially clinically, but, as I hope to demonstrate, I believe it is more clinically useful to think in terms of multiple selves, or self-states, rather than the singular cohesive self that Kohut's theory seeks to achieve and maintain.

So, whereas Kohut's self-psychology turns its primary clinical focus to the development, stabilization, and maintenance of the self (that is, the consolidation of a cohesive self-experience), in relational self-psychology, self-cohesion is best understood on a phenomenological level as a subjective experience of wholeness and integration: a sense of well being. This subjective experience of wholeness and integration is akin to what Bromberg (2012) writes about, that self-cohesion is the ability to feel like one self while actually being many selves. From my perspective, each person's experience includes multiple states of self-organization, each state including its own motives, history, needs, and affects. These states feel more or less stable, are more or less reachable, and are more or less coexistent and conversant with one another, depending on the degree to which dissociated aspects are maintained defensively as accessible or inaccessible to one another. Health, then, means having the ability to experience a sense of wholeness and at the same time being capable of maintaining multiple self-states more or less accessible or more or less dissociated: a view that is, to my mind, eminently consistent with relational theory (Black, 2007; Bromberg, 1996; Stern, 2004, 2010, 2015). This conceptualization is important to understanding trauma, as well as the self-state shifts that emerge in the clinical situation when change happens (Galatzer-Levy, 1995).

I turn now to a second basic assumption put forward by Kohut: the selfobject concept. This concept emerged from his postulate that dependence on, and even at times interdependence with, others, rather than independence from others, is a person's lifelong requirement and is the basis for Kohut's (1977, 1984) emphasis on the need for selfobject function in the self-selfobject matrix, serving both in the dyad of parent-child and in the dyad of analyst-patient. The selfobject function made possible by the selfobject other offers the individual (in this case, the patient) experiences of soothing, calming, self-delineating, affect articulating, affirming, and recognition; such experiences support the development, sustenance, and repair of the patient's self. The selfobject provider (here the analyst) is not conceptualized as a person in his or her own right, not there for the patient to feel curious about and interested in. Rather, the person serving in a selfobject role is there solely to respond to the patient's self needs: hence Kohut's own designation that self-psychology is a one person model. As Kohut wrote and also said, there is, in effect, only one person in the clinical situation – the patient – with the analyst being there not as a separate person but as a function.

Relational self-psychology, like all contemporary theories, is conceptualized as a two person model involving two individuals – analyst and patient – each with distinct and separate subjectivities, interacting bidirectionally and mutually influencing one another. In this intersubjective system, creative transformations of the patient's self-experience can emerge from interactions with the fully present analyst. However, as in the Kohutian conceptualization, in relational self-psychology the analyst can still provide necessary and significant selfobject experiences for the patient within that same bidirectional system. In my view, an adequate theory must maintain conceptual room for not only the essential selfobject experience that is dependent on a stance of empathic listening and responding, but also the equally essential collaborative dialogue that emerges between patient-analyst as two people mutually influencing and interacting with one another. My point is that by accepting the inestimable value of the selfobject concept in the clinical setting, the analyst is not limited to serving only that single function.

A third basic assumption in self-psychology is Kohut's (1959, 1971, 1977, 1981, 1984) introduction of the empathic, vicariously introspective mode of listening and responding in the psychoanalytic situation. He designated this mode as the fundamental listening perspective in psychoanalysis, honoring the patient's subjective experience as constituting the principal data source defining the field: a theoretical and clinical insight of lasting and inestimable value for the field in my estimation. Moreover, for Kohut (1971, 1977, 1981, 1984), empathy and its role in psychoanalysis was singularly important. He first discussed the concept in 1959, long before he invented self-psychology as a theory, and then again in two posthumously published papers. Yet, as he complained in a speech that preceded his death by only three days, no matter how often he tried to explain himself, no one ever understood what he meant by empathy. Kohut defined empathy as *the* way of *knowing* in psychoanalysis. It is not *sympathy* nor *intuition,* nor *kindness*, he said; rather, it is the very essence of the skilled analyst's ability to comprehend the patient by entering into the patient's point of view through vicarious introspection, and understanding the patient's perspective from that vantage point. Empathy can be used for either good or evil, Kohut emphasized, citing as a consummate example of effective empathy used for evil the Nazis' use of a shrieking whistle latched onto bombs falling in populated areas, the sound announcing to the potential victims what horror was coming their way, enhancing their terror as they waited for certain death and destruction to fall from the skies. That was empathy, Kohut taught: understanding of the other taken from the point of view of that other, the victim, informing the perpetrator as to what would be most unbearable for that victim to experience.

Empathic listening, therefore, is a listening stance characterized by entering into and experiencing the world from the patient's perspective, a listening stance designed to discover the patient's subjective truth. Moreover, experiencing sustained empathy is arguably a reparative, generative experience in and of itself for the patient. It may be contrasted with listening and responding from a position located outside of the patient's experience, representing, perhaps, the analyst's experience, or the experience of an other person in the patient's life as the analyst might imagine it: these are the alternative listening perspectives introduced by James Fosshage (2003).

I want to emphasize that I view empathic listening as essential to generative action in psychoanalysis. However, Kohut did not emphasize, nor even speak about, the fact that empathic perception – viewing the world of experience from the patient's perspective and not from the analyst's own – is inevitably influenced by and mediated through the analyst's own subjectivity (Stolorow, 1995). This realization, consistent with conceptualizing the analytic relationship as composed of two people mutually effecting and influencing one another, supports the contemporary relational concept of constructivism. That is, what happens in the dyad, whether in the patient's experience or even in the analyst's, is always co-constructed by analyst and patient together; the analytic relationship is defined as a fluid, mutual, bidirectional interaction and influence.

This recognition of mutual and bidirectional interaction, the inevitable influence of the analyst in the analytic process, seems to me to require expanding the listening perspective beyond the empathic-introspective mode so that the listening and responding position of the analyst can alternate among an effort to listen and respond empathically, listening and responding from the perspective of the patient; and an other-centered mode of listening, blending her empathic listening with an appreciation of her own other-centered experience of the patient's expression. In contrast, the analyst's decision as to how to *respond* to the patient, what she should focus on in the interaction, is based on a consideration of how the patient is able to experience her, whether the patient is experiencing her in terms of providing a selfobject function, or whether the patient is able to reflect on her as a separate person in her own right, a person whom the patient is interested in and curious about, and with whom the patient wants to share experience. The analyst's consideration as to how to respond is complex, and a discussion of it is beyond the scope of this paper, except to say that in her response, the analyst attempts to be optimally responsive to the patient's needs (Bacal, 1991, 1995).

In thinking about empathy, I am impressed by the provocative questions relationalists raise about the concept, questions that have first shaken and then reshaped my own views, particularly about what it might actually take for some patients, especially those who suffer from the after-effects of trauma, to experience empathy: that is, to really know that they have been heard and understood. Jessica Benjamin's (1988, 1991, 2004, 2006, 2017) version of intersubjectivity and empathy contends that for many patients, a more actively engaged level of responsiveness is required in order for the patient to feel understood. As I reflect on it, this is especially true of patients who have been traumatized.

The fourth basic assumption I abstract from self-psychological theory is that defenses that emerge in the patient in the analytic situation are conceptualized primarily as self-protective and self-preservative; they are not best understood as that patient's efforts either to disturb the therapeutic process or to thwart the analyst's efforts, as conceptualized in more traditional models. In self-psychology, defenses are thought of as the best option for the child to preserve his self-experience or, as Kohut would put it, these are the only remnants of self that had cohered as the child developed in the particular context in which he or she lived in the world. Clinically, this has meant that the analyst appreciates the patient's defenses as still feeling necessary to him in order to bring about self-state stability and are thus to be approached with respect and caution, even to the point of being left intact. The self-psychological hypothesis is that defenses will fall of their own weight once the patient experiences a sense of safety and security in the analytic setting. In my own work, too, I maintain this approach, but clearly there are times, with some patients or in some dyads, where interpreting the self-protective strategies of the patient becomes not only possible but also even *essential* for the patient's further psychoanalytic development, as can be seen in the following discussion of aggression.

The fifth basic assumption I glean from Kohut's self-psychology is that aggression, although conceptualized as inborn potential in the individual, is nevertheless viewed, when it makes an appearance, as primarily an emergent reaction to frustration and deprivation, not as drive expression. Thus the clinical focus is more on the *context* in which aggression is evoked or experienced and less on the aggressive self-state per se. The self-psychological clinician's goal is to strengthen the patient's self-experience through exploration and understanding of the conditions and threats to self-experience that motivate the emergence of an aggressive response. Ultimately by strengthening self-experience, it is postulated that the aggressive expression will be mitigated. Such a focus stands in contrast to much of contemporary psychoanalytic theory. For example, Mitchell (1995) asserted that the aggressive self is a separate self, one of multiple self-organizations, and, as such, is a self with its own history, worldview, values, and interests. In Mitchell's model, the clinician's best strategy would be to allow the aggressive self full expression in the transference so that the patient might claim his aggressive states of mind as valuable variants of himself, not as attempts to reconstitute a single self rendered vulnerable by an unresponsive surround. As such, Mitchell wrote, the patient's aggression should be confronted, clarified, interpreted, and accepted as an inextricable version of himself, a particular self or self-state, the aim being a resolution in which aggression becomes an enlivening and inevitable self-experience.

I appreciate the clarification of aggression and the expansion of clinical possibilities available to clinicians when treating aggression as encompassed in Mitchell's discussion. From my perspective, as with everything else that emerges in the therapeutic situation, the treatment of aggression must always be individualized as well as contextualized. I do see rageful, destructive aggression as a self-state shift often evoked by reactions to experiences of frustration or deprivation. Frequently my own therapeutic intent and effort would be directed towards helping the patient manage the intensity of his aggressive response by coming to understand his experience in context, reducing any accompanying shame or humiliation that emerges in the process.

However, I also recognize that such a listening stance is not always possible, or even desirable, especially with patients who manifest eruptive aggression (Lachmann, 2001). Enactments emergent in the analytic relationship with such patients may not only be unavoidable, they may also prove to be the most helpful of therapeutic engagements. Further, offering one's own perspective to the patient about the interactions between patient and analyst can be far more useful in the clinical process than the perennial maintenance of an empathic introspective stance, as Ehrenberg (1992), Davies (2004), Renik (1998a, 1998b, 1998c), and others have all illustrated in their theoretical and clinical work. I am convinced that always and perennially maintaining *any* one stance is not helpful; learning from Mitchell (1995), I believe there are times when looking at the aggressive *content*, and not just the context, may prove to be the most ameliorative approach. The important determination for me would be, in those moments when I *appear* to have a choice, to attempt to offer to that patient the response that would seem to be the most facilitative, most optimal one available to me (Bacal & Herzog, 2003).

The sixth and final assumption emphasized in Kohut's self-psychology is that the psychoanalytic process carries with it, along with reflective insight and understanding, a significant developmental power and thrust for both patient and analyst. This is beautifully illustrated in Slavin and Kriegman's (1998) article, "Why the Analyst Needs to Change." As indicated earlier, I have come to understand much of psychoanalytic theory, including development, in accord with a systems sensibility. Therefore, I conceptualize developmental attainment as an emergent phenomenon arising from within the patient-analyst system: self-organizing, nonlinear, bidirectional, and unpredictable. This view of development as a bidirectional system supports the contention, important in relational self-psychology, that psychoanalysis is development-enhancing for the analyst as well as for the patient.

I have now completed a review of the six basic assumptions I have drawn from Kohut's self-psychology, all of which, with the modifications I've just articulated, are foundational to our relational self-psychology (Magid & Shane, 2017). Many constitute ideas and empirical findings are drawn and integrated from attachment theory. Particularly important, I think, is the strong connection elaborated in attachment research between the establishment of a secure attachment in early childhood and the development in that context of the experience of a healthy, integrated sense of self with healthy capacities for intimacy with others. Current writings in attachment theory elaborate upon these ideas, focusing attention more particularly on just how a secure attachment can be seen to emerge in the parent-child relationship, with what I see as strong implications for the psychoanalytic process as well. For example, Lyons-Ruth (1999) described attachment research as demonstrating that the development of a cohesive and secure attachment bond, characterized by goodness of fit, is tied to participation in coherent forms of parent-child dialogue; it is only through coherent dialogue occurring between two persons, then, that a secure attachment can emerge. Lyons-Ruth defined coherent dialogue as truthful, clear, collaborative, and about "getting to know another's mind" (p. 588). Such a definition, she asserted, "may serve as . . . a . . . model for capturing essential attributes of dialogue in the . . . contemporary . . . two-person clinical situation" (p. 589). It brings to my mind Jessica Benjamin's (1988, 2017) contribution of mutual recognition.

Although there are other important sources from related disciplines that inform relational self-psychology, I barely have space to mention a particularly important influence for me, Gerald Edelman's global brain, from which Lucyann Carlton and Shane (2014) have developed an approach to brain-based psychoanalysis. We would argue that Edelman is important reading for psychoanalysts. Based on Edelman's wholly new brain model, as articulated in several of his works (Edelman, 1992, 2004; Edelman & Tononi, 2008), we have abstracted four arguments for the essential role of brain research in contemporary clinical theory and practice.

Very briefly, first, Edelman's brain model exposes the insufficiency of traditional psychoanalytic theories that are more or less premised on an epistemology of linear causality, positing universal, normative notions of the form and content of human motivation, development, health, illness, and cure. This is true of the traditional Freudian, Kleinian, and Kohutian perspectives, as examples. Brain research challenges such uniformity and predictability, establishing instead the undeniable distinctiveness of each person, with that distinctiveness emanating from that person's brain. Each brain, each cell of that brain, and all the neuronal connections of that brain, too, are unique to that person; no two people, even identical twins, are ever alike, and this is important: as they grow, their distinctiveness grows with them. We contend that any psychoanalytic theory that lacks a concomitant capacity for addressing the exquisitely unique individuality and capacity to change is, in that measure, inadequate.

Second, from current neuroscience we learn about the relationship between mind, with its attendant subjectivity and intersubjectivity, and brain. We learn that mind emerges from brain, and further the functioning of both mind and brain affects one another – brain affects mind and mind affects brain concomitantly. Brain and mind are inseparable, then, in the unified processes that give rise to both, but they are not the same, they do not merge. Phenomenology is useful, indeed essential, but it is not complete; it fails to account for what fundamentally influences subjective experience yet remains outside of subjective awareness. Knowing how brain affects mind increases understanding not only of conscious subjective experience but also of unconscious and nonconscious, bodily-based, procedural experience. As psychoanalysis privileges the mind's self-reflective capacities, knowledge of brain, the font of mind, becomes invaluable.

Third, brain theory shifts our level of theoretical attention from specific theory content to process generalizations or pattern organization. That is, there is a shift away from theories naming concrete structures (e.g., id, ego, superego, self) and defining concrete universal stages of development with a predictable end point, moving towards a theoretical focus on generalizations and principles of process that operate on a higher level of abstraction. Thus, a brain-based psychoanalytic perspective is premised on a systems understanding of life. Whereas phenomenology also operates at a systems level, brain-based theory offers brain-based generalities based on principles of pattern formation: that is, dynamic patterns that can be generalized, the generalizable in human experience. We offer three examples of such generalizations; the first is that people all create the worlds they live in to accord with their experience-based predictions of what the world is like. "The truth lies not in what we observe, but in what we create," said the Roman historian and philosopher Pliny the Elder, "making the only certainty uncertainty itself" (as cited in Carlton & Shane, 2014, p. 858). This ancient knowledge that resonates with contemporary brain-based knowledge assures people that the world they live both in and through is uniquely, largely, and inevitably of their own making, based on what they have learned to expect from a universe of possibilities. People anticipate what they have known and arrange their experience of it accordingly.

The second process generalization is based on Edelman's concept of the *econiche*: that is, the idea that anyone's perception of her world in a moment in time is always the perfect expression of her history of knowing her world over all of her time, as she herself is interwoven with and within her environment and as her environment is interwoven within her.

The third process generalization is that humans manifest two distinct levels of consciousness: primary consciousness, in which consciousness is restricted to what is immediately present, and higher order consciousness, in which consciousness includes a knowledge and experience of past, present, and future, with the ability to contextualize that experience rather than be overridden by it. The understanding of how higher order consciousness is erased in trauma, leaving only the terrors that the present moment has triggered, reveals how the brain works in trauma and in dissociation, derealization, and depersonalization. Given space limitations, I can only reference brain-based trauma related articles written by Lucyann Carlton and myself (e.g., 2014) for details.

I will conclude the argument for the brain's essential place in psychoanalytic understanding by noting that by putting together the three justifications I have outlined previously, what emerges is a profound shift in clinical attitude, and it is this shift that constitutes justification four for brain-based understanding in psychoanalytic theory and practice. Namely, it is an attitude that change can happen and that the analyst is integral to that change process. Given the exquisite uniqueness and ongoing creation of mindbrainbody, clinical uncertainty is inevitable, the potential for change is unknown, and hope is never discarded; again, change *can* happen.

Although there is much more to say about relational self-psychology, I will end by emphasizing that, in my view, the generative action in psychoanalysis occurs through empathic responsiveness in the two-person intersubjective relationship where positive new experience may emerge. As a relational self-psychologist, I am interested in creating with the patient through our intimate connection a relatively expanded experience of self that, paraphrasing Bromberg (2012), feels like one self while actually being many. This integrated experience of selfhood emerges in the context of an intersubjective system formed through my commitment to relationality, my focus on affective experience, and my dwelling with the patient within that affective experience, with all the pain and turmoil that may ensue (Atwood, Orange, & Stolorow, 2015; Atwood & Stolorow, 1994, 2014a, 2014b; Brandchaft, Atwood, & Stolorow, 2014; Stolorow, 2011a, 2011b; Stolorow & Atwood, 2018; Stolorow, Atwood, & Orange, 2002). These are all important tenets integrated in relational self-psychology. However, I want to make one final point; I believe that co-constructed, collaborative dialogue (Lyons-Ruth, 1999) is transformational and generates the positive new experience that I find essential to cure (Shane, Shane, & Gales, 1997).

In summary, it should be clear that relational self-psychology encompasses many theories in contemporary psychoanalysis and, in addition, borrows ideas from related disciplines outside the field. I believe that not only is this plurality and diversity of inspirational sources and the integration of theory and practice from other perspectives what constitutes the novelty and power in contemporary psychoanalysis, but also it represents one of the most important developments in psychoanalysis today. Further, and in particular, I believe that the introduction of Gerald Edelman's brain-based global theory to psychoanalytic understanding may provide a powerful potential for new understanding of our patients and an enhanced way to individualize our treatment of them.

References

Atwood, G. E., & Stolorow, R. D. (Eds.). (1994). *Faces in a cloud: Intersubjectivity in personality theory*. Northvale, NJ: Jason Aronson.

Atwood, G. E., & Stolorow, R. D. (2014a). *Contexts of being: The intersubjective foundations of psychological life*. New York, NY: Routledge.

Atwood, G. E., & Stolorow, R. D. (2014b). *Structures of subjectivity: Explorations in psychoanalytic phenomenology and contextualism*. New York, NY: Routledge.

Atwood, G. E., Orange, D., & Stolorow, R. D. (2015). *Working intersubjectively: Contextualism in psychoanalytic practice*. New York, NY: Routledge.

Bacal, H. A. (1991). Notes on the relationship between object relations theory and self psychology. *Progress in Self Psychology*, 7, 36–44.

Bacal, H. A. (1995). The centrality of selfobject experience in psychological relatedness: Response to editors' follow-up questions. *Psychoanalytic Dialogues, 5*, 403–410. https://doi.org/10.1080/10481889509539079

Bacal, H. A., & Herzog, B. (2003). Specificity theory and optimal responsiveness: An outline. *Psychoanalytic Psychology, 20*(4), 635–649. https://doi.org/10.1037/0736-9735.20.4.635

Beebe, B., & Lachmann, F. M. (1994). Representation and internalization in infancy: Three principles of salience. *Psychoanalytic Psychology, 11*(2), 127–165. https://doi.org/10.1037/h0079530

Benjamin, J. (1988). *The bonds of love*. New York, NY: Pantheon Books.

Benjamin, J. (1991). Father and daughter: Identification with difference: A contribution to gender heterodoxy. *Psychoanalytic Dialogues, 1*, 277–299. https://doi.org/10.1080/10481889109538900

Benjamin, J. (2004). Beyond doer and done to: An intersubjective view of thirdness. *Psychoanalytic Quarterly, 73*, 5–46. https://doi.org/10.1002/j.2167-4086.2004.tb00151.x

Benjamin, J. (2006). Crash: What we do when we cannot touch: Commentary on paper by Meira Likierman. *Psychoanalytic Dialogues, 16*, 377–385.

Benjamin, J. (2017). *Beyond doer and done to: Recognition theory, intersubjectivity and the third*. New York, NY: Routledge.

Black, M. J. (2007). Enhancing the therapeutic experience: A relational commentary on Judith Pickles's case. *Psychoanalytic Inquiry, 27*(1), 66–86. https://doi.org/10.1080/07351690701307363

Brandchaft, B., Atwood, G. E., & Stolorow, R. D. (2014). *Psychoanalytic treatment: An intersubjective approach*. New York, NY: Routledge.

Bromberg, P. M. (1996). Standing in the spaces: The multiplicity of self and the psychoanalytic relationship. *Contemporary Psychoanalysis, 32*(4), 509–535. https://doi.org/10.1080/00107530.1996.10746334

Bromberg, P. M. (2012). *The shadow of the tsunami and the growth of the relational mind*. New York, NY: Routledge.

Bucci, W. (1998). Transformation of meanings in the analytic discourse: A strategy for research. *Canadian Journal of Psychoanalysis, 6*(2), 233–260.

Bucci, W. (2001). Pathways of emotional communication. *Psychoanalytic Inquiry, 21*(1), 40–70. https://doi.org/10.1080/07351692109348923

Carlton, L., & Shane, E. (2014). Gerald Edelman's project: How Gerald Edelman's theory of consciousness completes Darwin's theory of evolution and provides a basis for a brain-based psychoanalytic perspective. *Psychoanalytic Inquiry, 34*(8), 847–863. https://doi.org/10.1080/07351690.2014.968032

Coburn, W. (2014). *Psychoanalytic complexity: Clinical attitudes for therapeutic change*. London, UK: Routledge.

Damasio, A. R. (1994). *Descartes' error: Emotion, rationality and the human brain*. New York, NY: Penguin.

Damasio, A. R. (1999). How the brain creates the mind. *Scientific American, 281*(6), 112–117. https://doi.org/10.1038/scientificamerican1299-112

Davies, J. M. (2004). Whose bad objects are we anyway? Repetition and our elusive love affair with evil. *Psychoanalytic Dialogues, 14*(6), 711–732. https://doi.org/10.1080/10481881409348802

Edelman, G. M. (1987). *Neural Darwinism: The theory of neuronal group selection*. New York, NY: Basic Books.

Edelman, G. M. (1989). *The remembered present: A biological theory of consciousness*. New York, NY: Basic Books.

Edelman, G. M. (1992). *Bright air, brilliant fire: On the matter of the mind*. New York, NY: Basic Books.

Edelman, G. M. (2004). *Wider than the sky: The phenomenal gift of consciousness*. New Haven, CT: Yale University Press.

Edelman, G., & Tononi, G. (2008). *A universe of consciousness: How matter becomes imagination*. New York, NY: Basic Books.

Ehrenberg, D. B. (1992). *The intimate edge: Extending the reach of psychoanalytic interaction*. New York, NY: W. W. Norton & Co.

Fosshage, J. L. (2003). Contextualizing self psychology and relational psychoanalysis: Bi-directional influence and proposed syntheses. *Contemporary Psychoanalysis, 39*, 411–448. https://doi.org/10.1080/00107530.2003.10747214

Galatzer-Levy, R. M. (1995). Psychoanalysis and dynamical systems theory: Prediction and self similarity. *Journal of the American Psychoanalytic Association, 43*(4), 1085–1114. https://doi.org/10.1177/000306519504300407

Greenberg, J., & Mitchell, S. A. (1963). *Object relations in psychoanalytic theory*. Cambridge, MA: Harvard University Press.

Kohut, H. (1959). Introspection, empathy, and psychoanalysis – An examination of the relationship between mode of observation and theory. *Journal of the American Psychoanalytic Association, 7*, 459–483. https://doi.org/10.1177/000306515900700304

Kohut, H. (1971). *The analysis of the self: A systematic approach to the psychoanalytic treatment of narcissistic personality disorders*. New York, NY: International Universities Press.

Kohut, H. (1977). *The restoration of the self*. New York, NY: International Universities Press.

Kohut, H. (1981, October). *Remarks on empathy*. Lecture presented at the Annual Conference on Self Psychology, Berkeley, CA.

Kohut, H. (1984). *How does analysis cure?* Chicago, IL: University of Chicago Press.

Lachmann, F. M. (2001). *Transforming aggression: Psychotherapy with the difficult-to-treat patient*. Northvale, NJ: Jason Aronson.

Lyons-Ruth, K. (1999). The two-person unconscious: Intersubjective dialogue, enactive relational representation, and the emergence of new forms of relational organization. *Psychoanalytic Inquiry, 19*(4), 576–617. https://doi.org/10.1080/07351699909534267

Magid, B., & Shane, E. (2017). Relational self psychology. *Psychoanalysis, Self and Context, 12*(1), 3–19. doi:10.1080/15551024.2017.1251176

Mitchell, S. A. (1995). *Hope and dread in psychoanalysis*. New York, NY: Basic Books.

Mitchell, S. A. (2000). *Relationality: From attachment to intersubjectivity*. Hillsdale, NJ: Analytic Press.

Renik, O. (1998a). The analyst's subjectivity and the analyst's objectivity. *The International Journal of Psycho-Analysis, 79*(3), 487.

Renik, O. (1998b). Getting real in analysis. *The Psychoanalytic Quarterly, 67*(4), 566–593. https://doi.org/10.1080/00332828.1998.12006066

Renik, O. (1998c). The role of countertransference enactment in a successful clinical psychoanalysis. In S. J. Ellman & M. Moskowitz (Eds.), *Enactment: Toward a new approach to the therapeutic relationship* (pp. 111–128). Northvale, NJ: Jason Aronson.

Shane, M., Shane, E., & Gales, M. (1997). *Intimate attachments: Toward a new self psychology*. New York, NY: Guilford Press.

Slavin, M. O., & Kriegman, D. (1998). Why the analyst needs to change: Toward a theory of conflict, negotiation, and mutual influence in the therapeutic process. *Psychoanalytic Dialogues, 8*(2), 247–284. https://doi.org/10.1080/10481889809539246

Stern, D. B. (2004). The eye sees itself: Dissociation, enactment, and the achievement of conflict. *Contemporary Psychoanalysis, 40*(2), 197–237. https://doi.org/10.1080/00107530.2004.10745828

Stern, D. B. (2010). *Partners in thought: Working with unformulated experience, dissociation, and enactment*. New York, NY: Routledge.

Stern, D. B. (2015). *Relational freedom: Emergent properties of the interpersonal field*. New York, NY: Routledge.

Stolorow, R. D. (1995). An intersubjective view of self psychology. *Psychoanalytic Dialogues, 5*(3), 393–399. https://doi.org/10.1080/10481889509539077

Stolorow, R. D. (2011a). *Trauma and human existence: Autobiographical, psychoanalytic, and philosophical reflections*. New York, NY: Routledge.

Stolorow, R. D. (2011b). *World, affectivity, trauma: Heidegger and post-Cartesian psychoanalysis*. New York, NY: Routledge.

Stolorow, R. D., & Atwood, G. E. (2018). *The power of phenomenology*. New York, NY: Routledge.

Stolorow, R. D., Atwood, G. E., & Brandchaft, B. (Eds.). (1994). *The intersubjective perspective*. New York, NY: Rowman & Littlefield.

Stolorow, R. D., Atwood, G. E., & Orange, D. (2002). *Worlds of experience: Interweaving philosophical and clinical dimensions in psychoanalysis.* New York, NY: Basic Books.

Tronick, E. Z., & Weinberg, M. K. (1997). Depressed mothers and infants: Failure to form dyadic states of consciousness. In L. Murray & P. J. Cooper (Eds.), *Postpartum depression and child development* (pp. 54–81). New York, NY: Guilford.

Chapter 9

Relational psychoanalysis
Origins, scope, and recent innovations

Steven Kuchuck

Birth of a movement

Jay Greenberg and Stephen Mitchell (1983) first coined the term relational (small r) as a way of identifying a common theme among a diverse group of theories that had not previously been considered connected or unified in any way. Each of the schools that appeared under the new umbrella of relational (which are primarily interpersonal, object relations, self-psychology, and intersubjective systems theory) emphasized a person's embeddedness in the social context (rather than the isolated individual) as the primary unit of study. According to these models, object relatedness (rather than drive discharge) is the common denominator for understanding human behavior and motivation. But it wasn't until Mitchell's first solo authored book (1988) that he began using the term relational to *also* refer to a newly developing perspective, which was in some ways overlapping with but also distinct from the earlier theories that he and Greenberg had included under the heading of relational psychoanalysis. Mitchell's new thinking arose from a melding of Fairbairn's object relations theory with interpersonal psychoanalysis, feminist, queer, gender, and other social theories. This theoretical turn is now sometimes referred to as the New York School or as North American Relational psychoanalysis. It also became referred to as "big R" Relational psychoanalysis in order to distinguish it from Mitchell's original use of the term relational (Kuchuck, 2017; Kuchuck & Sopher, 2017).

But it is not just the two different meanings of the word relational and other terms used within relational/Relational psychoanalysis[1] that can make understanding Relational psychoanalysis confounding. Further adding to the challenge of understanding this relatively new movement, there is no singular "school" of big R Relational psychoanalysis or individual founder, despite Mitchell's relatively solo initial contributions. For that reason, this way of thinking that Mitchell first identified a mere 30 years ago has often been referred to as a perspective rather than a theoretical school. There are a number of universal characteristics that he and his colleagues identified, including dialectical movement between intrapsychic and interpersonal, acknowledgment of intersubjectivity and the inevitable impact of the analyst's subjectivity, multiplicity/multiple self-states (Bromberg, 1996; Davies, 2012), co-construction (Hoffman, 1983), mutuality (Aron, 1996), judicious use of selective, deliberate self-disclosure (Aron, 1996; Kuchuck, 2009, 2014, 2016), and many other variables (Mitchell, 1981, 1988, 1998). Still, each Relational analyst defines and practices the perspective in his or her own particular way (Harris, 2011). It does warrant mention that Relational psychoanalysis has made huge strides in the development of trauma theory (Davies & Frawley, 1994; Davies, 2001; Boulanger, 2002) and understanding dissociation (Bromberg, 1996; Davies, 2012).

Some of these ideas were borrowed from interpersonal psychoanalysis, other psychoanalytic schools as mentioned, philosophy, and other studies. And some have become incorporated into contemporary Freudian theory and other schools of thought. One of the newer ways of approaching psychoanalytic plurality actually suggests a move away from thinking about and debating the merits of separate schools of thought. Relational analyst Steven Cooper uses the term bridge theory to address the numerous concepts that cross boundaries and become integrated into different orientations (Cooper, 2016).

I include this quite abbreviated historical overview and definition of Relational psychoanalysis as a common starting point for readers who might have less familiarity with this difficult-to-define perspective. It bears mention that from its inception—still relatively recent in the history of psychoanalysis—Relational psychoanalysis has been dismissed in many circles as being non-psychoanalytic. This is true in some cases regardless of whether or not it has been studied or fully enough understood (Aron, Grand, & Slochower, 2018a, 2018b). Additionally, this is a still relatively unknown way of thinking in some parts of the world outside North America, an idea that I will expand on towards the end of this chapter. This is all to say that Mitchell and his early colleagues felt themselves to be engaged in a revolution (Mitchell, 1988; Stolorow, Brandchaft, & Atwood, 1987). The tremors of aftershock of this revolution are still being felt, even though much of it has over time been disseminated as bridge theory.

For some psychoanalytic scholars both within and outside the Relational tradition, this continues to be an innovative, evolving framework. All the previously named characteristics of Relational psychoanalysis are still new when held in tension with classical theory, and all are undergoing refinement and subsequent evolution. As mentioned, the analyst's subjectivity (inclusive of gender, sexuality, specific life experiences, socio-political position, as well as other cultural factors) is widely recognized as integral to this way of thinking and practicing (Aron, 1991, 1996; Mitchell, 1998; Kuchuck, 2014). Also, recognizing relational psychoanalysis as a big tent (Harris, 2011; Stern & Hirsch, 2017) inclusive of "immigrants" from other theoretical orientations (Davies, 2012) rather than a singular, unified theory opens up endless possibilities for development as cultural factors shift and our understanding of gender, sexuality, and other aspects of the subjective self continue to expand.

Developments and innovation

What follows is a breakdown of what I view to be some of the newest and most important developments within Relational psychoanalysis. I suspect that many of my Relational (and differently identified) colleagues would likely include some of the same items on their lists. But I have no doubt that those lists would also vary greatly based on the numerous theoretical interests within the Relational paradigm and other subjective factors that determine which specific theories and techniques each of us is drawn to, modifies, or even originates.

The analyst's subjectivity, deliberate self-disclosure, and silent-disclosure

Joyce Slochower (2018) and others (for example, Mills, 2012, 2017) contend that the relational turn may have led at times to an overcorrection for classical models stuck in notions of analytic asymmetry and authoritarian hierarchy, positivism as expressed via an all-knowing, omniscient analyst, and the patient-as-baby metaphor. She suggests there is sometimes an over-focus on the analysis of enactment and assumed therapeutic action of the analyst's deliberate self-disclosure. This has only served to create new blind spots when at times we fail to explore the potentially problematic impact of certain analyst disclosures and complex, sometimes overwrought mutual analysis of enactment.

I agree with these concerns—offered by Slochower and others in the spirit of advancing Relational theory through self-critique (see later). In my writing, I've advocated for at least an attempt at "protecting our patients' psychic space and right not to know things about us" (Kuchuck, 2008, p. 430). In my most recent work, I suggest—as have others before me (Kuchuck, 2018; Harris, 2011; Aron, 1991)—that deep exploration of the analyst's subjectivity, albeit significantly hampered by limitations imposed by the unconscious, continues to be as crucial a part of conducting treatment as is close examination of the patient's subjective being. As a partial antidote to the problematic over-focus expressed by Slochower, I engage in as thorough-going an exploration of my impact on patients as consciousness will allow (see Ferro [1996]; Ferro and Basile [2008] on exploring the impact of interpretations), although I of course recognize that even potential solutions such as this can in some cases register as problematic for certain patients in particular moments (Kuchuck, 2014, 2016, 2018).

Like most contemporary analysts, I realize the value of selective, deliberate disclosure. These days though, I am particularly interested in certain newer aspects of this phenomenon. As just one part of a larger effort to carefully track the impact of the analyst's subjectivity, I approach the concept of the analyst's potential disclosures as a mostly internal process. Similar to silent interpretations, which have the powerful potential to become implicitly communicated and healing (Ogden, 1979; Atlas & Aron, 2018), I believe that the mere act of even *contemplating* whether or not to make a disclosure—whether it be biographical, sharing of an affect, thought, or insight of any kind—can become part of the therapeutic action. Maroda (2003) describes something similar when she differentiates between verbal self-disclosures, which run the risk of impinging on the patient's narrative and/or overstimulating the patient, and silent forms of affective disclosure that do not require words.

What I have come to call "silent-disclosure" (Kuchuck, 2018) might potentially operate similarly to Maroda's "silent form of affective disclosure" (2003, p. 116). While my use of this new term could include her description, I have another meaning in mind. That is, silent-disclosures often put us in contact with our otherwise inaccessible, possibly dissociated content. This might be our own historical or current psychic material, something disowned and perhaps projected by our patient, or some third medley of the two. In any case, the contemplation often emerges from or leads to a reverie akin to what Ogden and Ogden (2012) and others describe, and it becomes a way to recover otherwise lost subjective data.

This means that when time and consciousness allow, and when some awareness or chafing (Stern, 2004) registers, I'm sometimes moved to silently try on the words I contemplate saying to a patient as part of a deliberate disclosure. This exercise, not even always fully formulated, is not only intended as a way of evaluating whether or not I believe the disclosure has the possibility of being effective and/or whether or not I believe it is being offered (at least mostly) in service of the *patient's* perceived need (Kuchuck, 2009). Rather, I find that silent-disclosure often puts me in more conscious contact with certain affects and other cognitions, including the data these provide about intersubjective dynamics. In various ways, deliberate and inadvertent analyst disclosures as well as the silent ones can be mined as a way of understanding the impact of who we are in the room as much as to evaluate their merit as a treatment intervention. Here is an example of what I mean:

Jonathan is talking about his mother's illness and general deterioration. I feel a bit detached—as if outside and hearing him speak from a distance—I'm not with him as much as I would want to be. I find myself starting to think about my mother and some similar struggles she has been having. I remember that Jonathan likes to know more about me than I tend to deliberately share. On those rare occasions when I might disclose something more personal or otherwise biographical, he reports feeling appreciative of this and feels more connected to me. In remembering this, I decide I'm going to disclose a piece of current life with my mother, but I feel tears start to well up. At that point, I decide not to disclose—it would be too disregulating for me and possibly for my patient. Still, the contemplation itself has returned me to previously dissociated parts of myself, and therefore I'm now more present. One could also argue of course that an inadvertent disclosure—in this case via moistened eyes or other forms of nonverbal communication similar to Maroda's concept—has in fact occurred. But it is the silent-disclosure that has returned me to myself and therefore to my patient.

Reconceptualizing enactment

Relational psychoanalysis's focus on the inevitability and therapeutic value of enactments is one of its most important contributions to psychoanalysis.

Theodore Jacobs (1986) first introduced the term, but Sándor Ferenczi (1932) and much more recently Tony Bass (2003), Margaret Black (2003), and numerous other Relational analysts have contributed important writing on this topic. Theorists differ on how they define the term within the clinical context, but I would suggest that most of us come close to some approximation of the following: enactments involve analyst and patient unconscious, often dissociated content that—often through mutual projective identification and other means—leads to a clash and/or stalemate in the treatment. Living through and deconstructing these enactive processes are frequently fundamental to gaining an historic understanding and achieving psychic change.

With this in mind, there is a new, important development in Relational scholarship on enactment. Aron and Atlas (2015; Atlas & Aron, 2018) suggest that enactments are not only a means for accessing and working through otherwise dissociated, inaccessible *historical* material but also are a way of preparing for the *future* as well. They posit that unconscious hopes and dreams act as catalysts for fulfilling one's destiny via unconscious anticipation of and rehearsal for the future. They note that Jung's prospective function should not be confused with a prophetic one, but rather that people unconsciously imagine, look forward to, and construct future possibilities. Aron and Atlas approach a fuller, more contemporary understanding of the prospective function by relating this concept to enactment, the latter being a primary means by which patients and analysts enter into each other's psychic lives and find themselves to have become active participants within each other's psyches.

The authors maintain, therefore, that it is not only the actual resolution of otherwise problematic, often repetitive enactments that is therapeutic. Rather the enactments themselves may also be generative and growth enhancing as they not only repeat and work through the past but also help us to anticipate, rehearse, and work towards the future. This temporal shift in focus opens up new ways of working that emphasize a health, strength-based perspective rather than the more typical pathology-based model.

Psychotherapy integration and trauma treatment

A number of Relational writers stress the importance of accounting for the numerous external systems within which we must function alongside our patients on a regular basis (Altman, 2009; Benjamin, 1997; Layton, 2006). For many years, Paul Wachtel has critiqued psychoanalysis for privileging the intrapsychic at the expense of including these external systems issues in diagnostic and treatment formulations (2008). The efforts of these writers continue to this day, leading to the expansion of what we think of as curative within psychoanalysis and in some cases to the ongoing growth and development of applied and community-based psychoanalysis (Christian, Reichbart, Moskowitz, Morillo, & Winograd, 2014; Bassin, 2014). Wachtel has also championed the integration of cognitive behavioral therapy (CBT) with Relational psychoanalytic treatment, noting their areas of commonality even while remaining not only supportive but also critical of both paradigms (2018).

Likewise, Kenneth Frank (2013, 2015) stresses the importance of psychotherapy integration, like Wachtel focusing primarily on the integration of psychoanalysis with CBT, but also with focusing therapy, sensorimotor psychotherapy, somatic experiencing, and other mindfulness-based modalities. I would argue that any judicious attempts to broaden psychoanalytic treatment by including these and other alternative modalities, when done by a practitioner well-trained in more than one modality, has the potential to enhance therapeutic action (Frank & Bernstein, 2012; Wachtel, 2012). This may be especially true for highly traumatized patients, who from the time of Freud's rejection of his seduction theory and prior to the recovery of Ferenczi's work and other interpersonal and Relational advances, were mostly outsourced to non-psychoanalytic practitioners (Foa, Steketee, & Rothbaum, 1989; Najavits, 2002). Likewise, there has been a proliferation of trauma training programs in relational psychoanalytic training institutes, including but not limited to New York City institutes such as the National Institute for the Psychotherapies, The Institute for Contemporary Psychoanalysis, and Manhattan Institute for Psychoanalysis.

Race, gender, and sexuality

Intersectionality refers to the ways in which race, class, gender, sexual orientation, age, religion, and other social markers impact personal experience and social interaction (Harris & Bartlow, 2015). It would be difficult to name an area within psychoanalysis more in need of a theoretical overhaul. And I would suggest that Relational psychoanalysis has done more to advance psychoanalytic thinking in the areas of race, gender, and sexuality than any other contemporary psychoanalytic framework.

Beginning with Stephen Mitchell's first published article (1981), he becomes one of the very first analysts to challenge the notion of pathologizing same sex object choice, a mere seven years after homosexuality was removed from the DSM. Relational colleagues who followed in his footsteps similarly overturned older definitions of perversion in favor of a much wider, if not limitless scope of "valid" sexual options (Stein, 2005; Dimen, 2001; Saketopolou, 2014a). And in very recent years, sexual orientation and gender identity, separate but related phenomena, are now assumed by most Relational thinkers to be non-binary, fluid states of being that intersect with each other as well as with race, class, and other social factors (Saketopolou, 2011a).

Much of this more current writing about gender and sexuality builds on Jessica Benjamin's scholarship. Benjamin's early books and articles made significant advances in these areas, helping to assure that from the beginning, Relational psychoanalysis would incorporate feminist theory and gender studies into its theory-base and metatheory (Benjamin, 1988, 1995, 1996, 1997, 2004; Benjamin & Atlas, 2015). Most recently, Benjamin has advanced her thinking about gender, sexuality, mutual recognition, and intersubjectivity in an important new work (2018). Among numerous others, she cites Galit Atlas, whose influential (2016a) volume addresses sexual (primarily female) desire and longing in the context of what she terms enigmatic and pragmatic knowing. Atlas's contributions to the psychoanalytic literature on female sexuality make her one of the most important and prolific contemporary Relational writers on this topic (2011a, 2011b, 2012, 2013, 2015, 2016a, 2016b).

Adrienne Harris's contributions to Relational psychoanalysis are many and varied. Her 2005 book and numerous other publications (1991, 1999, 2000) address postmodern concepts of gender by challenging traditional notions of linear development, as do most relational writers. Harris argues that children become gendered in multiply configured contexts and views gender as a less essentialist than constructed concept. Likewise, Virginia Goldner (1991, 2011), Ken Corbett (1993, 1996, 2011), Katie Gentile (2009, 2011, 2015), Jill Gentile (2016a, 2016b), and Steven Kuchuck (2012, 2013) all address particular elements of gender, sexual orientation and expression, and desire. Focusing on notions of essentialism, embodiment, cultural norms, and taboos, a handful of Relational writers have also begun to engage in the still new study of transgender identities and psychoanalytic treatment. Avgi Saketopolou (2011b, 2014a, 2014b), Sandra Silverman (2015), Virgina Goldner (2011), Melanie Suchet (2011), Griffin Hansburry (2005a, 2005b, 2011), and Adrienne Harris (2005, 2011), among others, have all made important contributions to this emerging literature.

In writing about race, Melanie Suchet (2004) examines the transference-countertransference dynamics between an African-American patient and herself, a white analyst born in South Africa. Racial trauma circulated throughout the analysis, as elements of slavery became enacted in the treatment. And in a 2007 paper, Suchet deconstructs whiteness from historical, political, and psychoanalytic perspectives in which socially constructed racial identities are examined and challenged. These are among the very few contemporary psychoanalytic papers about race and certainly the only few I am aware of that also address whiteness as a racial issue.

Like Dorothy Holmes (2016), Cleonie White (2016), in discussing Holmes's paper, focuses on the under-addressed psychological impact of disruptive, traumatizing effects of socio-cultural events. With regard to race (amongst other socio-cultural phenomena), Holmes and White address theoretical deficits that might otherwise help us to understand developmental and treatment issues—including trauma reactions—that arise for people of color. Steven Knoblauch (2015, 2017), writing primarily about affect regulation and embodiment—the latter yet another innovative area of study in Relational psychoanalysis—also addresses issues of race and culture within and outside the treatment room. Lama Khouri (2018) writes as a woman of color, a Palestinian living in Trump's United States. And speaking at the 2017 annual conference of the International Association for Relational Psychoanalysis and Psychotherapy (IARPP), Cynthia Chalker delivered a plenary presentation entitled Living and Working from the Centre: Reflections by a Black American Analytically Trained Therapist, now also in press with the journal *Psychoanalytic Perspectives*.

In addition to their examination of the under-theorizing of race in psychoanalysis, Holmes and White highlight the reluctance of psychoanalytic training institutes to address race per se or the trauma of racism. I can note that some institutes are just beginning to form or revitalize previously inactive diversity committees, a change often driven by psychoanalytic candidates much as or more than members and faculty. These committees, in conjunction with curriculum and training committees, are charged with seeing to it that readings better reflect notions of "Otherness" (an important concept in current Relational psychoanalysis [Goodman & Severson, 2016; Binder, 2006]) and therefore increase the inclusion of writing by and about people of color as well as other traditionally marginalized groups. Some of this effort has likely been galvanized by the Black Psychoanalysts Speak conferences and videos (Winograd, 2014). Relational psychoanalysis is certainly not the only theoretical perspective that is attempting to address issues of racial disparities and underrepresentation on faculties, supervisory staffs, in candidate bodies, and in curriculum representation. I suspect that at least within the psychoanalytic literature, it may be at the forefront.

Critiquing from within

If I had to choose a single new, exciting, and even unprecedented development within psychoanalysis, it would be an effort spearheaded by Lewis Aron, Sue Grand, and Joyce Slochower. Together, the three have co-edited a two-volume set of books for Routledge's Relational Perspectives Book Series. *De-Idealizing Relational Theory: A Critique from Within* (2018a) and *Decentering Relational Theory: A Comparative Critique* (2018b). Their project is an ambitious one and, as they contend, not one that has ever been tried before in psychoanalysis.

The editors of these collections remind us that the patient's *self-examination* is fundamental to psychoanalytic treatment and is a mainstay of therapeutic action. In 1996, Lewis Aron wrote that it was only by soliciting the patient's examination of the analyst through inviting direct and honest feedback and critique that the analyst could begin to examine the impact of his or her subjectivity on the patient and examine the blind spots that each clinician is impeded by. It is our patients, Aron contended, that often have the most accurate read on who we are in the treatment room and beyond. Related, the patient longs to know his analyst's mind in much the same way that the child longs to know their parent's. We must therefore invite and even encourage them to tell us what they see in order to fully explore the transference-countertransference field. The "eye cannot see itself" (Stern, 2004, p. 225; Frank, 2012).

Within the field, however, psychoanalysts haven't sufficiently utilized their own methodology or subjected their own preferred theories and practice techniques to systematic and critical, ongoing self-examination. On the contrary and from the beginning of psychoanalytic time, writers and clinicians of all theoretical persuasions have too often responded to criticism with defensiveness. In some extreme but not uncommon scenarios, such criticism has resulted in institutional splits rather than openness and self-reflection on either side of the critique (Reeder, 2004; Berman, 2004; Kuchuck, 2008). Rather than automatically assuming that critics of Relational (or any) theory are always wrong and distorting or misunderstanding the Relational premise, each of the Relationally-identified editors and authors in these volumes asks the questions: in what ways does Relational theory lend itself to specific criticisms, and (as with our patients) how might these critiques illuminate blind-spots and highlight new areas of focus and growth?

Many of the contributors also offer their own critiques of the Relational perspective. As noted earlier, Joyce Slochower's (2018) chapter addresses the Relational ideal and its actual limits. She notes that we analysts are not always mindful enough of how much our own need for privacy and self-protection impacts the clinical work and what we can realistically offer our patients. Slochower, and in individual chapters Steven Seligman (2018), Ken Corbett (2018), and Robert Grossmark (2018), all reflect on various aspects of the fact that Relational work may at times similarly miss the patients' profound sense of vulnerability and wish not only for relatedness and engagement but also a deep need for alone interiority. I would agree that as practiced by some, Relational work does not always privilege the analyst's restraint as much as it does explicit, often articulated, overt expressions of relatedness and/or subjectivity that run the risk of impingement.

Donnel Stern (2018) takes up the question of mutual influence – and the lack thereof. He is rightly worried about psychoanalysis's isolationist tendencies and notes that Relational psychoanalysis has remained somewhat obscured from the views of both European and Latin American psychoanalysis. They experience "us" as marginalizing "them." As noted in my earlier words about perceptions of what constitutes a "real" analyst, many Relational analysts feel the same way. Otherness, as many of the authors in these volumes discuss, forecloses dialogue and subsequent opportunities for mutual learning. Stern challenges this collapse of dialogue by addressing what relational psychoanalysis can gain through respectful conversation and non-defensive openness to the critiques leveled at Relationalists by these colleagues. We have a chance to learn from and engage our critics by reading their work and considering their critiques. We can only challenge them effectively if we understand them. Of course we might hope for this to happen on both sides of the debate.

Final thoughts

Similar to Stern's (2018) commentary, in volume one of the critique on Relational theory (Aron et al., 2018a) and in an earlier paper (see Aron, 2017), Lew Aron offers a model for how psychoanalysis might stay relevant and evolve rather than stagnate. He introduces and expands upon Karl Popper's notion of critical rationalism, the contention that *scientific knowledge grows not by accumulating supporting evidence but by subjecting our beliefs to the most severe criticism we can garner*. Aron advocates that we therefore approach psychoanalysis with an attitude of reflexive skepticism and critical pluralism, in which

> we can gain the most from the diversity of psychoanalytic theories by moving beyond mutual respect and tolerance toward a genuine appreciation of others, for the critical perspective that they can offer to us and that we can offer to them. The other school, viewpoint, or orientation can provide a function that we cannot do for ourselves nor they for themselves.
>
> (2017, p. 271)

To the extent that Relationalists and all analysts can begin to incorporate this way of approaching our theories, along with holding the tension between theoretical plurality on the one hand and bridge theories on the other, I would suggest that this might be the single most important, recent, overarching development in psychoanalysis today. It is a crucial correction to the isolation and splitting of theoretical schools that has existed since the time of Freud, making it difficult, at times even impossible, for us to cross-fertilize ideas and learn from one another.

Relational psychoanalysis continues to evolve and develop new ideas through the incorporation of a younger generation's changing cultural values and norms – including but not limited to a rapidly evolving understanding of gender, sexual orientation, and sexual and relationship expression. Postmodern perspectives also continue to expand in other realms and are becoming more familiar to us and an increasingly larger segment of the population, more extensively integrated even into mainstream society. An older generation's accumulated wisdom also contributes to this evolution of Relational and all schools of psychoanalysis.

As mentioned, the Relational perspective and other contemporary models and versions of psychoanalysis place particular value on sociocultural and political issues as well as other external systems. Also, Relational (and contemporary) psychoanalysis in particular focuses much more on a move away from the one-size-fits-all paradigm that typifies some older versions of classical psychoanalysis. With every advance and just the mere passage of time, more questions arise. I can't help but wonder, for example, what the impact will be over time of a still new, incoming generation of Relationally-trained students and analysts who, unlike the founders and first or second generation of Relational psychoanalysis, are not in fact immigrants from other theoretical lands or only white and heterosexually identified.

Ours is truly a perspective that seeks to examine analyst and patient subjectivity, transient self-states, and intersubjective dynamics. The unique, co-constructed spaces that every analytic dyad inhabits are situated on shifting terrain, the result of intrapsychic and cultural change and growth. As such, Relational psychoanalysis, though not alone in this pursuit, will by definition continue to reinvent itself in new and exciting ways that can barely be imagined, much less predicted.

Acknowledgments

With great appreciation to my dear friend, teacher and colleague, the late Lewis Aron, Galit Atlas, Sharyn Leff, and Annelisa Pedersen for their close reading and valuable contributions to this chapter.

Note

1 For example, intersubjective (or intersubjectivity) refers not only to a separate theoretical school that has some overlap with relational and Relational psychoanalysis, but also to a concept—defined differently by different theorists—within r/Relational psychoanalysis (Kuchuck & Sopher, 2017; Kuchuck, 2017).

References

Altman, N. (2009). *The analyst in the inner city: Race, class, and culture through a psychoanalytic lens* (2nd ed.). Hillsdale, NJ: Analytic Press.

Aron, L. (1991). The patient's experience of the analyst's subjectivity. *Psychoanalytic Dialogues*, *1*, 29–51.
Aron, L. (1996). *A meeting of mind: Mutuality in psychoanalysis*. Hillsdale, NJ: Analytic Press.
Aron, L. (2017). Beyond tolerance in psychoanalytic communities: Reflexive skepticism and critical pluralism. *Psychoanalytic Perspectives*, *14*(3), 271–282.
Aron, L., & Atlas, G. (2015). Gains and loss in translation. *Contemporary Psychoanalysis*, *51*(4), 767–775.
Aron, L., Grand, S., & Slochower, J. A. (2018a). *De-idealizing relational theory: A critique from within*. New York, NY: Routledge.
Aron, L., Grand, S., & Slochower, J. A. (2018b). *Decentering relational theory: A comparative critique*. New York, NY: Routledge.
Atlas, G. (2011a). Attachment abandonment murder. *Contemporary Psychoanalysis*, *47*(2), 245–259.
Atlas, G. (2011b, Fall 11). The bad father, the sinful son and the wild ghost. *Psychoanalytic Perspectives*, *8*(2), 238–251.
Atlas, G. (2012). Sex and the kitchen: Thoughts on culture and forbidden desire. *Psychoanalytic Perspectives*, *9*(2), 220–232.
Atlas, G. (2013). What's love got to do with it? Sexuality, shame and the use of the other. *Studies in Gender and Sexuality*, *14*(1), 51–58.
Atlas, G. (2015). Touch me, know me: The enigma of erotic longing. *Psychoanalytic Psychology*, *31*(1), 123–139.
Atlas, G. (2016a). *The enigma of desire: Sex, longing, and belonging in psychoanalysis*. New York, NY: Routledge.
Atlas, G. (2016b). Breaks in unity: The caesura of birth. *Studies in Gender and Sexuality*, *17*, 201–204.
Atlas, G., & Aron, L. (Eds.). (2018). *Dramatic dialogue: Contemporary clinical practice*. London: Routledge.
Bass, A. (2003). Enactments in psychoanalysis: Another medium, another message. *Psychoanalytic Dialogues*, *13*, 657–676.
Bassin, D. (2014). The mourning after. *PEP Video Grants*, *1*(1), 12.
Benjamin, J. (1988). *The bonds of love: Psychoanalysis, feminism and the problem of domination*. New York, NY: Pantheon Books.
Benjamin, J. (1995). *Like subjects, love objects: Essays on recognition and sexual difference*. New Haven, CT: Yale University Press.
Benjamin, J. (1996). In defense of gender ambiguity. *Gender and Psychoanalysis*, *1*(1), 27–43.
Benjamin, J. (1997). *Shadow of the other: Intersubjectivity and gender in psychoanalysis*. New York, NY: Routledge.
Benjamin, J. (2004). Beyond doer and done-to: An intersubjective view of thirdness. *Psychoanalytic Quarterly*, *73*, 5–46.
Benjamin, J. (2018). *Beyond doer and done to: Recognition theory, intersubjectivity and the third*. New York, NY: Routledge.

Benjamin, J., & Atlas, G. (2015). The "too muchness" of excitement: Sexuality in light of excess, attachment and affect regulation. *International Journal of Psychoanalysis, 96*, 39–63.

Berman, E. (2004). *Impossible training: A relational view of psychoanalytic education*. Hillsdale, NJ: Analytic Press.

Binder, P. (2006). Searching for the enriching sense of otherness: The psychoanalytic psychotherapist as a meaning-bearing other. *International Forum of Psychoanalysis, 15*(3), 162–168.

Black, M. (2003). Enactment: Analytic musings on energy, language, and personal growth. *Psychoanalytic Dialogues, 13*(5), 633–655.

Boulanger, G. (2002). Wounded by reality: The collapse of the self in adult onset trauma. *Contemporary Psychoanalysis, 38*, 45–76.

Bromberg, P. (1996). Standing in the spaces: The multiplicity of self and the psychoanalytic relationship. *Contemporary Psychoanalysis, 32*, 509–535.

Cooper, S. (2016). *The analyst's experience of the depressive position: The melancholic errand of psychoanalysis*. New York, NY: Routledge.

Corbett, K. (1993). The mystery of homosexuality. *Psychoanalytic Dialogues, 10*, 345–357.

Corbett, K. (1996). Homosexual boyhood: Notes on girlyboys. *Gender and Psychoanalysis, 1*, 429–462.

Corbett, K. (2011). *Rethinking masculinities*. New Haven, CT: Yale University Press.

Corbett, K. (2018). The analyst's private space: Spontaneity, ritual, psychotherapeutic action, and self-care. In L. Aron, S. Grand, & J. Slochower (Eds.), *De-idealizing relational theory: A critique from within* (pp. 150–166). New York, NY: Routledge.

Chalker, C. (In press). Living and working from the centre: Reflections by a black American analytically trained therapist. *Psychoanalytic Perspectives*.

Christian, C., Reichbart, R., Moskowitz, M., Morillo, R., & Winograd, B. (2014). Psychoanalysis in El Barrio. *PEP Video Grants, 1*(1), 10.

Davies, J. (2001). Back to the future in psychoanalysis: Trauma, dissociation, and the nature of unconscious processes. In M. Dimen & A. Harris (Eds.), *Storms in her head: Freud and the construction of hysteria* (pp. 245–264). New York, NY: Other Press.

Davies, J. (2012). Getting cold feet, defining "safe-enough" borders: Dissociation, multiplicity, and integration in the analyst's experience. *The Psychoanalytic Quarterly, 68*(2), 184–208.

Davies, J., & Frawley, M. G. (1994). *Treating the adult survivor of childhood sexual abuse: A psychoanalytic perspective*. New York, NY: Basic Books.

Dimen, M. (2001). Perversion is us? Eight notes. *Psychoanalytic Dialogues, 11*(6), 825–860.

Ferenczi, S. (1932). *The clinical diaries of Sándor Ferenczi* (M. Balint & N. Z. Jackson, Trans.). Cambridge, MA: Harvard University Press, 1988.

Ferro, A. (1996). *In the analyst's consulting room* (P. Slotnik, Trans.). New York, NY: Brunner-Routledge.

Ferro, A., & Basile, R. (2008). Countertransference and the characters of the psychoanalytic session. *Scandinavian Psychoanalytic Review, 31*(1), 3–10.

Foa, E., Steketee, G., & Rothbaum, B. O. (1989). Behavioral/cognitive conceptualizations of post-traumatic stress disorder. *Behavior Therapy, 20*(2), 155–176.

Frank, K. (2012). Therapeutic action. *Psychoanalytic Perspectives, 9*, 75–87.

Frank, K. (2013). Psychoanalysis and the 21st century: A critique and a vision. *Psychoanalytic Perspectives, 10*, 300–334.

Frank, K. (2015). Psychoanalysis and the twenty-first century: A critique and a vision. In J. Bressler & K. Starr (Eds.), *Relational psychoanalysis and psychotherapy integration: An evolving synthesis. Relational psychoanalysis book series*. New York, NY: Routledge, Taylor and Francis Group.

Frank, K., & Bernstein, K. (2012). Therapeutic action: An introduction and overview. *Psychoanalytic Perspectives, 9*(1), 1–19.

Gentile, J. (2016a). Between the familiar and the stranger: Attachment security, mutual desire, and reclaimed love. *International Journal of Psychoanalytic Self Psychology, 11*, 193–215.

Gentile, J. (2016b). Naming the vagina, naming the woman. *Division/Review, 14*, 23–29.

Gentile, K. (2009). The collective artistry of activism: A review of making trouble: Life and politics. By Lynne Segal. *Studies in Gender and Sexuality, 10*(4). London: Serpents Tail.

Gentile, K. (2011). What about the patriarchy? Response to commentaries by Zeavin and Layton. *Studies in Gender and Sexuality, 12*(1), 72–77.

Gentile, K. (2015). Temporality in question: Psychoanalysis meets queer time. *Studies in Gender and Sexuality, 15*(1).

Goldner, V. (1991). Toward a critical relational theory of gender. *Psychoanalytic Dialogues, 1*, 249–272.

Goldner, V. (2011). Trans: Gender in free fall. *Psychoanalytic Dialogues, 21*, 159–171.

Goodman, D, & Severson, E. (2016). *The ethical turn: Otherness and subjectivity in contemporary psychoanalysis*. New York, NY: Routledge.

Greenberg, J., & Mitchell, S. (1983). *Object relations in psychoanalytic theory*. Cambridge, MA: Harvard University Press.

Grossmark, R. (2018). The unobtrusive relational analyst and psychoanalytic companioning. In L. Aron, S. Grand, & J. Slochower (Eds.), *De-idealizing relational theory: A critique from within* (pp. 167–190). New York, NY: Routledge.

Hansburry, G. (2005a). The middle men: An introduction to the transmasculine identities. *Studies in Gender and Sexuality, 6*(3), 241–264.

Hansburry, G. (2005b). Mourning the loss of the idealized self: A transsexual passage. *Psychoanalytic Social Work, 12*(1), 19–35.

Hansburry, G. (2011). King Kong & goldilocks: Imagining transmasculinities through the trans-trans dyad. *Psychoanalytic Dialogues, 21*(2), 210–220.

Harris, A. (1991). Gender as contradiction. *Psychoanalytic Dialogues, 1*(3), 243–248.

Harris, A. (1999). Making genders: Commentary on paper by Irene Fast. *Psychoanalytic Dialogues, 9*(5), 663–673.

Harris, A. (2000). Gender as soft assembly: Tomboys' stories. *Studies in Gender and Sexuality, 1*, 223–250.

Harris, A. (2005). *Gender as soft assembly.* Hillsdale, NJ: Analytic Press.

Harris, A. (2011). The relational tradition: Landscape and canon. *Journal of the American Psychoanalytic Association, 59*(4), 701–736.

Harris, A., & Bartlow, S. (2015). Intersectionality: Race, gender, sexuality, and class. In J. DeLamater & R. F. Plant (Eds.), *Handbook of the sociology of sexualities* (pp. 261–271). New York, NY: Springer.

Hoffman, I. Z. (1983). The patient as interpreter of the analyst's experience. *Contemporary Psychoanalysis, 19*, 389–422.

Holmes, D. (2016). Come hither, American psychoanalysis: Our complex multicultural America needs: What we have to offer. *Journal of the American Psychoanalytic Association, 64*(3), 569–586.

Jacobs, T. (1986). *Blood brothers: Siblings as writers* (N. Kiell, Ed., p. 434). New York, NY: International Universities Press, Inc., 1983, *Psychoanalytic Quarterly, 55*, 168–170.

Khouri, L. (2018). Through Trump's looking glass into Alice's wonderland: On meeting the house Palestinian. *Psychoanalytic Perspectives, 15*(3).

Knoblauch, S. (2015). A culturally constituted subjectivity: Musically and beyond: A discussion of three offerings from Aron, Ralph, and White. *Psychoanalytic Dialogues, 25*(2), 201–207.

Knoblauch, S. (2017). The fluidity of emotions and clinical vulnerability: A field of rhythmic tensions. *Psychoanalytic Perspectives, 14*(3), 283–308.

Kuchuck, S. (2008). In the shadow of the towers: The role of retraumatization and political action in the evolution of a psychoanalyst. *Psychoanalytic Review, 95*, 417–436.

Kuchuck, S. (2009). Do ask, do tell? Narcissistic need as a determinant of analyst self-disclosure. *The Psychoanalytic Review, 96*, 1007–1024.

Kuchuck, S. (2012). Please (don't) want me: The therapeutic action of male sexual desire in the treatment of heterosexual men. *Contemporary Psychoanalysis, 48*, 544–562.

Kuchuck, S. (2013). Reflections on the therapeutic action of desire. *Studies in Gender and Sexuality, 14*, 133–139.

Kuchuck, S. (Ed.). (2014). *Clinical implications of the psychoanalyst's life experience: When the personal becomes professional.* New York, NY: Routledge.

Kuchuck, S. (2016). Challenging fathers: Margarethe Lutz's consultation with Sigmund Freud. *Psychoanalytic Perspectives, 13*(3), 305–310.

Kuchuck, S. (2017). Postscript to: "Critique of Relational Psychoanalysis" by Jon Mills. In R. E. Barsness (Ed.), *Core competencies of relational psychoanalysis: A guide to practice, study and research*. New York, NY: Routledge.

Kuchuck, S. (2018). The analyst's subjectivity: On the impact of inadvertent, deliberate, and silent disclosure. *Psychoanalytic Perspectives, 15*(3), 265–274.

Kuchuck, S., & Sopher, R. (2017). Relational psychoanalysis out of context: Response to Jon Mills. *Psychoanalytic Perspectives, 14*(3), 364–375.

Layton, L. (2006). Racial identities, racial enactments, and normative unconscious processes. *Psychoanalytic Quarterly, 75*, 237–269.

Maroda, K. (2003). *Seduction, surrender, and transformation: Emotional engagement in the analytic process*. New York, NY: Routledge.

Mills, J. (2012). *Conundrums: A critique of relational psychoanalysis*. New York, NY: Routledge.

Mills, J. (2017). Challenging relational psychoanalysis: A reply to my critics. *Psychoanalytic Perspectives, 15*(1), 2–9.

Mitchell, S. A. (1981). The psychoanalytic treatment of homosexuality: Some technical considerations. *International Review of Psychoanalysis, 8*, 63–80.

Mitchell, S. A. (1988). *Relational concepts in psychoanalysis: An integration*. Cambridge, MA: Harvard University Press.

Mitchell, S. (1998). The analyst's knowledge and authority. *The Psychoanalytic Quarterly, 67*(1), 1–31.

Najavits, L. (2002). *Seeking safety: A treatment manual for PTSD and substance abuse*. New York, NY: The Guilford Press.

Ogden, B. H., & Ogden, T. H. (2012). How the analyst thinks as clinician and as literary reader. *Psychoanalytic Perspectives, 9*(2), 243–273.

Ogden, T. H. (1979). On projective identification. *International Journal of Psychoanalysis, 60*, 357–373.

Reeder, J. (2004). *Hate and love in psychoanalytic institutions: The dilemma of a profession*. New York, NJ: Other Press.

Saketopolou, A. (2011a). Minding the gap: Intersections between gender, race, and class in work with gender variant children. *Psychoanalytic Dialogues, 21*(2), 192–209.

Saketopolou, A. (2011b). Consent, sexuality and self-respect: Commentary on Skerrett's essay. *Studies in Gender and Sexuality, 12*, 245–250.

Saketopolou, A. (2014a). Mourning the body as bedrock: Developmental considerations in treating transsexual patients analytically. *Journal of the American Psychoanalytic Association, 62*(5), 773–806.

Saketopolou, A. (2014b). To suffer pleasure: The shattering of the ego as the psychic labor of perverse sexuality. *Studies in Gender and Sexuality, 15*(4), 254–268.

Slochower, J. (2018). Going too far: Relational heroines and relational excess. In L. Aron, S. Grand, & J. Slochower (Eds.), *De-idealizing relational theory: A critique from within* (pp. 8–34). New York, NY: Routledge.

Seligman, S. (2018). *Relationships in development: Infancy, intersubjectivity, attachment*. New York, NY: Routledge.

Silverman, S. (2015). The colonized mind: Gender, Trauma, and mentalization. *Psychoanalytic Dialogues, 25*, 51–66.

Stein, R. (2005). Skimming the milk, Cajoling the Soul – Embodiment and obscenity in sexuality: Commentary on Muriel Dimen's paper. *Studies in Gender and Sexuality, 6*(1), 19–31.

Stern, D. (2004). The eye sees itself: Dissociation, enactment, and the achievement of conflict. *Contemporary Psychoanalysis, 40*, 197–237.

Stern, D. (2018). Otherness within psychoanalysis: On recognizing the critics of relational psychoanalysis. In L. Aron, S. Grand, & J. Slochower (Eds.), *Decentering relational theory: A comparative critique* (pp. 27–48). New York, NY: Routledge.

Stern, D., & Hirsch, I. (Eds.). (2017). *The interpersonal perspective in psychoanalysis, 1960s-1990s: Rethinking transference and countertransference*. New York, NY: Routledge.

Stolorow, R., Brandchaft, B., & Atwood, G. (1987). *Psychoanalytic treatment: An intersubjective approach*. Hillsdale, NJ: The Analytic Press.

Suchet, M. (2004). A relational encounter with race. *Psychoanalytic Dialogues, 14*, 423–438.

Suchet, M. (2007). Unraveling whiteness. *Psychoanalytic Dialogues, 17*(6), 867–886.

Suchet, M. (2011). Crossing over. *Psychoanalytic Dialogues, 21*, 172–191.

Wachtel, P. (2008). *Relational theory and the practice of psychotherapy*. New York, NY: The Guilford Press.

Wachtel, P. (2012). Reflections on the therapeutic process. *Psychoanalytic Perspectives, 9*(1), 88–117.

Wachtel, P. (2018). Toward a more fully integrative and contextual relational paradigm. In L. Aron, S. Grand, & J. Slochower (Eds.), *Decentering relational theory: A comparative critique* (pp. 73–91). New York, NY: Routledge.

White, C. (2016). I am, you are, we . . . are . . . us! Discussion of "Culturally imposed trauma: The sleeping dog has awakened: Will psychoanalysis take heed?" by Dorothy Evans Holmes, Ph.D. *Psychoanalytic Dialogues, 26*(6), 673–677.

Winograd, B. (2014). Black psychoanalysts speak. *PEP Video Grants, 1*(1), 1.

Chapter 10

Phenomenology speaks
From intersubjectivity to the ethical turn

Donna M. Orange

In the presence of received ideas, established theories, or even knee-jerk opposition, philosophers tend to squirm. After a century that saw certainties and dogmatisms destroy human beings worldwide on a scale not previously dreamed, some understandably squirmed into postmodernism. Not only was God dead, but so was any reality or theory we could rely on. Every theory might become a mighty murderer of human souls.

Psychoanalysis, as Aner Govrin (Govrin, 2016) has recently written, was born in the era of grand theories. Freud's "followers," amazed and fascinated with the territory he was "discovering," put all their creative energy into promoting and expanding his revolution. Freud himself, though, studying for five terms with Franz Brentano, the grandfather of phenomenology, and translating John Stewart Mill into German, had dreamed as a young man of being a philosopher. Once Austrian anti-Semitism made it clear to him that he would never have a career in the university, and once Freud became intoxicated with the grand theories to which he passionately devoted the rest of his life, he had to turn away from philosophy. Philosophy, and in particular the philosophies of Schopenhauer and Nietzsche permeating the air Freud breathed in turn-of-the-century Vienna, would have made him skeptical. So, explicitly modeling psychoanalysis on the empirical sciences so wildly successful in his day, he claimed that psychoanalysis had nothing to do with philosophy.

Yet philosophy has returned to psychoanalysis in at least two important forms. Postmodern skepticism has pervaded relational psychoanalysis, for good and ill. Its conviction that nothing can be foundational, that there is no bedrock (Poland, 2018), that many voices – or at least two – count, that reality emerges, that description may be more important than definition, and so on, has helped to install in contemporary psychoanalysis a salutary humility and a listening ear. My own suggestion, borrowed from the American pragmatists, to hold our theories lightly, comes in this spirit. Postmodern skepticism keeps us wondering if there may be another side to every story, a constantly needed questioning central to the psychoanalytic spirit from its very beginnings. Postmodern skepticism, sometimes related to what phenomenologist Paul Ricoeur (1970) named the "hermeneutics of suspicion," attributing this attitude to Marx, Freud, and Nietzsche, has importantly contributed to undoing the essentialisms of patriarchy, colonialism, heterosexism, and so on.

Still, postmodernism has its dark sides, to which we will return in the final section of this chapter. It may understate the traumatic effects of war, genocide, torture, and child abuse. It may miss the ethical demand on each and all of us. My immediate task, to highlight the new and creative psychoanalytic contributions in intersubjectivity and ethics, requires the descriptive hat of the phenomenologist. In my view, the phenomenology of trauma and the "ethical turn" constitute the two areas of development most clinically important to emerge from phenomenological intersubjectivity.

The intersubjectivities in psychoanalysis

The 1980s were a fascinating time to be joining the psychoanalytic world, especially for those of us trained in philosophy. Not surprisingly, we turned to the intersubjectivities, whether the more Hegelian form developed and articulated by Jessica Benjamin (Benjamin, 2004) or to the more phenomenologically inclined form found in the work of Stolorow, Atwood, and Brandchaft (Stolorow, Atwood, & Branchaft, 1994; Stolorow, Brandchaft, & Atwood, 1987; Orange, Atwood, & Stolorow, 1997), and best developed just now by Chris Jaenicke (Jaenicke, 2008, 2011). In the first years of the twenty-first century, lively debates – perhaps owing something to the varying sensibilities of some relationalists and self-psychologists – raged about the relative merits of these forms of intersubjectivity in psychoanalysis. Meanwhile, the tremendously creative work of Thomas Ogden, an intersubjectivist in his own way, continued to develop from a very traditional form of practice.

But much of the energy has now disappeared from these debates, it seems. Why? First, we have, dialogically, attempted to listen to each other, to hear each other's concerns, to give each other the benefit of the doubt, to see what the other is attempting to say that needs to be said and may be missing from our own perspective. Of course, true to the worst legacy of our psychoanalytic history, analysts remain ready to give each other the cold shoulder, to refuse to speak with those with whom they disagree, to describe those with whom they disagree as harmful to patients. We are no saints, and our human frailties limit our prospects in this direction.

And yet our psychoanalytic thinking, either linking the consulting room to its larger context or feeling the intrusion of the "outside" world into clinical work, has been shifting focus. We hear talk of an "ethical turn" in psychoanalysis. Suddenly relationality involves more than two people: it evokes world poverty, racism, economic inequality, climate crisis, and much more. You find Jessica Benjamin deeply involved with injustices to the Palestinians; I have been writing about "suffering strangers" not only in the consulting room but also those being destroyed by climate crisis and dire poverty. We intersubjectivists of all stripes have been called out into an ethical turn.

Why has intersubjective systems theory, even held fallibilistically in a Peircean spirit, been so compelling for us phenomenologists? This theory, to start abstractly and formally, examines the field – two personal worlds of experience in the system they create and from which they emerge – both in human development and in any form of psychoanalytic treatment. Because of this focus, intersubjectivity theory also implies a complex contextualist view of development and of pathogenesis, describing the emergence and modification of subjectivity (phenomenologists often call this the experiential world) and defining all these processes as irreducibly relational. As observers and participants, we focus on the evolving psychological field constituted by the interplay between the differently organized experiential worlds of child and caregivers, patient and analyst, and so on. Informally, this means I am always trying not only to describe experience (yours, mine, and ours) in this temporal-relational context but also to understand in what relational contexts we became the people who participate and experience as we do.

This use of the terms intersubjective and intersubjectivity differs from some related ideas. In our usage (Atwood & Stolorow, 2014; Orange, 1995; Orange et al., 1997; Stolorow & Atwood, 1992; Stolorow, Atwood, & Brandchaft, 1987; Stolorow, Atwood, & Orange, 2002), "intersubjective," describing the emergent relatedness between any two or more people, does not refer primarily to a developmental achievement. Daniel Stern's earlier work (Stern, 1985), for example, names as "the intersubjective self" a stage and process of recognition of another's subjectivity as connected and responsive to one's own. This mutual recognition, also brought center stage in Benjamin's work (Jessica Benjamin, 1995), may be a late achievement in the intersubjective field of an analysis, especially in patients, such as those described by Ferenczi, Guntrip (1968), and Kohut (1971). Though both have value, mutual recognition intersubjectivity differs from our contextualist conception of an intersubjective field. Instead this mutual-recognition intersubjectivity may occur within an always already existing intersubjective world (Orange, 2008). I see intersubjective systems theory as one form of American relational theory – a variant more rooted in continental philosophies of phenomenology and hermeneutics.

This point of view links to more basic convictions, a "web of belief" (Quine & Ullian, 1970), and thus can sound circular. These include:

1 Personal experience takes form, is maintained, and transforms itself in relational contexts. What we call experience could not yet be experience without its interpretation by the explicit or implicit community. I become I – with my characteristic ways of thinking, feeling, believing, and living with others – only within complexly nested and overlapping systems: infant caregiver, family, culture, religion, lifeworlds (Husserl, 1970; Merleau-Ponty, 1962), and so on. How I experience myself and the otherness of the other depends upon these systems. When I bring my organization of experience to a relational situation, I bring a range of expectancies, emotional convictions, and ways I am prepared to respond or react. This range may be narrower or wider, depending on my whole life history in relational contexts and on the possibilities of therapeutic transformation available to me so far. This specific situation re-evokes particular aspects of my organized experience with more or less intensity, creating new interpretive possibilities. This view of experience need not exclude many kinds of prereflective self-awareness or self-familiarity (Zahavi, 2005). What I bring is just an enduring set of possibilities and leanings, nothing actual until I meet you. What I experience in the situation with you is not something inside of me but is, instead, my participation in the world we inhabit together. Levinas (1969) would have said that I become myself only in response to the face of the other, the widow, the orphan, the stranger, in a word, to the destitute. But here I am getting ahead of my story.

2 All experience is interpretive and thus perspectival. This means no one and no group of people can take more than a partial view of anything – not even those claiming that all is constructed! Our horizons of possibility of experiencing are limited, both spatially and temporally. This means that I have no God's eye authority to say that the patient is projecting or that I know an enactment is going on around here. Even a community's view, be it classical Freudian, ego psychological, Kohutian, Kleinian, Sullivanian, or anything else, can only provide a partial access to complex and plural truths. Our only possibility is to search together for understandings, always provisional.

3 The inherent temporality of experience means that development and change – despite our longings for stability, reliability, and certainty – are as important as what endures. In the psychoanalytic situation, for example, mutually regulated experiences form unstable, though past-loaded, systems. These are always organizing and reorganizing themselves, both continually and in fits and starts, as the developmentalists (Beebe & Lachmann, 2001; Sander, 1995; Thelen & Smith, 1994) teach us. At the same time, this conviction differentiates intersubjective systems phenomenologists from those relationalists tending to disparage a developmental emphasis in psychoanalysis. To think developmentally does not require a linear stage theory, nor does it necessarily infantilize but simply refuses the atomism of the single moment.

4 Human being is *embodied* spirit (Merleau-Ponty, 1945/1962). There is only one of me. My Cartesian mind does not take my material body out to ride my bicycle; rather, I go out for a ride. Nor do my brain mechanisms drive me to do this, even though the neuroscientists (not only their brains) may, in part, be able to explain why I am able to do it. Human being is describable in more mentalist or more physicalist language, but systems theories encourage inclusiveness of description and resist reductionism in all its forms.

5 As a perspectival realist (Orange, 1995), I see consciousness and unconsciousness as qualities of personal and relational experience, primarily as dependent on the conditions of relationality for individuals and communities (Stolorow et al., 2002). Thus consciousness and unconsciousness are not locations; nor do they sharply divide experience. Often it is a question of more or less. At times, depending on many forms of context, I can tell you things about myself, about my

patients, about those closest to me that I seem not to know at other times. Even Freud's dynamic unconscious was accessible within the psychoanalytic conversation. His concept of "working through" is one of several that points to the incompleteness of the conscious-unconscious dichotomy. Relational and systems theories suggest that both are shifting properties of relational processes.

6   The uniqueness and unrepeatability of each human being distinguishes this view from the asocial conception that my collaborators and I have called the "Cartesian isolated mind." In every life there is an indefinitely large combination of relational and implicitly relational micro and macro events. From this myriad, each person continually self-organizes into a personality that can never be reduced to a formula or category. I inhabit my experiential world as it inhabits me (Orange, 2001). Most of what is wonderful, and strange, and difficult in life and art results from this always-emergent individuality – selfness when it is mine and otherness when it is yours. To claim that individuals are unique and can know themselves by a kind of intimate familiarity or *Selbstvertrautheit* (Frank, 1991) is not to return to the monism, without windows (Leibniz & Latta, 1948), of the Cartesian mind.

7   A fallibilistic attitude that holds theory lightly, and warns us never to be too sure, protects us against theoretical and clinical rigidity. As dogma, fallibilism is, as George Atwood often warns me, impossible to hold consistently "all the way down" because it would itself have to be brought into question. As an attitude, however, it can keep us humble, unpretentious, and ready to learn.

Finally, intersubjective systems psychoanalysis includes what I most value in other psychoanalytic theories without obligating me to accept those aspects I find unacceptable. Here is a very brief summary. Freudian psychoanalysis brings us the search for meaning as a way of healing troubled lives. Object relations theories focus a sharp lens on the priority of relatedness in the formation of personal experience, providing concepts such as the holding environment and transitional experience. Self-psychology contributes a clinical sensibility that places understanding and developmental thinking at the center of its process and of its theory of curative efficacy. American relationalists demonstrate how completely inevitable is the mutual participation in the psychoanalytic process and how to value and embrace this mutuality while also always living an ethical asymmetry

(Levinas, 1981; Aron, 1996). All these gifts, and doubtless more, can be embraced by an intersubjective systems phenomenology and sensibility.

Intersubjective systems theory, above all, both informs and results from my experience of daily clinical work and supervision. This aspect, however, is most difficult to articulate without seeming to discredit clinicians who think and practice differently. Probably analysts and other psychotherapists of every school can tell stories of patients untreated or mistreated by colleagues who practice differently and who seem to be much better treated according to another approach. I try to remember that previous treatment narratives come constituted by the intersection of at least three subjective worlds – the patient's, the previous therapist's, and mine – but I know that such stories have influenced me. Even more, reading and hearing psychoanalysts describing their work, I imagine myself as their patient and thus create yet another virtual intersubjective system. Recognizing that clinical style varies with the practitioner, I have tried to develop a theory and sensibility that, golden-rule-wise, I would want as a patient myself.

No distinct body of clinical theory or of "technical" recommendations derives from intersubjectivity theory. Rather an intersubjective perspective introduces a more general characterization of all psychoanalytic work from within any specific clinical theory. Because each treatment includes an analyst with a point of view, different kinds of intersubjective fields develop in classical, interpersonal, or self-psychological treatments as well as in each psychoanalytic pair. From a clinical point of view, intersubjectivity is not so much a theory as it is a sensibility. It is an attitude of continuing sensitivity to the inescapable interplay of observer and observed. It assumes that instead of entering and immersing ourselves in the experience of another, we accompany the other in the intersubjective space-time. Each participant in the psychoanalytic dialogue brings an emotional history to the process. This means that although the analysis is always for the patient, the emotional history and psychological organization of patient and analyst are equally important to the understanding of any clinical exchange. What we inquire about, or interpret, or leave alone depends upon who we are. The analytic process, as relational theorist Lewis Aron (1996) has explained, is mutually constituted but asymmetrical. One participant bears more responsibility. The other chiefly seeks relief from emotional suffering. (The Latin root of "patient" means to suffer, undergo, or bear.) In the developmental process that we name psychoanalysis, one is primarily respondent, inquirer, and guide, while the other seeks to organize and reorganize experience in less painful and more creative ways. Nevertheless, each is a full participant and contributor to the process that emerges.

There are, however, chiefly three attitudes that characterize our clinical work: (1) a concentration on the emotional convictions (organizing principles) that pattern a person's experiential world, (2) radical engagement, that is, a self-reflective awareness of the clinician's constant and unavoidable participation, and (3) a refusal to argue about reality, that is, to assume an authoritarian "knowing" attitude. The principal components of subjectivity, first of all, are the organizing principles, whether automatic and rigid or reflective and flexible. These principles, often unconscious, are the emotional conclusions a person has drawn from lifelong experience of the emotional environment, especially the complex mutual connections with early caregivers. Until these principles become available for conscious reflection, that is, until they emerge in dialogue, and until new emotional experience leads a person to envision and expect new forms of emotional connection, these old inferences will thematize the sense of self. This sense of self includes convictions about the relational consequences of possible forms of being. A person may feel, for example, that any form of self-articulation or differentiation will invite ridicule, sarcasm, exclusion, or loss.

The identification and working through of these emotional organizing principles is the daily bread of ordinary clinical work. Although much of the childhood experience may be easily remembered, the full power of the shaming conviction that one is defective ("the village idiot"), or degraded, comes to conscious awareness in dialogue with an analyst or therapist who can hear and respond. Such a therapist's very interest in the relational origins of such emotional convictions tends to call them into question and to open the possibility of experiencing oneself in other ways.

By radical engagement, secondly, we mean the self-reflexive awareness of our own implication in what we come to understand with the patient. Our own emotional history, clinical theories, gender, race or ethnicity, social class, sexual orientation, various forms of embeddedness in larger cultural contexts, and attitudes towards difference will be present and influential throughout the intersubjective system that we form with the patient. Further, our very choice of psychoanalytic theory will be shaped by these same factors.

To engage radically with the other, thirdly, requires a therapist or an analyst willing to know and acknowledge deeply ingrained bias, an indispensable aspect of a fallibilistic attitude. Hans-Georg Gadamer's hermeneutic concept of dialogic understanding significantly underlies my sense of the day-to-day and moment-to-moment process in psychoanalysis. He wrote,

> The person with understanding does not know and judge as one who stands apart and unaffected; but rather, as one united by a specific bond with the other, he thinks with the other and undergoes the situation with him.
>
> (Gadamer, 1975, p. 288) WM, 306

In conversation and dialogue, we try to make sense together of this patient's experiential world – whether of trauma, exclusion, discrimination, or any other relational experience – and to find out how past experience continues to organize the expectancies for future experience. Suspending interest in "the facts" without denying the patient's perspective and attending to emotional meanings, a fallibilistic analyst may create with the patient a world that supports understanding, dignity, and further personal development. Suspending attachment to our own perspectives, personal and theoretical, as superior and privileged, we may listen in the service of the other (Poland, 2018). This fallibilistic and hermeneutic discipline, not radically constructivist, at least as rigorous and demanding as the abstinence and neutrality of former years, requires us to acknowledge the reality of worlds of experience that differ from our own. Intersubjective phenomenology simply reminds us that we have no privileged access to reality. It gives up the search for certainty (including diagnosis and treasured generalizations) in favor of the search for understanding.

Trauma

Retrieving Freud's early emphasis on trauma and newly provided with Ferenczi's indispensable texts, staggered by the wars, genocides, torture, and child abuse of the twentieth century, psychoanalysis has once again given voice and witness to those suffering from psychological trauma. Outside psychoanalysis, Cathy Caruth (Caruth, 1995) and Judith Lewis Herman (Herman, 1992) have helped us emerge from our theoretical fogs to hear their suffering. Psychoanalytic colleagues like Dori Laub and Shoshana Felman (Laub, 1992) have preserved and explained the testimony of holocaust survivors. Robert Stolorow (Stolorow, 2007), a psychoanalytic phenomenologist, has brought trauma into context and experience. Françoise Davoine and Jean-Max Gaudillière (Davoine & Gaudillière, 2004) have taught us to hear madness as a saner account of history than what ordinarily seems normal. Psychoanalysis, perforce confronted with horrors, has been transformed by these and many other leaders. Clinical distance, the old gold standard, not only becomes impossible when both patient and analyst meet in traumatic spaces but also the clinical turn towards trauma makes the second great innovation – the ethical turn – unavoidable.

Ethical turn

Given the intersubjectivists' emphasis on the unrepeatable, irreplaceable other, never to be violated by generalizing reductionisms, but to be received and treated dialogically, it seems a short step into a phenomenological ethics of responsibility and solidarity. Many of us had studied the virtue ethics of Aristotle, the duty ethics of Kant, the cost/benefit ethics of the utilitarians, and the mixed social contract/neo-Kantian social ethics of John Rawls and Jürgen Habermas. These two emphasized inclusion and recognition, without exception and preference, as foundational to social ethics. In addition, in relational psychoanalysis we have found the Hegelian recognition mentioned earlier. But now Judith Butler, writing of "precarious life" (Butler, 2000, 2004), at least hints that another kind of otherness than that available in the Hegelian recognition discourse may be needed for the ethical. She writes:

> A vulnerability must be perceived and recognized in order to come into play in an ethical encounter, and there is no guarantee that this will happen.... [V]ulnerability takes on another meaning at the moment it is recognized, and recognition wields the power to reconstitute vulnerability.... [N]orms of recognition are essential to the constitution of vulnerability as precondition of the "human."
>
> (2004, p. 43)

She goes on to note that she is perhaps offering a "version of Hegel" (p. 44), one, she hopes, that offers hope that struggles for recognition may have non-violent outcomes because they are rooted in something more primary than recognition of the "I" or the "you."

First though, let us notice the possibility that we may, in Wittgenstein's terms, be switching language games. Some would say levels of discourse – everyday, clinical, theoretical, philosophical – are at stake. I prefer Wittgenstein's language games. Each game has equal dignity with its grammar, integrity, rules, and possibilities for development, as well as its resistance to easy translation. Most probably the grammar of the mutual recognition game will persist, for example. At the same time, the ethics as fairness (Rawls, 1999) game has its part to play, but the "ethics beyond ethics" is another language game, to which we now turn. As Lisa Baraitser (Baraitser, 2008) notes, we are now in "another register":

> Self-recognition that relies on recognition by another subject will perhaps always run into difficulties with how to prevent a collapse of alterity due to the colonizing impulse that is inherent not only in "knowing" another but in recognizing too. In contrast, describing the relationship with the Other as an ethical relationship prior to self, a relationship that establishes the subject as a responsible subject before being a subject at all, Levinas redefines both the notion of the subject and the Other, as well as the nature of their relationship and that of recognition itself.
>
> (p. 102)

We hear in Baraitser echoes of Emmanuel Levinas, philosopher/prophet of asymmetrical responsibility. Levinas addressed two besetting sins: evasion and indifference, that is, bystandership. Hearing in his reading of Dostoevsky and the Hebrew scriptures the right answer to Cain's insolent question, "Am I my brother's keeper?," he contested Western philosophy on every form of egoism. Claiming that ethics is an optics, he challenged us to see human suffering without turning away. A five-year Nazi labor camp survivor who lost all his Lithuanian family, he wrote:

> that face facing me, in its expression – in its mortality – summons me, demands me, requires me as if the invisible death faced by the face of the other – pure alterity, separate, somehow, from any whole – were "my business." [As if I were, always already, my brother's and sister's keeper.] As if, unknown by the other whom already, in the nakedness

> of its face, it concerns, it "regarded me" before its confrontation with me, before being the death that stares me, myself, in the face. The death of the other man puts me on the spot, calls me into question, as if I, by my possible indifference, became the accomplice of that death, invisible to the other who is exposed to it; and as if, even before being condemned to it myself, I had to answer for that death of the other, and not leave the other alone to his deathly solitude. It is precisely in that recalling of me to my responsibility by the face that summons me, that demands me, that requires me – it is in that calling into question – that the other is my neighbor.
>
> (Levinas, 1999, pp. 24–25)

The miserable other *interpellates* (calls on me) me, traumatizing me, taking me hostage, calling me to subjection, to substitution (Levinas, 1981), to the only kind of meaningful suffering, that taken on for the sake of the other. Levinas used "interpellate" in its precise philosophical meaning of "to bring into being or give identity to," as well as "to command." Precisely in responding to the command that the other's suffering imposes on me, I am brought to subjectivity, constituted as subject, in his view. No masochism here, no pleasure in this suffering. But of course no one can live up to the infinite demand, the endless responsibility, so like Dostoevsky, I am forever guilty for all, before all. Though the ethic of responsibility – framed in response to extreme situations and full of traumatic memory – often sounds extreme, it grounds itself in everyday proximity to those unexpected situations that ethically call us out.

Simon Critchley (2007) comments that infinite responsibility to the other creates what Levinas liked to call "the curvature of intersubjective space" in which the other always occupies the high point. "When I am within the relation, then the other is not my equal, and my responsibility towards [the other] is infinite" (Critchley, 2007, p. 60). Levinas makes the extreme claim that my relation to the other is not some benign benevolence, compassionate care, or respect for the other's autonomy, but is the obsessive experience of responsibility that persecutes me with its sheer weight. I am the other's hostage, taken by them and prepared to substitute myself for any suffering and humiliation that they may undergo. I am responsible for the persecution I undergo and even for my persecutor; a claim that, given the experience of Levinas's family and people during the Second World War, is nothing less than extraordinary (pp. 60–61). Meanwhile, the discourse of responsibility – often dismissed by feminists because of Levinas's admittedly unwise use of gender categories, and because, perhaps, women have long enough borne the care of others – returns in the voice of Judith Butler. She hears the ethical call in the affirmation of the precarious, the vulnerable, and the traumatized.

> [I]f they [the unnamable and ungrievable lives] do not appear in their precariousness and their destruction, we will not be moved. We will not return to a sense of ethical outrage that is distinctively for an Other, in the name of an Other. We cannot, under contemporary conditions of representation, hear the agonized cry or be compelled or commanded by the face.
>
> (Judith Butler, 2004, p. 150)

She worries that our ethical subjectivity becomes systematically occluded by media manipulation.

The ethical constitution of subjectivity

Suppose we grant to developmental and intersubjective psychoanalysts that subjectivity, or a sense of selfhood, originally emerges – absent significant developmental trauma – from the harmonious interpenetrating mixup (Balint, 1979); maternal care (Winnicott, 1965); self-selfobject relatedness (Kohut, 1977); primordial density (Loewald, 1980); the intersubjective field (Stolorow et al., 1987); or relationality (Mitchell, 2000). The daily work of psychotherapists involves understanding and responding to those many in our world whose early and later trauma and other trouble brings them to our door.

But what constitutes our own subjectivity, our own moral center or *hegimonikon*, as the ancient Greeks and Romans would have called it? Where do we hear the voice of the *daimon*, of conscience, of responsibility? Judith Butler (Museum, 2011) suggests that the precarious face of the suffering other faces us daily on television, in our newspapers, and on our handheld devices, infinitely close and infinitely distant.

How does one respond? Some join Doctors without Borders, surely a life without recognition. In 1939, theologian Dietrich Bonhoeffer returned to Germany to rejoin other German Christians in the plot against Hitler's life – his twin sister had married a Jew so he knew well what was happening – instead of remaining in New York, as colleagues advised him to do. He spent much of the war in prison and was hanged before its end. Witold Pilecki, as we now know from his newly available account (Pilecki, 2012), volunteered to be a prisoner in Auschwitz, where he remained for three years, attempting to organize resistance and to communicate to the outside world about the nature of the place. He tried to keep his name unknown to protect others. He was tortured, tried, and executed by the Communist government of Poland in March, 1948. Likewise many journalists have died in their recent effort to tell the stories of oppression and violence.

But many serve humbly and scarcely know themselves that they simply do what they must. French theorist Gilles Deleuze writes:

> To say something in one's own name is very strange, for it is not at all when we consider ourselves as selves, persons, or subjects that we speak in our own name. On the contrary, an individual acquires a true proper name as the result of the most severe operations of depersonalization, when he opens himself to the multiplicities that pervade him and the intensities which run through his whole being.
> (P. 114, "I have nothing to admit," trans. *Semiotext(e)* *19772:3111–116*, quoted in Baraitser, 2008, p. 86)

So to begin with, we must never expect to be recognized in our own name. Multiplicities run us through. Moreover, as Dostoevsky understood once he had been to Siberia, morality is no abstraction. The other – possibly ugly, disgusting, demanding, and grotesque, at least in need of my care – is my sister or brother. The colicky infant who can give me nothing requires me to respond. The patient disparaged by others as a schizophrenic or a borderline becomes my sister or brother. The clinician becomes not distant but quiet and unobtrusive. Responsibility replaces recognition in the world of the ethical. Recognition, sought as an end in itself, may collapse into the world social contract philosopher Thomas Hobbes believed natural to humans: solitary, poor, nasty, brutish, and short. When recognition arrives by chance, it seems to me a gift to be humbly received and passed on to others.

To conclude, witness to trauma and ethical response to the devastated, allowing ourselves to be traumatized and called out by their suffering, these two elements have transformed clinical psychoanalysis today.

References

Aron, L. (1996). *A meeting of minds: Mutuality in psychoanalysis.* Hillsdale, NJ: Analytic Press.

Atwood, G. E., & Stolorow, R. D. (2014). *Structures of subjectivity: Explorations in psychoanalytic phenomenology and contextualism* (2nd ed.). London and New York, NY: Routledge, Taylor & Francis Group.

Balint, M. (1979). *The basic fault: Therapeutic aspects of regression.* New York, NY: Brunner-Mazel.

Baraitser, L. (2008). Mum's the word: Intersubjectivity, alterity, and the maternal subject. *Studies in Gender and Sexuality, 9,* 86–110.

Beebe, B., & Lachmann, F. M. (2001). *Infant research and adult treatment: A dyadic systems approach.* Hillsdale, NJ: Analytic Press.

Benjamin, J. (1995). *Like subjects, love objects: Essays on recognition and sexual difference.* New Haven, CT: Yale University Press.

Benjamin, J. (2004). Beyond doer and done to: An intersubjective view of thirdness. *Psychoanalytic Quarterly, 73,* 5–46.

Butler, J. (2000). Longing for recognition. *Studies Gender & Sexual, 1*(3), 271–290.

Butler, J. (2004). *Precarious life: The powers of mourning and violence.* London and New York, NY: Verso.

Caruth, C. (1995). *Trauma: Explorations in memory.* Baltimore: Johns Hopkins University Press.

Critchley, S. (2007). *Infinitely demanding: Ethics of commitment, politics of resistance.* London and New York, NY: Verso.

Davoine, F., & Gaudillière, J-M. (2004). *History beyond trauma: Whereof one cannot speak, thereof one cannot stay silent.* New York, NY: Other Press.

Frank, M. (1991). *Selbstbewusstsein und Selbsterkenntnis : Essays zur analytischen Philosophie der Subjektivität.* Stuttgart: P. Reclam.

Gadamer, H.-G. (1975). *Truth and method.* London: Sheed & Ward.

Govrin, A. (2016). *Conservative and radical perspectives on psychoanalytic knowledge: The fascinated and the disenchanted.* London and New York, NY: Routledge.

Guntrip, H. (1968). *Schizoid phenomena, object-relations, and the self.* New York: International Universities Press.

Herman, J. L. (1992). *Trauma and recovery.* New York, NY: Basic Books.

Husserl, E. (1970). *The crisis of European sciences and transcendental phenomenology: An introduction to phenomenological philosophy.* Evanston: Northwestern University Press.

Jaenicke, C. (2008). *The risk of relatedness: Intersubjectivity theory in clinical practice.* Lanham, MD: Jason Aronson.

Jaenicke, C. (2011). *Change in psychoanalysis: An analyst's reflections on the therapeutic relationship.* New York, NY: Routledge, Taylor & Francis Group.

Kohut, H. (1971). *The analysis of the self: A systematic approach to the psychoanalytic treatment of narcissistic personality disorders*. New York: International Universities Press.

Kohut, H. (1977). *The restoration of the self*. New York, NY: International Universities Press.

Laub, D. (1992). An event without a witness: Truth, testimony and survival. In S. Felman & D. Laub (Eds.), *Testimony: Crises of witnessing in literature, psychoanalysis, and history* (pp. 75–92). New York, NY: Routledge.

Leibniz, G. W., & Latta, R. (1948). *The monadology and other philosophical writings*. London: Oxford University Press.

Levinas, E. (1969). *Totality and infinity: An essay on exteriority*. Pittsburgh: Duquesne University Press.

Levinas, E. (1981). *Otherwise than being: Or, beyond essence*. Hague: Boston; Hingham, MA: M. Nijhoff; Distributors for the U.S. and Canada: Kluwer Boston.

Levinas, E. (1999). *Alterity and transcendence*. New York, NY: Columbia University Press.

Loewald, H. W. (1980). *Papers on psychoanalysis*. New Haven, CT: Yale University Press.

Merleau-Ponty, M. (1962). *Phenomenology of perception*. London and New York, NY: Routledge.

Mitchell, S. A. (2000). *Relationality: From attachment to intersubjectivity*. Hillsdale, NJ: Analytic Press.

Museum, N. (Producer). (2011). *Judith Butler: Precarious life: The obligations of proximity*. Retrieved from www.youtube.com/watch?v=KJT69AQtDtg

Orange, D. M. (1995). *Emotional understanding: Studies in psychoanalytic epistemology*. New York, NY: Guilford Press.

Orange, D. M. (2001). From Cartesian minds to experiential worlds in psychoanalysis. *Psychoanalytic Psychology*, *18*(2), 287–302.

Orange, D. M. (2008). Recognition as: Intersubjective vulnerability in the psychoanalytic dialogue. *International Journal of Psychoanalytic Self Psychology*, *3*(2), 178–194.

Orange, D. M., Atwood, G. E., & Stolorow, R. D. (1997). *Working intersubjectively: Contextualism in psychoanalytic practice*. Hillsdale, NJ: Analytic Press.

Pilecki, W. (2012). *The Auschwitz volunteer: Beyond bravery* (1st ed.). Los Angeles, CA: Aquila Polonica Pub.

Poland, W. S. (2018). *Intimacy and separateness in psychoanalysis*. New York, NY: Routledge.

Quine, W. V., & Ullian, J. S. (1970). *The web of belief*. New York: Random House.

Rawls, J. (1999). *A theory of justice* (Rev. ed.). Cambridge, MA: Belknap Press of Harvard University Press.

Ricoeur, P. (1970). *Freud and philosophy: An essay in interpretation*. New Haven, CT: Yale University Press.

Sander, L. W. (1995). Identity and the experience of specificity in a process of recognition: Commentary on Seligman and Shanok. *Psychoanalytic Dialogues*, 5(4), 579–593.

Stern, D. N. (1985). *The interpersonal world of the infant: A view from psychoanalysis and developmental psychology*. New York, NY: Basic Books.

Stolorow, R. D. (2007). *Trauma and human existence: Autobiographical, psychoanalytic, and philosophical reflections*. New York, NY: Analytic Press.

Stolorow, R. D., & Atwood, G. E. (1992). *Contexts of being: The intersubjective foundations of psychological life*. Hillsdale, NJ: Analytic Press.

Stolorow, R. D., Atwood, G. E., & Branchaft, B. (1994). *The intersubjective perspective*. Northvale, NJ: Jason Aronson.

Stolorow, R. D., Atwood, G. E., & Brandchaft, B. (1987). *Psychoanalytic treatment: An intersubjective approach*. Hillsdale, NJ: The Analytic Press.

Stolorow, R. D., Atwood, G. E., & Orange, D. M. (2002). *Worlds of experience: Interweaving philosophical and clinical dimensions in psychoanalysis*. New York, NY: Basic Books.

Stolorow, R. D., Brandchaft, B., & Atwood, G. E. (1987). *Psychoanalytic treatment: An intersubjective approach*. Hillsdale, NJ: The Analytic Press.

Thelen, E., & Smith, L. B. (1994). *A dynamic systems approach to the development of cognition and action*. Cambridge, MA: MIT Press.

Winnicott, D. W. (1965). *The maturational processes and the facilitating environment: Studies in the theory of emotional development*. New York: International Universities Press.

Zahavi, D. (2005). *Subjectivity and selfhood: Investigating the first-person perspective*. Cambridge, MA: MIT Press.

Chapter 11

Self-medication, anaclitic and introjective personality styles, drug of choice, and the treatment of people with substance use disorders

Theoretical and clinical implications of the empirical research

William H. Gottdiener

The self-medication hypothesis of substance use disorders (SUD) argues that people abuse and become dependent on alcohol and other drugs (AOD) to tolerate unpleasurable affective experiences (Johnson, 1999; Khantzian, 1985; Khantzian & Albanese, 2008). The inability to tolerate unpleasurable affects is the consequence of a significant history of traumatic events. The self-medication hypothesis also posits that people with an SUD discover that specific classes of drugs appear to ameliorate their psychological suffering better than others, leading most people with an SUD diagnosis to have a drug or drugs of choice.

What processes are involved in self-medication? Self-medication is the result of ungratified wishes that are born from intrapsychic conflict. The core conflictual relationship theme method (CCRT, Luborsky & Crits-Christoph, 1990) is an operationalized method of understanding and measuring transference (Freud, 1912, 1917), and transference is understood as a basic personality process. Transference has three components to it in the CCRT. The first is a person's wish (W) that they want gratified in relation to another person. The other person will either gratify it fully, gratify it partially, or not at all. The response of the other person is called the response of the other (RO). The RO can either be an actual response from another person, or it can be a response that exists in fantasy or in dreams. The result of the wish being gratified or not leads the person with the wish to respond with feelings, thoughts, and behaviors, and these are called the response of the self (RS). If the wish is gratified, then people tend to feel joy and think and act accordingly. If the wish is only partially gratified or not gratified at all, then people tend to feel sad, scared, angry, and any combination of painful emotions. They tend to have congruent thoughts and behaviors that go along with those thoughts and feelings. Some RS reactions might be pathological, reflecting symptoms and signs of psychopathology.

The triangle of conflict helps to explain what happens when the RS occurs (Coughlin, 2016). The triangle of conflict states that our symptoms and signs of psychopathology are the result of the action of maladaptive defenses being used to avoid awareness of feelings that are experienced as dangerous. In this model, any emotion can be experienced as dangerous or threatening to the sense of self due to super ego injunctions. The dangerous emotion gives rise to anxiety, which in turn gives rise to defense mechanisms. In the case of psychopathology, such as an SUD, the primary defense mechanisms that will be used are maladaptive defenses (e.g., denial, rationalization, projection; Bornstein, Gottdiener, & Winarick, 2010; Khantzian & Wilson, 1993; Prout, Gottdiener, Carmago, & Murphy, 2018; Prout, Gerber, & Gottdiener, 2015). Thus feelings that are dangerous to the sense of self are what are being medicated. The AOD that people use aims to reduce awareness of the dangerous dysphoric feelings they have. Alcohol and other drugs are used in the service of maladaptive defense mechanisms.

The use of AOD is an attempt to cope with unbearably disturbing feelings, and their use works. The problem is that the effects of AOD are temporary, and like any medication, new doses need to be taken. The rub for AOD is that people develop a tolerance to their use, and larger doses of AOD are needed to get the same effects as the original dose. In addition, AOD use brings with it iatrogenic physical, psychological, and social problems, which lead to more dysphoric emotions that also need to be self-medicated. Thus the self-medication hypothesis explains why SUDs develop and why they can be so intractable for so many people.

The self-medication hypothesis was created from Khantzian's psychoanalytically oriented treatments of people with a wide range of SUDs. It is a model born from clinical experience and not from empirical research. Yet it is one of the most influential models of SUD even among cognitive-behavioral therapists. It is also a controversial model, especially among empirical researchers (Khantzian & Albanese, 2008).

There is agreement that people over-indulge in AOD to cope with emotional pain. But Khantzian also argued that the idiosyncratic nature of a person's emotional pain leads them to prefer certain classes of drugs over others because some drugs are more effective at being able to reduce a person's emotional pain than other drugs (Khantzian & Albanese, 2008). In other words, drugs of choice are pharmacospecific to the kind of emotional pain a person experiences. He argued that people with an opioid use disorder diagnosis have considerable rage, and they cope with it via opioids because that class of drugs is most effective at ameliorating their rage. Stimulant users, however, are those who have problems with feeling deflated and anergic and use stimulants to become energized (Khantzian & Albanese, 2008). Some stimulant users are energetic people and use stimulants to keep them in that energetic state.

Research support for the pharmacospecificity aspect of the self-medication hypothesis has been uneven (see for example Green, Adyanthaya, Morse, & Davis, 1993; Khantzian & Albanese, 2008). It is possible that drugs of choice are matched to affective states that typically manifest themselves in the context of specific personality styles, rather than drugs of choice being matched to affective states linked to various forms of psychopathology, a hypothesis that seems more plausibly supported by available clinical reports and empirical research.

Clinical observation (Khantzian, 1985) and research have found that individuals with opiate dependence manifest behaviors and cognitive and affective processes that are consistent with an introjective personality style (Blatt & Berman, 1990, 2004; Blatt, Rounsaville, Eyre, & Wilbe, 1984; see also Blatt, McDonald, Sugarman, & Wilber, 1984 for a review of research and psychoanalytic theorizing on opiate dependence), whereas individuals with cocaine dependence manifest behaviors and cognitive and affective processes that are consistent with an anaclitic personality style (Khantzian, 1985; Spotts & Shontz, 1977).

The possibility that different drugs of choice are associated with different personality styles has significant treatment implications because Blatt and his colleagues have found that individuals with introjective and anaclitic personality styles manifest differential treatment responses in non-SUD treatments (Blatt, 1992; Blatt & Ford, 1994; Blatt, Zuroff, Quinlan, & Pilkonis, 1996; Shahar, Blatt, & Ford, 2003; Blatt & Shahar, 2004a, 2004b). Introjective patients respond more positively to higher dosage treatments (those with three or more weekly psychotherapy sessions and of an open-ended nature) across a variety of types of psychotherapies (including psychoanalysis), whereas anaclitic patients respond more positively to lower dosage treatments (those with one or two weekly psychotherapy sessions and of relatively short duration). Therefore, it would be plausible to hypothesize that individuals with SUDs would show differential treatment responses as a function of their personality styles.

Empirical research on the self-medication hypothesis

Results of empirical research on the self-medication hypothesis have been mixed. Empirical research largely supports the notion that people use AOD as a way of ameliorating dysphoric emotions (Darke, 2012; Smith, Feldner, & Badour, 2011; Khantzian & Albanese, 2008). The empirical research shows uneven support for the part of the model that posits that people gravitate towards specific classes of drugs to help them cope with specific kinds of dysphoric affect (Khantzian & Albanese, 2008). It is important to note, however, that the research that fails to find support for why people prefer one class of AOD over another has not been investigated effectively with psychoanalytic theory in mind or with qualitative methods that are more akin to those found in typical psychoanalytic clinical participatory activity (Khantzian & Albanese, 2008).

I would, therefore, like to offer the possibility that we might be able to learn something about the self-medication hypothesis and its clinical implications by considering the positive treatment outcomes of two people who suffered from comorbid substance use and posttraumatic stress disorders (SUD-PTSD). I would like to consider the possibility that the positive treatment outcomes in two cases of SUD-PTSD, one with a presumed introjective personality style and a heroin dependency and the other with a presumed anaclitic personality style and a methamphetamine dependency, were the result of each individual obtaining successful treatment outcomes via treatments that suited his personality style. Here I use the single case-study method to investigate the potential interaction between personality and treatment outcome in individuals who were diagnosed with SUD-PTSD and to see if the results are consistent with the self-medication hypothesis, including whether drug of choice and treatment outcome are related to personality style.

Relevance of the case study for understanding SUD-PTSD treatment

Clinical case studies have a long and distinguished history in psychoanalysis and related disciplines. They have contributed and continue to contribute to the development of psychological theories and to the development of therapeutic interventions. According to McAdams and West (1997), case studies can serve three purposes. First, they can be used to "exemplify" a theory. The researcher employs case studies as an illustration of a theoretical construct. McAdams and West argue that the case studies made famous by Sigmund Freud are examples of using the case study method to exemplify psychoanalytic theories. Second, case studies can be used to discover new theoretical constructs. In this way, researchers employ methods similar to those embodied by grounded theory (Henwood & Pidegeon, 2003). The methods of grounded theory enable researchers to derive new theoretical understanding of a phenomenon from data that is not based on pre-existing theoretical constructs. Third, case studies can be used to compare different theoretical views to try to determine which theory best explains available data. In this way, a comparison of different theories is similar to hypothesis testing.

I briefly mention the different uses of case study research because I want the reader to be clear that I will discuss the cases in this chapter as *examples* of the self-medication hypothesis using Blatt's theory of introjective and anaclitic personality styles. I use Blatt's theory because it predicts how people with different personality styles will respond to any kind of psychological treatment. Furthermore, Blatt's research and theorizing allow the possibility that AOD of choice is not solely due to the need to defend against certain emotions but also that the AOD of choice fits the overall workings of the personality. Those overall workings can be considered as defensive processes unto themselves (Shapiro, 1965).

I also use Blatt's work in the hope that the conclusions I draw provoke readers to think about their own cases in similar terms and to try to provoke readers to develop hypotheses to test in the clinic and in the laboratory, either through further case-study research or via quantitative research.

The cases

Patient J. H.: history of opiate abuse and PTSD

Following is a case study of an individual who had previously been diagnosed and treated for opioid dependence and PTSD. As with both cases to be presented in this chapter, the information was obtained via an interview that was conducted by a research assistant. The interview with J.H. was conducted on April 5, 2005.

The following participant is a Caucasian male of Italian and Anglican descent. He was born in 1957 and was 49 years old at the time of the interview. J.H. stated that he is heterosexual and has been married four times. Although he was not married at the time of the interview, J.H. was in a romantic relationship. He works as an iron worker.

According to the interviewer, J.H. appeared slightly older than his stated age. His hands clearly indicate hard manual labor. He wore jeans, a T-shirt, a jean jacket, and a cap. He was large, muscular, and experienced by the interviewer as slightly imposing.

The interviewer found the participant to be alert, oriented, and easy to talk with, though he appeared to have some difficulty expressing his feelings. He maintained good eye contact throughout the interview. J.H. reported several traumatic events in his life that appear related to his SUD-PTSD diagnoses. The traumas include the death of his father at age 14, the death of a close friend in the 1980s, and the trauma that he experienced as a result of working at Ground Zero, the site of the September 11, 2001, terrorist attack on The World Trade Center in New York City. J.H. worked as an iron worker at Ground Zero for one year.

J.H. described himself as someone with thrill-seeking tendencies. In fact, his first use of heroin was intravenously (IV). His first encounter with heroin is notable because he recognized immediately that he found the drug's effects extremely attractive. J.H. also described himself as having an "addictive personality" because when he ends one particular addiction, he quickly finds a replacement addiction, either another psychoactive substance or a behavior. In this light it is important to note that the participant was on methadone for six years from 1996 to 2002.

J.H. was born and raised in Connecticut. He has one brother who is 10 years his senior, and he has one sister who is 13 years his senior. He maintains contact with his sister, but not with his brother. Both of his parents are deceased. His father was an alcoholic, though he remembers getting along well with him. J.H. says his mother was a "disciplinarian." She remarried shortly after his father died. He attended parochial school till the tenth grade; then he left and eventually obtained his Graduate Equivalency Diploma (GED). He entered a trade union for iron working at the age of 22.

J.H. has been addicted to a number of different drugs. He first became addicted to amphetamines while he was still in high school. He quit once things got out of hand (after about a month using every day) with little difficulty. He became addicted to heroin in the 1980s following a work-related injury. His heroin addiction appeared to start as an addiction to opiate-based analgesic medications that he took to ease the pain caused by his injury. From pain killers he moved to heroin.

J.H. has a long and complicated history involving work, relationships, and drug use. As stated previously, he began using heroin in the 1980s and used continuously through the early 90s. When he used heroin, he used almost exclusively on his own, and for a long time he was able to keep his work and drug use separate. However, eventually he began using throughout the day, though he claims this did not affect his job performance. Following the death of a close friend in the late 1980s – a death J.H. in part blamed himself for – his heroin use intensified, and he eventually entered a methadone maintenance program. J.H. was clean from heroin from about 1997 onwards, though he detoxed off the methadone following his experience at Ground Zero. J.H. was first diagnosed with PTSD in 2002 following his experience working at Ground Zero, though it is arguable that earlier traumas are equally as significant to the PTSD diagnosis. Finally, J.H. has been in individual psychotherapy since 2002 and has been clean from heroin and methadone since then too, though he smokes cannabis regularly and indicated he has other addictive behaviors.

Proximal precipitating episode to treatment

According to J.H.'s history, the precipitant to his entering methadone treatment was the death of his close friend, which he felt at least somewhat responsible for. Although J.H. was able to stop using heroin, he continued to require the use of opiates in the form of methadone from 1997 until 2002. It was his experience working at Ground Zero that seemed to precipitate his cessation of methadone and his subsequent entrance into individual psychotherapy for the treatment of his PTSD.

Stage of readiness to change in each treatment episode

What is interesting about his decision to stop using heroin and his decision to stop using methadone is that he has never been able to become abstinent from all psychoactive substances. He traded heroin for methadone, stopped methadone, but remains a regular marijuana smoker. Because of his continued use of methadone when he stopped heroin and his continued use of marijuana when he stopped methadone, it is hard to determine what stage of change J.H. was in when he entered each treatment episode.

If stopping heroin is considered as a discrete act or set of actions, then it is possible that he was in the action stage when he decided to stop, and that his use of methadone was a clear indication that he was in the maintenance stage. His stopping methadone and entrance into psychotherapy could be viewed in parallel. Even his use of marijuana could have instrumental value in that he uses marijuana, in part, to maintain his abstinence from methadone.

Yet the transtheoretical model of change (Prochaska, DiClemente, & Norcross, 1992) is hard to apply to J.H.'s behaviors because he continues to use psychoactive substances regularly. As a result, it could be argued that despite giving up opiates, he remains in a continuous state of contemplation. Because of J.H.'s continuous use of psychoactive substances, the transtheoretical model of change seems not very usefully applicable.

Comorbidities and their role in the course of the disorder

J.H. is a person who is diagnosable with a comorbid SUD-PTSD. It is plausible to surmise that the grief that J.H. suffered from his father's death caused a destabilizing influence in his life and in his personality organization. It is also possible that having an alcoholic father and a mother whom he experienced as strict could have been the diathesis that led J.H. to be less capable of regulating his own affects to start with and that his father's death was the stressor that led to his need to find some way of regulating his unpleasurable affects from grieving via the uses of psychoactive substances that resulted from his grief over this loss.

Case analysis

It is always hard to conduct arm-chair evaluations of the treatment an individual received. An impossible number of details are inevitably missing. Nonetheless, it is possible to describe in broad strokes how I would approach J.H. if he showed up to my office.

Theoretical perspective

J.H.'s SUD-PTSD symptoms are consistent with the self-medication hypothesis of SUDs (Khantzian, 1985). In addition, theoretical discussions of SUDs from a neuropsychoanalytic perspective argue that clinical observation and neuroscience research strongly support the notion that SUDs reflect deficits in affect regulation (Johnson, 2001).

As stated previously, heroin dependent individuals have been found to manifest introjective personality styles (Blatt, McDonald, et al., 1984). There exists a core depressive experience among such individuals. Depressive experiences in introjective individuals are frequently experienced as anger and rage, along with vegetative signs, and not as sadness or crying. Khantzian (1985) observed that individuals who are opiate dependent use opiates to defend against their experience of rage. Such rage makes for stormy relationships and poor self and affect regulation. Hence it is plausible to conjecture that J.H. is an individual with an introjective personality style who has used heroin to defend against the experience of a core depression in himself. In addition, his continued use of marijuana, which has also been observed to help individuals defend against depression and rage (Khantzian & Albanese, 2008; Sugarman & Kurash, 1982), suggests that he continues to need help with self and affect regulation surrounding the depressive core of his personality.

Another important aspect to introjective individuals is that they often have problems with intimate relationships because they are more concerned with how things impact themselves and their self-image. That J.H. began methadone maintenance following the death of a close friend, a death that he partly blamed himself for, indicates that his reaction was to improve himself.

Finally, treatment outcome is possibly affected by patient personality style. Blatt and colleagues (Blatt et al., 1996; Blatt & Shahar, 2004a, 2004b) found that introjective individuals have significantly better treatment outcomes when they are treated in relatively high dosage open-ended psychotherapies. Blatt and colleagues found these results in psychodynamic, psychoanalytic, cognitive-behavioral, and interpersonal therapies. On the other hand, individuals with anaclitic personalities have significantly better treatment outcomes when they are treated in low dosage short-term psychotherapies. Blatt hypothesizes that individuals with introjective personalities need high-dosage open-ended treatments because they do not form a strong therapeutic alliance quickly or easily. They tend to be detached from their therapists and need the high dosage to form a strong therapeutic alliance and for them to become engaged in the therapeutic process. Anaclitic individuals, because they are concerned with interpersonal relations more than introjective individuals are, form strong therapeutic alliances more quickly and are more interested in doing what is needed to satisfy the therapist and therefore do not need to be coaxed into treatment. They want to do what the therapist wants, do it, and get done with it. Finally, it is important to point out that Blatt found specifically that individuals who were diagnosed with a depressive disorder had much better treatment outcomes if the treatment matched their personality style.

Treatment choice and possible course of treatment

Given that J.H. has always been involved in outpatient treatments for his SUD (and SUD-PTSD), and given the clinical and research findings about introjective individuals, I think that the best choice of a behavioral therapy would be a high-dosage, open-ended, outpatient harm-reduction psychoanalytically oriented psychotherapy.

I do not think that the particular course of treatment that I would have offered J.H. would have been that much different than he has already taken. Perhaps by having a therapist attending to his defensive processes – his estrangement from his own attitudes and feelings towards himself (see Shapiro, 1989) – he would have been able to discuss the impact of traumatic experiences sooner in his life than he did. This might have helped him reduce his opioid use sooner or stopped it and all other psychoactive drugs. Perhaps he would have had fewer conflictual romantic relationships than he did. A psychoanalytically oriented therapist could have helped him become aware of some of his maladaptive behaviors via transference analysis and could have also served to help develop the therapy as a role-model for an intimate relationship. However, given that he seems to be an introjective individual, I have no doubt that his treatment would have been marked by slow but relatively steady progress and likely continued use of psychoactive substances.

I think a psychotherapeutic treatment with a frequency of two or more sessions weekly would have been acceptable by J.H. I base this on his having been in methadone maintenance treatment for five years. Methadone maintenance requires an individual to appear at a clinic for daily dosages. Therefore, methadone is a high-frequency treatment that lasts indefinitely until the patient weans off of it. It seems reasonable to extrapolate from J.H.'s use of methadone maintenance therapy to conjecture that he would accept a high-dosage long-term psychotherapeutic treatment.

Although I would have initiated psychotherapeutic treatment immediately with J.H., I would have also encouraged him to participate in methadone maintenance therapy to help stabilize his life and to reduce the potentially serious harms caused by injection drug use. This recommendation is also based on empirical research. Supportive-expressive psychodynamic therapy, which focuses on transference analysis, was effective in helping people who were diagnosed with opioid use disorder when combined with methadone (Woody, 2003). However, if he had been unable or unwilling to participate in methadone maintenance therapy, I would have encouraged him to make sure that he was using safe-injecting and safe-drug use practices, especially those developed by organizations such as the Harm Reduction Coalition.

Because J.H. was able to work while he was heroin dependent, I would not encourage him to enter into any sort of residential treatment program. Working appears to have been an important aspect of his life, and participation in a residential program could have caused him to lose his job, perhaps compounding his problems with a sense of loss of self-respect or purpose. Such a loss could have contributed to relapse rather than to harm reduction.

The case of A.A.: SUD-PTSD with ecstasy, cocaine, and alcohol abuse

Following is a case study of an individual who had previously been diagnosed and treated for abuse of ecstasy, cocaine, alcohol, and comorbid PTSD. The information for this case was also obtained via an interview that was conducted by a research assistant. The interview with A.A. was conducted on May 4, 2006.

The following participant is a Caucasian male of Italian descent. He was 32 years old at the time of the interview. A.A. stated that he is homosexual and in a relationship. His occupation is as a financial planner.

A.A. appeared at the interview very well dressed in a suit, clearly coming to the interview following work. He was articulate and easy to engage in conversation, though he had some difficulty accessing and describing emotionally-tinged thoughts and experiences. Notably, he made no mention of his PTSD diagnosis or its connection to his substance use history during his phone screening prior to the in-person interview, even though the interviewer had requested information about history of psychological disorders. In addition to the history of PTSD, A.A. also stated that he has a history of a mild eating disorder, which manifests in weight fluctuations.

A.A.'s relevant personal history

He was born and raised on Long Island, the middle of five children (two older and two younger sisters). His parents own and run a restaurant. He has overall very positive memories from his childhood. A self-described over achiever, A.A. excelled academically in high school and went to college at an Ivy League university where he received two bachelor's degrees in five years (B.A. in sociology and B.S. in hotel administration/management). Notably, A.A. now believes that his personal relationships suffered as a result of his desire to do well in school.

A.A. told his family that he is a homosexual while he was in college. He stated that his family accepts his sexual orientation. Furthermore, he did not show any discomfort when talking about sexual issues.

Following college, A.A. moved up the ladder in the finance and business sector in New York City. He eventually found a job he felt well suited for in financial planning, which was housed in a building next to the World Trade Center. On September 11, 2001, A.A. was walking to work when the terrorist attack that destroyed the World Trade Center occurred. His recollection of the day of the attack was very detailed and had a fresh, almost recently experienced quality to it. While A.A. feels he has resolved his PTSD in therapy, there was some indication that some aspects remain unresolved. In addition to the detailed recounting of the attack, supporting the conjecture that A.A. might still be suffering from residual PTSD symptoms, is his current difficulty describing his emotional experiences, which suggests that he became alexithymic as a result of his PTSD. Furthermore, alexithymia is a common consequence of PTSD (see Verhaeghe & Vanheule, 2005).

A.A. returned to work a couple of months after the terrorist attacks and tried to avoid thinking about how the attacks affected him: he said he shut down his feelings and that he avoided talking about his experiences.

However, in the middle of 2002, he began experiencing PTSD symptoms, including nightmares, panic attacks, fear of construction sites, and vomiting in his sleep. These symptoms persisted for about a year. In late 2002 and early 2003, his friends, family, and colleagues began voicing their concern about his symptoms to him. At around the same time, he had begun to dramatically increase his use of psychoactive substances, which included ecstasy, cocaine, and alcohol. During 2003 and 2004, this pattern of PTSD symptoms and substance use increased in severity. A.A. reports having no desire to address his problems at the time; when friends suggested he seek help through therapy, he refused to do so; hence clearly in a stage of precontemplation according to the transtheoretical model of change (Prochaska et al., 1992). At the height of his drug use, A.A. was doing ecstasy every weekend night, then cocaine on Monday and Tuesday nights, and drinking often in conjunction with those drugs.

A.A.'s boss eventually told him he needed to take a leave of absence or be fired – he chose the leave of absence and chose to seek help, which coincided with him reaching what he called a "rock bottom" in his substance abuse. He sought psychotherapy primarily to get relief from his PTSD symptoms. In psychotherapy, he found it helpful to address how he was self-medicating his PTSD symptoms with substance abuse.

It seems clear from A.A.'s interview that he had a very tough time seeking help and that he remained in the precontemplation stage of change for some time. However, according to the interview, when he finally admitted to himself that he did in fact need help, he quickly moved to the action stage of change by making a commitment to getting better. In fact, A.A. threw himself into his psychotherapy and he also began attending A.A. meetings. He pointed out that his condition improved rapidly.

A.A. reported that he is abstinent from ecstasy and cocaine, but that he still occasionally drinks alcohol (wine) socially. He had also returned to work. Finally, he stated that he finished his psychotherapy treatment six months before the interview because his PTSD symptoms had abated. However, he said that he would be more likely to return to therapy sooner if he needed it in the future.

Case analysis

The case of A.A. seems to fit well with Blatt's anaclitic personality style and that such individuals respond best to relatively shorter-term treatments.

In addition, individuals with anaclitic personality styles are people most concerned with interpersonal relationships. In contrast, introjective individuals are primarily concerned with individuation. Some research on SUDs supports the hypothesis that individuals who primarily use stimulants, such as ecstasy and cocaine, are more anaclitic, and those who use opiates like heroin are more introjective.

Ecstasy is mainly taken because of its "dramatic and consistent ability to induce a profound feeling of attachment and connection in the user" (McDowell, 2005, p. 163). Therefore, it makes sense that ecstasy would appeal to individuals with an anaclitic personality style. Because A.A. reported feeling withdrawn emotionally, it is plausible to hypothesize that ecstasy helped to counteract that feeling.

The relative brevity of A.A.s psychotherapy treatment also supports the possibility that A.A. has an anaclitic personality style. Because anaclitic individuals tend to have better treatment outcomes when they are in short-term circumscribed treatments rather than open-ended treatments, it is possible to surmise that A.A. did well in his treatment, in part, because it lasted less than one year. Supportive-expressive therapy has been found to benefit people who have a cocaine use disorder, as does dynamic deconstructive psychotherapy, both of which have been empirically tested as relatively short-term psychotherapies (Gottdiener & Suh, 2015).

Possible course of an alternative treatment

If A.A. has an anaclitic personality style, as I think he does, then I would likely suggest a similar treatment to the one he had, which was a relatively short-term individual psychotherapy such as the briefer version of supportive-expressive therapy with concomitant self-help group meetings.

Discussion

The self-medication hypothesis states that individuals abuse psychoactive substances to manage unpleasure (Khantzian, 1982, 1985, 1997, 1999, 2002; Khantzian & Albanese, 2008; Johnson, 1999). The self-medication hypothesis also states that an individual's primary drug of choice is largely determined by the type of emotional unpleasure that he or she desires to control. This observation is called the pharmacospecificity hypothesis. Past research has generally not supported the pharmacospecificity hypothesis (Green et al., 1993). An alternative way of understanding pharmacospecificity in SUDs is to view drugs of choice as largely determined by the type of personality style that the individual has rather than the type of emotional unpleasure that he or she desires to control. Indeed, a modest amount of research supports this view (Blatt, McDonald, et al., 1984; Blatt & Berman, 1990). Individuals who abuse opiates are more likely to have an introjective personality style, and individuals who abuse strong stimulants like amphetamines and cocaine are more likely to have an anaclitic personality style (Spotts & Shontz, 1977). The case analyses in this chapter are consistent with this perspective on the pharmacospecificity hypothesis.

Linking personality style, transference, and therapeutic technique

How do personality style, transference, and therapeutic technique connect? According to Blatt (2004), transference manifests somewhat differently in anaclitic and introjective personality styles. People with an anaclitic personality style are more concerned with interpersonal relations, and those with an introjective personality style are more concerned with self-definition. As a result, transference phenomena tend to feature themes that are related to these basic personality factors of interpersonal relating and self-definition, respectively. The transference themes will change as patients improve (Crits-Christoph, Cooper, & Luborsky, 1988). Importantly, the therapist would use the same basic therapeutic technique regardless of the patient's personality style, but the intensity and duration of the treatment is likely to differ in people with different personality styles (Blatt, 2004).

Future research should aim to determine if personality style interacts with intensity and duration of treatment for people with an SUD, as is suggested by the case analyses in this chapter. Therefore, new research needs to be conducted to address this issue. If personality style predicts treatment outcome in people with an SUD, then modifications of existing treatments could occur. It is plausible that individuals with anaclitic personality styles would require less costly treatments (because they would be of a less intense and shorter duration) and that those with introjective personalities would require more costly treatments (because they would be of a more intense and longer duration).

The case analyses presented in this chapter are limited in that they are based upon the retrospective reports of the patients themselves. I do not mean to imply that the reports are necessarily invalid. Rather, data from retrospective self-reports are limited because there is no way to understand the individuals' lives from other vantage points. But the apparent weakness of the case report being retrospective is also a strength because it enables us to understand how a person sees themselves now through the lens of the interviewer or therapist (see Ogden, 2005 for a similar view).

It is also important to note that each treatment also fits comfortably under the rubric of harm reduction psychotherapy (HRP, Denning, 2000; Tatarsky, 2002; see also Kellogg & Kreek, 2005 for a similar view), in which the main aim of treatment is to reduce the potential harms caused by SUDs and where treatment outcomes can range from safer substance use (e.g., using clean needles) to sobriety. J.H. and A.A. each went into treatment and used it effectively when they were ready to make changes in their lives. In addition, each patient shows success from a harm reduction perspective, with J.H. still using marijuana at the end of his treatment despite being abstinent from heroin and all other psychoactive substances and A.A. being abstinent from all psychoactive substances, with the exception of drinking wine socially. These outcomes also underscore the reality that total abstinence from all psychoactive substances is not a realistic goal for all individuals with an SUD. However, gradual progression to reduced substance abuse or abstinence can be acceptable goals, and these two outcomes might make it more realistic for clinicians to engage individuals with SUDs patiently and empathically. Finally, these outcomes are consistent with the psychoanalytic observation that sublimation of drives is not possible for all patients as an outcome. Johnson (2003) has hypothesized that SUDs can be viewed as a drive akin to aggression and libido. If he is right, then full sublimation of an addictive drive might only be possible in some individuals at any one time in their lives.

Psychoanalytic treatment of SUD is a complex process. Previous research, clinical observation, and the case analyses presented in this chapter suggest that a successful treatment outcome might depend on matching treatment intensity and duration with a patient's personality style. Introjective patients would require longer and more intense treatments, and anaclitic patients would require shorter and less intense treatments. Thus there is not a one-size-fits-all treatment, and the search for a single magic bullet to slay the addictive monster is possibly nothing more than a pipe dream. There are considerable implications for clinical practice and public health policy from the perspective put forth in this chapter, that if correct, would save lives, make the lives of those affected by SUD more enjoyable, and potentially target treatment funding more efficiently and accurately. The treatment considerations discussed herein link the self-medication hypothesis, empirical research, and clinical practice, thereby strengthening the basis for the self-medication hypothesis and working with patients in a psychoanalytically informed manner.

References

Blatt, S. J. (1992). The differential effect of psychotherapy and psychoanalysis on anaclitic and introjective patients: The Menninger psychotherapy research project revisited. *Journal of the American Psychoanalytic Association, 40*, 691–724.

Blatt, S. J. (2004). *Experiences of depression: Theoretical, clinical, and research perspectives*. Washington, DC: American Psychological Association.

Blatt, S. J., & Berman, W. (1990). Differentiation of personality types among opiate addicts. *Journal of Personality Assessment, 54*, 87–104.

Blatt, S. J., & Ford, R. (1994). *Therapeutic change: An object relations perspective*. New York, NY: Plenum.

Blatt, S. J., & Shahar, G. (2004a). Psychoanalysis: For what, with whom, and how: A comparison with psychotherapy. *Journal of the American Psychoanalytic Association, 52*, 393–447.

Blatt, S. J., & Shahar, G. (2004b). Stability of the patient-by-treatment interaction in the Menninger Psychotherapy Research Project. *The Bulletin of The Menninger Clinic, 68*, 23–36.

Blatt, S. J., Berman, W., Bloom-Feshbach, S., Sugarman, A., Wilber, D., & Kleber, H. D. (1984). Psychological assessment of psychopathology in opiate addicts. *Journal of Nervous and Mental Disease, 172*, 156–165.

Blatt, S. J., McDonald, C., Sugarman, A., & Wilber, C. (1984). Psychodynamic theory of opiate addiction: New directions for research. *Clinical Psychological Review, 4*(2), 159–189.

Blatt, S. J., Rounsaville, B. J., Eyre, S., & Wilber, C. (1984). The psycho-dynamics of opiate addiction. *Journal of Nervous and Mental Disease, 172*, 342–352.

Blatt, S. J., Zuroff, D. C., Quinlan, D. M., & Pilkonis, P. A. (1996). Interpersonal factors in brief treatment of depression: Further analyses of the National Institute of Mental Health Treatment of Depression Collaborative Research Program. *Journal of Consulting and Clinical Psychology, 64*, 162–171.

Bornstein, R. F., Gottdiener, W. H., & Winarick, D. J. (2010). Construct validity of the relationship profile test: Links with defense style in substance abuse patients and comparison with nonclinical norms. *Journal of Psychopathology and Behavioral Assessment, 32*, 293–300.

Coughlin, P. (2016). *Maximizing effectiveness in dynamic therapy*. New York: Routledge.

Crits-Christoph, P., Cooper, A., & Luborsky, L. (1988). The accuracy of therapist's interpretations and the outcome of dynamic psychotherapy. *Journal of Clinical and Consulting Psychology, 56*(4), 490–495.

Darke, S. (2012). Pathways to heroin addiction: Time to re-appraise self-medication. *Addiction, 108*, 659–667.

Denning, P. (2000). *Practicing harm reduction psychotherapy: An alternative approach to addictions*. New York, NY: The Guilford Press.

Freud, S. (1912/1958). The dynamics of transference. In J. Strachey (Ed. and Trans.), *The standard edition of the complete works of Sigmund Freud* (Vol. 12, pp. 99–108). London: Hogarth Press.

Freud, S. (1917/1963). Transference: In introductory lectures on psychoanalysis: Lecture 27. In J. Strachey (Ed. and Trans.), *The standard edition of the complete works of Sigmund Freud* (Vol. 16, pp. 431–447).

Gottdiener, W. H., & Suh, J. J. (2015). Substance use disorders. In P. Luyten, L. C. Mayes, P. Fonagy, M. Target, & S. J. Blatt (Eds.), *Handbook of psychodynamic approaches to psychopathology* (pp. 216–233). New York, NY: The Guilford Press.

Green, R., Adyanthaya, A., Morse, R., & Davis, L. (1993). Personality variables in cocaine- and marijuana-dependent patients. *Journal of Personality Assessment, 61*, 224–230.

Henwood, K., & Pidegeon, N. (2003). Grounded theory in psychological research. In P. M. Camic, J. E. Rhodes, & L. Yardley (Eds.), *Qualitative research in psychology: expanding perspectives in methodology and design*. Washington, DC: American Psychological Association.

Johnson, B. (1999). Three perspectives on addiction. *Journal of the American Psychoanalytic Association, 47*(3), 791–815.

Johnson, B. (2001). Drug dreams: A neuropsychoanalytic hypothesis. *Journal of the American Psychoanalytic Association, 49*(1), 75–96.

Johnson, B. (2003). Psychological addiction, physical addiction, addictive character, and addictive personality disorder: A nosology of addictive disorders. *Canadian Journal of Psychoanalysis, 11*(1), 135–160.

Kellogg, S. H., & Kreek, M. J. (2005). Gradualism, identity, reinforcements, and change. *International Journal of Drug Policy, 16*(6), 369–375.

Khantzian, E. J. (1982). Psychological (structural) vulnerabilities and the specific appeal of narcotics. *Annals of the New York Academy of Sciences, 398*, 24–32.

Khantzian, E. J. (1985). The self-medication hypothesis of addictive disorders. *American Journal of Psychiatry, 142*(11), 1259–1264.

Khantzian, E. J. (1997). The self-medication hypothesis of addictive disorders: A reconsideration and recent applications. *Harvard Review of Psychiatry, 4*, 231–244.

Khantzian, E. J. (1999). *Treating addiction as a human process*. Northvale, NJ: Jason Aronson.
Khantzian, E. J. (2002). Forward. In M. Weegmann & R. Cohen (Eds.), *The psychodynamics of addiction*. London: Whurr.
Khantzian, E. J., & Albanese, M. J. (2008). *Understanding addiction as self-medication: Finding hope behind the pain*. Lanham, MD: Rowman & Littlefield.
Khantzian, E. J., & Wilson, A. (1993). Substance abuse, repetition, and the nature of addictive suffering. In A. Wilson & J. E. Gedo (Eds.), *Hierarchical concepts in psychoanalysis: Theory, research, and clinical practice* (pp. 263–283). New York: Guilford.
Luborsky, L., & Crits-Christoph, P. (1990). *Understanding transference: The CCRT method*. New York, NY: Basic Books.
McAdams, D. P., & West, S. G. (1997). Personality psychology and the case study: Introduction. *Journal of Personality, 65*(4), 757–783.
McDowell, D. (2005). Marijuana, hallucinogens, and club drugs. In R. J. Frances, S. I. Miller, & A. H. Mack (Eds.), *Clinical textbook of addictive disorders* (3rd ed., pp. 157–183). New York: Guilford.
Ogden, T. H. (2005). On psychoanalytic writing. *The International Journal of Psychoanalysis, 86*, 15–29.
Prochaska, J. O., DiClemente, C. C., & Norcross, J. C. (1992). In search of how people change: Applications to addictive behaviors. *American Psychologist, 47*(9), 1102–1114.
Prout, T. A., Gerber, L., & Gottdiener, W. H. (2015). Trauma and substance abuse: The role of defenses and religious engagement. *Mental Health, Religion, & Culture, 18*(2), 123–133.
Prout, T. A., Gottdiener, W. H., Carmago, A., & Murphy, S. (2018). The relationship between defense mechanisms and religious coping using a new two-factor structure of the defense style questionnaire-40. *The Bulletin of the Menninger Clinic, 82*(3), 224–252.
Shahar, G., Blatt, S. J., & Ford, R. Q. (2003). Mixed anaclitic-introjective psychopathology in treatment-resistant inpatients undergoing psychoanalytic psychotherapy. *Psychoanalytic Psychology, 20*(1), 84–102.
Shapiro, D. (1989). *Psychotherapy of neurotic character*. New York: Basic Books.
Shapiro, D. (1965). *Neurotic styles*. New York, NY: Basic Books.
Smith, R. C., Feldner, M. T., & Badour, C. L. (2011). Substance use to regulate affective experiences in posttraumatic stress disorder: A review of laboratory-based studies. *Journal of Experimental Psychopathology, 2*(1), 3–27.
Spotts, J. V., & Shontz, F. C. (1977). *The life styles of nine American cocaine users*. Washington, DC: National Institute on Drug Abuse.
Sugarman, A., & Kurash, C. (1982). Marijuana abuse, transitional experience, and the borderline adolescent. *Psychoanalytic Inquiry, 2*(4), 519–538.

Tatarsky, A. (2002). *Harm reduction psychotherapy: A new treatment for drug and alcohol problems*. Northvale, NJ: Jason Aronson.
Verhaeghe, P., & Vanheule, S. (2005). Actual neurosis and PTSD: The impact of the other. *Psychoanalytic Psychology, 22*(4), 493–507.
Woody, G. E. (2003). Research findings on psychotherapy of addictive disorders. *The American Journal on Addictions, 12*, S19–S26.

Chapter 12

Bodies and screen relations

Moving treatment from wishful thinking to informed decision-making

Gillian Isaacs Russell and Todd Essig

When the words psychoanalysis, technology, and innovation are considered together, one might reasonably expect that the innovation then discussed would be a realization of technology's shimmering promise: psychoanalytic treatment for anyone, anywhere, anytime. Such technologically mediated treatment heralds democratization, continuity, convenience, and cost-effectiveness. The promise includes psychoanalysis reestablishing its relevance in the mental healthcare delivery system, a place where psychoanalysts have long been struggling to keep a relevant foothold. But we believe, and will argue in this chapter, that such techno-dreams of remote therapy are not innovative. That promise is empty. It expresses yesterday's future, not today's. Instead, innovation in psychoanalysis and technology is the next step of championing "local therapy," both clinically and culturally, while keeping "remote therapy" as a better-than-nothing compromise. Innovation involves making the radical differences between physical co-presence and technologically mediated presence, i.e., between being bodies together and screen relations (Isaacs Russell, 2015), central in clinical decision-making.

Psychoanalytic innovation with technology is part of a larger story being told in the wider culture. We are not the only ones advocating for the intimacies and self-experiences only possible when people are bodies together. Many who were active as creators and promoters of various technology "revolutions," along with scholars of communication and technology, now caution about the damage being done to solitude, reverie, attention, empathy, relatedness, and intimacy when we trade physical co-presence for screen relations (e.g., Carr, 2011, 2015; Harris, 2017; Lanier, 2018; Sax, 2016; Turkle, 2011, 2015). While we focus this chapter on the differences between two treatment contexts in psychoanalysis, local and remote, those differences resonate across all our connections and relationships, both in-person and on screen. The experience of having enthusiastically embraced technology's shimmering promises only to end up surprised and disappointed by realities that fall far short of that promise is increasingly common among all age groups. In other words, our view on psychoanalytic innovation is part of an emerging cultural trend to expect more from each other and less from technology.[1]

As illustration of this emergence, consider a 2018 advertisement from Audi, the car company. Set in the near future, it has a successful grey-haired senior executive leaving the office for the back seat of his slightly futuristic self-driving car. He settles in, saying, "Evening Clara, home please" as an elegant cup filled with hot coffee rises from the arm rest. It's an ideal image of techno-convenience. But Clara, sounding very much like the granddaughter of Siri or Alexa, senses something amiss and asks what's on his mind. Looking wistful, sad even, he answers, "there was a time I used to sit up there." Images of him driving older Audis appear as the scene transitions to a boring, lonely evening at home – until he's had enough. He smashes his evening's drink to the ground as rock music accelerates to a frenzy. He jumps into the driver's seat of a revved-up Audi sports car and peels away into the night. "Progress is seizing every moment" flashes across the screen. Audi's innovative message is that once juxtaposed, techno-convenience just can't compare to the thrill of the open road, that technology allows some experiences while blocking others, and that new gadgets involve necessary loss. Our aim here is to do something similar with the conveniences of remote treatment compared to the depth of experience and functional consequences of local treatment. Innovation today is understanding gadget-use, not how to use gadgets.[2]

Not everyone agrees. The shimmering promise of new technologies, like a luxurious self-driving car or high-definition video-conference platforms, has left a seductive patina of innovation over much thinking about remote therapies. You see it in the work of Carlino (2011), Fishkin and Fishkin (2011), and Gordon and Lan (2017). Lemma (2017) and many contributors to the *Psychoanalysis Online* series (2013, 2015, 2017) struggle with it, sometimes successfully and sometimes not. Claims of not just feasibility but inevitability are made. Scharff wrote, "Technology is driving their [digital natives] choices, and their lifestyle is driving their need for technology, including the need for technology-assisted psychoanalysis to maintain the optimum frequency of analytic sessions for in-depth analytic work" (2013, p. 65). Some suggest current technologies have effected a radical transformation of mind and its perception of and relation to the body, "to which psychoanalysts must now adapt their treatment approach" (Scharff, ibid.). Organizations like the IPA and the APA host webinars teaching how to make the most of these new technologies. But we agree with those like Jaron Lanier who maintain that such a patina is an illusion of innovation ultimately serving primarily the needs of Silicon Valley investors (Kulwin, 2018).

It is important to remember that innovation is not synonymous with the merely new, nor is it about gadgets. In fact, genuine innovation is found, or not, in the human consequences, both experiential and functional, of whatever new practices, actions, and understandings new technologies allow. As Nicholas Carr wrote, "The real sentimental fallacy is the assumption that the new thing is always better suited to our purposes and intentions than the old thing. That's the view of a child, naive and pliable" (2015, p. 231). As such, genuine innovation in psychoanalysis and technology requires removing that patina by becoming as aware as possible of the differences between being bodies together and screen relations, with the specific case of the differences between local therapies and remote therapies of immediate clinical relevance. To accomplish that aim, we will discuss the concepts of "affordance" and "presence" before turning to specific psychoanalytic processes radically transformed when the treatment relationship is mediated by a communications technology, be it audio or video.

Differences between local therapy and remote therapy

Understanding how the two treatment contexts differ starts with comparing what is possible in the two contexts, i.e., comparing their "affordances." This is a concept from the ecological study of perception developed by J. J. Gibson. Gibson writes, "the affordances of the environment are what it offers . . . what it provides or furnishes, either for good or ill" 1979, p. 56). People do not perceive the world by taking in disembodied information that is then related to a pre-existing representational structure. Instead, and this is why this conceptual framework is so useful, people perceive the world's action potentials. They are not inferred from a world one perceives abstractly. People engage the world directly based on the opportunities it presents to fulfill desires and manifest intentions. Affordances are the possibilities a specific context offers a specific person. For example, when an analysand walks by their analyst sitting in a chair, they do not perceive her lap by noting an abstract arrangement of approximately perpendicular geometrical shapes. They perceive, among other things, a potential place to sit. So when accounting for the influence of a new technology, such as widely available video conferencing, one must account for the affordances provided and the ones not present, like a lap. That means looking at both what the new technology makes possible and the experiences and consequences it does not afford, as well as the necessary losses attendant on its use.

When the question is then asked of how the two treatment contexts afford different experiences and consequences, three broad areas emerge (Essig, 2015a). These differences will be apparent throughout the following sections of this chapter. The first difference is risk. The functional consequences of safety in the presence of actual risk are vastly different than the absence of risk. As one patient commented ruefully in Isaacs Russell's ethnography of screen relations based treatments, in remote treatment there is no opportunity to "kick or kiss" (2015, p. 39). The context does not afford such possibilities. The second difference is repleteness or richness. In-person experience is replete with infinite possibility. In contrast, technologically mediated moments are limited by the design of the technology. Rather than being replete with infinite possibility, the depth of experience is set by the decisions of the technology's designers. Think of the differences in repleteness (as well as risk) between a video war-game and an actual war. In addition, inevitable mediation artifacts introduce affordances not present in person (Branham, 2017). The third difference concerns relational embodiment. The two contexts are differentially embodied, not that one is embodied and the other disembodied. Each context affords different possibilities for using one's body to manage the relationship, e.g., handshakes and hugs or their rule-governed avoidance versus clicking on a window to activate a video image. Despite the AT&T advertisements for long-distance that were ubiquitous in the 1980s, you really can't reach out and touch someone during a telephone call.

In talking about these differences at conferences and with colleagues, we often hear some version of "but it all feels the same, at least sometimes." That is not a surprise. One of our central themes is that technology is designed to be a trickster. It's designed to make us think we are there with an other when really sitting all alone with a screen. So the crucial question is the different affordances, not the felt similarities. For example, people report similar feelings of interactive competition playing video-game tennis and actual tennis. But it's the differences that matter. Similarly, the two treatment contexts are functionally different even when participants feel them to be the same or similar. To quickly illustrate this separation of functional significance from perceived similarity, consider a 2016 study of medically unexplained pain (MUP) treated with intensive short-term dynamic psychotherapy either in-person or via video-conference (Chavooshi, Mohammadkhani, & Dolatshahee, 2017). Both groups, in-person and on screen, rated the treatments as equally credible and satisfying: there was no clinically significant difference in how the two groups experienced the different contexts. But the in-person group had significantly less pain both immediately following the treatment and at a 12-month follow-up. Plus they also reported "significant decreases in depression, anxiety and stress as well as a greater increase in emotion regulation functioning, mindfulness and quality of life" (p. 133). These are patients who reported similar experiences while also manifesting significant outcome differences. The innovation should be asking why this difference exists rather than championing less effective treatments just because they use cutting-edge technology and feel similar. In fact, what we are working towards is a future in which understanding what local therapy affords that remote therapy cannot will increasingly be seen as an innovative, cutting-edge, and culturally relevant practice that champions core psychoanalytic values of intimacy, relatedness, and reflection.

Presence is key for understanding difference

Presence is the other concept important in understanding how the two treatment contexts afford different experiences and functional consequences. As emerging technologies rapidly transformed the wider culture, researchers in information science, communication technology, and cyberpsychology focused efforts on studying how to maintain the illusion that a mediated experience was not mediated, a concept called "(tele)presence" (Lombard & Ditton, 1997). A goal was to understand how, if at all, a technologically mediated simulation of being in the same place at the same time could reproduce the experience of actually being together

(Mantovani & Riva, 1999; Riva, 2006, 2009; Riva & Waterworth, 2003; Riva, Waterworth, & Waterworth, 2004; Riva, Anguera, Wiederhold, & Mantovani, 2006; Riva, Waterworth, Waterworth, & Mantovani, 2009; Waterworth & Waterworth, 2003). This work included new approaches in cognitive science and neuroscience suggesting that minds require bodies, that cognition is influenced and largely determined by experiences in the physical world (Damasio, 1999, 2005, 2012; Lakoff & Johnson, 2003). No longer were experiences seen as coming from the manipulation of abstract symbols isolated in the brain. Instead mind itself was embodied, firmly lodged in a bedrock of sensorimotor processing (Clark, 1998).

Just as our minds are situated in the body, our experience of presence is situated, either in the risky repleteness of physical co-presence or the constrained realities of a screen or a speaker. These experiences of presence result from intentional actions for which one receives temporally appropriate feedback that the intention had achieved its goal. For example, when you say hello in greeting, you expect some immediate acknowledgment. And if you receive properly timed feedback, you feel like the two of you are present with each other, be it in text or face-to-face. If you have to wait so that the temporal pattern is not similar to being face-to-face, then you do not experience presence, like with letter writing, faxes, or being ghosted. A good illustration is the facial micro-attunements so carefully studied by infant development researchers (Beebe, Knoblauch, Rustin, & Sorter, 2005; Stern, 1985; Tronick, 1989). When the parent's feedback does not come as expected, like in Tronick's "still face" experiments (1989), the baby loses the feeling of being present with an other, and their mood crashes. But properly timed feedback for an intentional action generates a sense of presence. A basic experience of presence contributes to the development of self-experience and to allowing others to be recognized as separate selves with their own goals and purposes. It is through presence that we experience both self and others as intentional selves with inner worlds distinct from behavior. This is the case both in the developing infant and in the adult, as the sense of self and one's boundaries between self and other are continually being redefined throughout life.

Recognizing that the two treatment contexts afford different experiences of presence is key. Presence varies in intensity, quality, and consequence. It is also important to note that presence is not the same thing as emotional engagement, absorption, or the degree of technological immersion. Researchers consider presence to be a core neuropsychological phenomenon: a sense of presence comes from an organism's capacity to locate itself in the external, including interpersonal, world according to the intentional actions that can be done (Riva et al., 2009). For human relationships, these actions specifically include someone's ability to interact with someone else in a shared external environment. With a sense of presence, the nervous system can recognize that one is in an environment that is outside one's self and not just a product of one's inner world (i.e., being awake, not dreaming). As illustration, consider the following from a blind patient interviewed as part of Isaacs Russell's (2015) study of remote treatment:

> Despite the fact that I am unable to see my analyst even during live sessions, I feel a loss when we are not together. I was very interested to realize that, no, it's not just being able to 'see' the person. There's something about being in the room with them. There's something not visual, and not necessarily auditory.
>
> (p. 29)

That "something" is presence, and it includes all the possibilities for what people can do to and with each other, and it is limited by what people cannot do to and with each other.

Therapeutic presence and psychoanalysis

Therapeutic presence, "bringing all of yourself to the encounter and being present on multiple levels: physically, emotionally, cognitively, spiritually, and relationally" (Geller, 2017, p. 4), is central in all psychotherapies and especially so for psychoanalysis, including experiences emerging from being bodies together. Transference and countertransference, discovering dissociations in enactments, re-invigorating stalled developmental processes, and even just being together in reverie and quietude (Little, 2015; Ogden, 2004) have always been seen to play out on a stage set by the realities of physical co-presence: "the presence and engagement of the self in the analytic process is inherently bodily in all its manifestations" (Meissner, 1998, p. 278). From Freud's famous early comment that "(t)he ego is first and foremost a bodily ego" (1923b, p. 26) to, for example, Sletvold's contemporary work on embodiment showing how the "analyst's own body is the nexus of experiencing and communicating in the analytic situation"

(2014, p. 186), being bodies together in the analytic encounter has been central. It is what affords possibilities for experiencing one's self as intentional agent giving meaning to behavior as well as imbuing the other's behavior with expressive meaning regarding their inner world.

In a remarkable overlap, both psychoanalysts and computer-science presence researchers (Isaacs Russell, 2015; Riva, 2006) similarly conceptualize what Winnicott called "unit status" (1965, p. 91). Both literatures document that experiencing the presence of another is grounded in embodied perception and co-present interaction with a physically present other and that this is what affords the growth of interiority/exteriority, self, identity, and personhood. Celenza (2005) recently asks, "Where is analysis?" and responds: "The physical presence of both the analyst and the analysand is the foundation through which the experience of the analytic process is mediated . . . making the location of bodies a potentially anchoring metaphor for therapeutic action" (p. 1647). Thus it should not be a surprise that radically changing the experience of presence by moving it from a shared environment (i.e., physical co-presence) to a technologically mediated illusion of non-mediation (i.e., telepresence) will inevitably lead to correspondingly radical changes in psychoanalytic processes and functional consequence, and it is to those specific changes we now turn.

Clinical process differences

Difference is found both in familiar processes being qualitatively altered or lost and in newly emergent processes and factors that result from the realities of technological mediation. We contend that the central innovation in psychoanalysis and technology is keeping these differences in mind while deepening understanding of what the two contexts afford. While a full understanding of difference is aspirational since there is always more to learn, the current understanding of difference is developed enough that it should directly inform both whether and how to conduct remote therapy (Isaacs Russell, 2015).

A facilitating, holding environment

Winnicott famously listed the necessary conditions for creating a "facilitating environment" (1955, p. 21). Balint (1950) spoke of "creating a proper atmosphere for the patient by the analyst" (p. 123). Obviously, when a shared physical environment is lost, patients must instead provide their own atmosphere. This is a problem. Asking patients to provide their own safe space forecloses areas of potential healing and growth while restricting the range of psychoanalytic treatment to those who already know such safety and can construct it for themselves.

Furthermore, the demands of constant connection and distraction present in emerging technoculture make it especially important for analysts to provide a shared space. By providing patients with the safety of a shared environment, analysts provide both a traditional "good-enough" holding environment for healing psychic damage and fostering psychic change and a space Turkle (2011) has described as a "sacred space . . . a place where we recognize ourselves and our commitments" (p. 47). It is "where we are fully present to each other or to ourselves, where we're not competing with the roar of the Internet" (Turkle & Tippett, 2012). Even with technological wonders enlivening imagination, we still believe people can feel most fully themselves when physically together in such a shared sacred space. It is where both analyst and patient have the freedom to be just as they need to be in order to find joint analytic understanding. In fact, the security of a shared environment, a protected external space, just may be what makes possible a similarly secure internal space (Parsons, 2014).

Being alone in the absence of the other

Telepresence is fragile. Both the necessary psychological conditions of attention, desire, and imagination and technological conditions of interactivity and reliability must be maintained. Because of this, remote sessions afford a new experience that can be called being alone in the absence of the other (cf. Winnicott, 1958) and have a significantly lower threshold for exiting the session.

Someone lost in rage or sadness silently staring off into the distance of their office or home (or wherever they happen to be) would no longer be attending to any of the information signaling the presence of the other. They might even actively be wanting to erase the other. When this happens, the necessary psychological conditions for telepresence evaporate, and there is no longer a technologically mediated presence of an other. Someone would simply be angry or sad and alone with some random piece of technology in the background. For example, Bollas (2015) describes a remote session with a woman who for 30 minutes psychotically raged through her house fighting a hallucinated dragon before returning to the phone. During that time, she was alone in the absence of the other, forced into a solitary fight with her demons that could be considered cruel and dangerously risky (Essig, 2015c). Other less dramatic or lengthy examples of being alone in the absence of the other occur frequently in remote sessions, often unnoticed.

Remote sessions are also remarkably easy to leave. Among the interviews with remote treatment participants cited in her book, Russell writes of analysts discussing the difference in quality and significance between angry patients storming out of a shared environment session or simply disconnecting from a Skype session. "The ease of exit is really problematic: exiting from a session by the flick of a switch," says Charles, a Boston psychoanalyst. In contrast, "It takes courage to enter a room and walk out of a room" (p. 34).

Technological glitches can also impose experiences of being alone in the absence of the other as well as terminating a session when the glitches block the experience of presence. Just about everyone who has worked remotely has had experiences of misbehaving technology rendering the illusion of non-mediation impossible. The therapeutic dyad then finds themselves alone with a relatively inert piece of technology either momentarily or for the duration of the session. With the exception of fire drills, burst pipes, or some other rare calamity, imposed session terminations hardly ever happen in person.

Free-floating attention and reverie replaced by focused attention and continuous partial attention

Attention is deployed differently in local and remote sessions. Maintaining a technologically mediated sense of presence requires focused attention frequently in conflict with analytic listening and attention. First, participants must keep from awareness all the environmental affordances extraneous to relational contact. When the local does intrude, as it inevitably does, the illusion of non-mediation is lost as awareness of the separateness of the environments intrudes. To keep that from happening, participants must focus on the speaker or screen mediating the contact. In fact, the intensity of attentional effort decreases the sense of presence and undermines free-floating attention (Campanella, Bracken, &

Skalski, 2010, p. 187). Second, the devices themselves compel continuous partial attention, which also must be managed. Even when email, texting, and social media programs are closed, they are lurking there in the same machine, creating an interpersonal shadow. As a result, feeling the presence of a technologically mediated other requires tremendous amounts of attentional work unnecessary in person, where one encounters an interpersonal field so rich one can only avoid it with tremendous effort.

While changes in how psychoanalysts have traditionally deployed attention will reverberate through all clinical processes related to the act of fully listening, shared reverie (Ogden, 2004) is especially vulnerable. Such open receptivity to self and other that moves empathy and understanding forward is strangled by the attentional demands screen relations require. What one experiences is something fundamentally different. Shared reverie in screen relations would inevitably include moments in which the participants are alone in the absence of the other.

Memory changes

Differences in risk, repleteness, and relational embodiment diminish the salience of treatment experiences. As a result, as documented in studies of actual remote therapy participants (Isaacs Russell, 2015; Trub & Magaldi, 2017), there is a functionally significant weakening of memories. Remote therapy is just less memorable. For example, patients report that the journey to and away from the consulting room can be an important aid in remembering the session. But turning off a computer or immediately trying to catch up on the texts or social media posts that accumulated during the session is not such a facilitative journey. Other research documents how mediation flattens and levels the experience (Jackson, 2007; Carr, 2011). A patient in Isaacs Russell's study even commented: "[Leaving a Skype session] with a click of a mouse is like having a Caesarean instead of a natural birth." Analysts also directly report weakened memory in remote treatments, including uncharacteristic difficulties in remembering both the times and actual content of sessions. As a way to compensate, some analysts who never took notes in co-present sessions found themselves taking extensive notes in mediated sessions (Isaacs Russell, 2015).

Mediation artifacts and the introduction of a "technological unconscious"

Mediation artifacts are powerful additions to the psychoanalytic process unique to remote treatments. Branham (2017), a computer scientist who became a psychoanalyst, describes how "[a]ll sensors, video screens, speakers, transmission channels, quantization and sampling methods, and encoding/decoding schemes introduce noise, distortions, and other artifacts, and all are limited in the range of signals they are capable of capturing, processing, and transmitting." (145) As a result, the "transmission process" "changes the unconscious expressions of human subjectivity, producing impressions that have nothing to do with the subject yet are often unconsciously confused with" them (139). For example, inevitable "audio/video mismatches and discrepancies can be unconsciously deceptive and disruptive, perturbing the feeling tones produced by the client's subtle and unconscious communications" (153). Consequently, remote sessions inevitably include subtle versions of Tronick's "still face" experiments introduced by the technology but experienced as coming from one of the participants. These confusing unconscious communications are what we're calling a "technological unconscious."

This all takes place when technological mediation is working as intended. The time and distance it takes for a signal to travel, zigzagging through myriad nodes, and the signal processing that occurs along the way as analogue is converted to digital and then back again affects the quality of communication in subtle but significant ways. Throughout the audio/video transmission process, distortions are introduced; errors detected; and enhancements made to sharpen signals, heighten colors, suppress noise, and augment missing data. For example, removing intrusive noise creates a silence that is experienced perceptually as a disconnection, so "comfort noise" is synthesized and inserted back into the transmission to be unconsciously reassuring. Human psychology then makes this even more consequential. Fieldwork in the area of human-computer interaction shows that participants are unaware of difficulties with communication devices. Microanalysis of transcripts of mediated interaction show that distortions from mediation artifacts contribute to serious shifts in meaning, with neither participant being aware of the miscommunication (Ruhleder & Jordan, 1999, 2001). People experience the technological unconscious as coming from the person.

In addition, there are still inevitable glitches, dropped connections, and network slowdowns. Even occasional breaks in the reliability of the technology can cause ongoing anxiety. This constant anticipation of disruption or potentially traumatic rupture, as can be the case when connections are dropped in the midst of emotionally heightened exchanges, is obviously consequential. Fear of disconnection forces the analytic couple to engage in attempts to establish, maintain, and prolong a communication connection, disrupting the silences required to create a space for reverie.

Potential for regressive experiences shrinks as the therapeutic alliance becomes a "therapeutic collusion"

In general, technologically mediated communication sharply attenuates the multi-layered richness and consequential riskiness of physically co-present conversation, thereby inclining participants towards concrete, practical information. In treatment, therapists find themselves talking more, giving advice, and focusing on external events in ways they do not do co-presently. As Isaacs Russell wrote reporting from a group of clinicians who met regularly to discuss their remote treatment experiences: "We did more talking with our patients about the comparative times and weather. We did more talking in general, as silences were not so easy" (2015, p. 5). This is understandable; people talk so they can stay connected with the therapeutically unfortunate consequence of inclining relationships away from potentially healing transferential regressions. She continued, "We felt less in touch, less intuitively connected" (p. 5).

Furthermore, different psychoanalytic schools, and all forms of effective psychotherapy, include a bond based on therapist attunement to patients' subjective experience. This is also true in screen relations based treatments. Even when treatment is conducted remotely, therapist and patient are constantly trying to read and respond to each other. There is a moment-by-moment adaptation to what the technological mediation affords with the over-arching goal of maintaining that attunement-based bond – above all else, stay connected. But on screen that bond is as fragile as the telepresence on which it depends. Consequently, and the authors have repeatedly seen this in their own work, that of their colleagues, and from supervisees, screen relations based treatments include a collusion to avoid the dark and dangerous that would put telepresence at risk. As a result, the anxiety gradients remote treatment dyads surf are often much shallower. Such treatments become more like strolls through gently rolling hills rather than climbing anxiety gradients with sharp peaks and valleys. The medium not only allows analysts to "coast in the countertransference" (Hirsch, 2008), it powerfully pulls for such a collusive leveling of experience.

Plus technologically mediated communications afford a new experience that further shrinks possibilities for regressive experiences in the transference/countertransference pulling the analyst and the patient into a therapeutic collusion. Specifically, using technology is easier than being bodies together. As one therapist said: "Sometimes I am filled with profound countertransference reactions, like terror or grief. It's easier with Skype: [patients] can hurt you less – and they're probably saying the same thing!" (Isaacs Russell, 2015, p. 27).

It takes effort and sacrifice to be "much more reliable than people are in ordinary life," to provide the safe, holding environment, to project many months ahead for breaks, to bear the anger and anguish that patients feel when we are away (Winnicott, 1955, p. 21). The discovery that distance makes therapeutic relationships easier is embedded in technology's transformations of relationships in the wider culture. We text rather than talk, we edit and curate our communications in social media, we protect ourselves from vulnerability, distancing ourselves from the spontaneous, messy, uncontrolled encounters in co-present conversation. We are colluding to move away from the demands of intimate relationships.

Consequences for practice

The innovation of understanding the different experiences and functional consequences of remote psychoanalytic care and physically co-present local treatment directly influences clinical decision-making. We'd like to offer the following suggestions concerning whether and how to conduct a remote session or treatment. But because all situations and analytic dyads are unique, it is not useful to offer specific "rules" like, for example, "x-number of in-person sessions are necessary." Instead we offer a set of general principles that can guide clinical decision-making. In addition, this innovation has significant consequence beyond the consulting room. We believe it provides psychoanalysts with a platform for productively engaging the wider culture, hopefully helping the field regain some lost stature.

Limit the better-than-nothing to better than nothing

Providing psychoanalytic care via technological mediation to those who have no other option is certainly important and useful. However, as already noted, technology is a trickster. Its current is strong. What starts out better-than-nothing soon slips into being thought of as routinely good-enough and then better than anything else (Turkle, Essig, & Isaacs Russell, 2017; Essig, Isaacs Russell, & Turkle, 2018). Both authors have encountered numerous examples where the merely inconvenient becomes a rationale for starting remote work. But how much travel time is too much or how inclement does the weather have to be? Other uses of remote treatment indicate a wish to participate in something "new" or "edgy." Another example of slippage is occasionally offered by well-meaning senior, expert clinicians. They want to use technology to project expertise not just to where other options are not available but also with the idea that everyone should have access to those considered to be the best clinicians. However, this ignores the significant differences between the two contexts, evincing not clinical wisdom but someone entrapped by the simulations technology provides. It is as though someone asserted it is better to learn tennis by playing a video-game version with Serena Williams than to take lessons from one's local club pro. All three rationales illustrate how technology's pull requires that one remain mindful that the better-than-nothing really does need to stay better than nothing.

Accept the inevitability of loss and limit

One of technology's empty seductions is being able to escape loss. Too often remote treatment is used to avoid difficult, even painful, yet necessary experiences of loss. When members of a therapeutic dyad relocate, or just want something different from life like more travel, remote treatment is seen as a way to maintain therapeutic continuity even when other excellent local options exist. Such a comforting thought ignores the reality of loss because in such situations continuity actually is impossible. What is possible is choice of loss: the loss of shared embodiment with one's therapist or the loss of a specific therapist. There is no loss free option. We owe our patients the opportunity to mourn, whether in the form of an in-person goodbye or an on screen experience of the different and diminished possibilities of remote treatments.

Setting a remote session frame

Because the local and remote are such radically different contexts, setting the frame for remote treatment is critical. The Appendix has a handout useful for doing this.

Sharing states of mind is not sharing states of being

After a decision is made to begin remote treatment, listening for unconscious material around distance and the loss/absence of shared embodiment is crucial. It is also very difficult. Analysts are used to attending to their internal states as they are made manifest in the relationship and in a shared external environment. We bring not just our thoughts, but our entire state of being to the work. When working remotely, clinicians have the added burden of trying to be aware of the influence of the now separate settings as well as the technology itself on themselves as well as on their patients. The pull to shut down and have a seemingly interesting conversation about mental states is strong. But this does not provide patients with the immersive, potentially transformative experience psychoanalysis promises.

Attend to differences in risk, repleteness, and relational embodiment

Rather than remaining entrapped in a technologically mediated simulation of being bodies together, an awareness of difference helps anchor experience in the realities of connection over distance. These three dimensions of difference discussed earlier provide clinicians with ways to experience and understand aspects of remote treatment that might otherwise be missed.

Cherish the unique possibilities of "local therapy"

Technoculture continues to accelerate (Harari, 2016; Kurzweil, 2010). The siren call of constant connection threatens to change how we experience each other and ourselves (Turkle, 2011, 2015). But psychoanalytic local therapy provides a unique corrective. Our legacy of valuing introspection, intimacy, and empathy, of aspiring to transformative healing and personal freedom, is worth cherishing whether one is dealing with a specific clinical challenge or thinking about participating with the culture at large.

Our innovative future: local therapy

Technological innovation in general and specifically in psychoanalysis now includes reclaiming and reasserting the unique value of body-with-body relating (Lanier, 2011; Turkle, 2015). People are learning that technology is a trickster, that it is designed to replace bodies with screens (Alter, 2017). Experience and research increasingly show that despite apparent success – and even reports of emotional satisfaction – the consequences of intimate communication in technologically mediated contexts are sharply limited (Sax, 2016; Chavooshi et al., 2017; Aghajan et al., 2015). We contend that the future of psychoanalysis depends on embracing this innovation. It depends on cultivating awareness of the differences between the local and remote treatment contexts. Delivering treatment mediated by screens may provide moments of experience that feel functionally equivalent. But they are not. Bodies need time together to experience presence that fosters the deep transformations at the core of psychoanalytic work. Without shared experiences of actual presence, opportunities to experience a space of internal and external reality are lost, as is an intermediate space useful for joint play and the creation of symbols. At the extreme, technological mediation makes inauthentic the potentially symbolic because it is not balanced by the experience of body-to-body communication, with all the palpable potentiality that it implies.

Our bodies are not just incidental in opening up experiences technoculture is closing. Turkle wrote: "The culture of therapy affects our culture as a whole. How we seek help, what we expect help to look like, changes our values in a broader way. Right now digital culture closes down the questions that talk therapy knows how to open up" (2016). We agree. The path to authentically being alive cannot fully travel along cables nor be confined to two-dimensional screens or even to three-dimensional virtual reality environments, despite the significant allure of such contexts. At some point, patients need to test the analyst's capacity to bear the impact of their love and their hate in flesh not protected by the barrier of a screen. The truth of these experiences needs to be lived, not simulated.

Ongoing innovations in psychoanalysis and technology will recognize the unique affordances of both local therapy and remote therapy without shying away from the inevitable losses and limitations distance requires. Practice in the two contexts needs to be fully differentiated, in part by seeing remote therapy as the better-than-nothing compromise it must always be. Of course, technology can be a useful adjunct in some areas of treatment, just as is the case with all tools. But we must dictate the terms and know the limitations. Tools are to be used with good judgment by people who create them and not the reverse: the tools should never be in charge. Simply put, remaining mindful of difference so as to appreciate the unique value of being bodies together is the next step in the relationship between psychoanalysis and technoculture.

Notes

1 This phrase takes the subtitle of Turkle's (2011) *Alone Together: Why We Expect More from Technology and Less from Each Other* and turns it around to make it consistent with the activist stance we want to present that was also central in her later (2016) work, *Reclaiming Conversation*.
2 Readers please note that like the man in the ad who has lots of experience with the techno-conveniences Clara provides, both authors are technophilic users who are coming to this comparison after extensive experience with the promise and perils of remote treatment (Essig, 2015b).

References

Aghajan, Z. M., Acharya, L., Moore, J. J., Cushman, J. D., Vuong, C., & Mehta, M. R. (2015). Impaired spatial selectivity and intact phase precession in two-dimensional virtual reality. *Nature neuroscience*, *18*(1), 121.

Alter, A. (2017). *Irresistible: The rise of addictive technology and the business of keeping us hooked*. New York, NY: Penguin.

Balint, M. (1950). Changing therapeutical aims and techniques in psycho- analysis. *International Journal of Psychoanalysis*, *31*, 117–124.

Beebe, B., Knoblauch, S., Rustin, J., & Sorter, D. (Eds.). (2005). *Forms of inter-subjectivity in infant research and adult treatment*. New York, NY: Other Press.

Bollas, C, (2015, October 17). A conversation on the edge of human perception. *New York Times*. Retrieved November 7, 2018, from https://opinionator.blogs.nytimes.com/2015/10/17/a-conversation-on-the-edge-of-human-perception/

Branham, S. (2017). Comparison of in-person and screen-based analysis using communication models: A first step towards the psychoanalysis of telecommunications and its noise. *Psychoanalytic Perspectives*, *14*, 1–21.

Campanella Bracken, C., & Skalski, P. D. (Eds.). (2010). *Immersed in media: Telepresence in everyday life*. New York, NY: Routledge.

Carlino, R. (2011). *Distance psychoanalysis: The theory and practice of using communication technology in the clinic* (J. Nuss, Trans.). London: Karnac.

Carr, N. (2011). *The shallows: What the internet is doing to our brains*. New York, NY: W. W. Norton.

Carr, N. (2015). *The glass cage: How our computers are changing us*. New York, NY: W. W. Norton.

Celenza, A. (2005). Vis-à-vis the couch: Where is psychoanalysis? *International Journal of Psychoanalysis, 86*, 1645–1659.

Chavooshi, B., Mohammadkhani, P., & Dolatshahee, B. (2017). Telemedicine vs. in-person delivery of intensive short-term dynamic psychotherapy for patients with medically unexplained pain: A 12-month randomized, controlled trial. *Journal of Telemedicine and Telecare, 23*(1), 133–141.

Clark, A. (1998). *Being there: Putting brain, body, and the world together again*. Cambridge, MA: MIT Press.

Damasio, A. (1999). *The feeling of what happens: Body and emotion in the making of consciousness*. London: Vintage.

Damasio, A. (2005). *Descartes' error*. New York, NY: Penguin.

Damasio, A. (2012). *Self comes to mind: Constructing the conscious brain*. New York, NY: Vintage.

Essig, T. (2015a). The gains and losses of 'screen relations': A clinical approach to simulation entrapment and simulation avoidance in a case of excessive internet pornography use. *Contemporary Psychoanalysis, 51*(3).

Essig, T. (2015b). The full training illusion and the myth of functional equivalence. *Round Robin Newsletter, 30*(2). Retrieved July 16, 2017 http://internationalpsychoanalysis.net/wp-content/uploads/2015/05/RoundRobin2Essig2015FINAL.pages.pdf

Essig, T. (2015c, October 31). A conversation on the edge of being irresponsible about talk therapy and schizophrenia. *Forbes*. Retrieved November 7, 2018, from www.forbes.com/sites/toddessig/2015/10/31/a-conversation-on-the-edge-of-being-irresponsible-about-talk-therapy-and-schizophrenia/

Essig, T., Isaacs Russell, G., & Turkle, S. (2018). *Sleepwalking towards artificial intimacy: How psychotherapy is failing the future*. Forbes. Retrieved from www.forbes.com/sites/toddessig/2018/06/07/sleepwalking-towards-artificial-intimacy-how-psychotherapy-is-failing-the-future/

Fishkin, R., & Fishkin, R. (2011). The electronic couch: Some observations about Skype treatment. In S. Akhtar (Ed.), *The electrified mind* (pp. 99–111). Lanham, MD: Jason Aronson.

Freud, S. (1923b). The ego and the id. *S.E., 19*, 1–66. London: Hogarth.

Geller, S. M. (2017). *A practical guide to cultivating therapeutic presence*. Washington, DC: American Psychological Association.

Gibson, J. J. (1979). The theory of affordances. In *The ecological approach to visual perception* (pp. 127–143). Boston: Houghton Mifflin.

Gordon, R. M., & Lan, J. (2017). Assessing distance training: How well does it produce psychoanalytic psychotherapists? *Psychodynamic Psychiatry, 45*(3), 329–341.

Harari, Y. N. (2016). *Homo Deus: A brief history of tomorrow*. New York: HarperCollins.

Harris, M. (2017). *Solitude: In pursuit of a singular life in a crowded world*. New York: Thomas Dunne Books.

Hirsch, I. (2008). *Coasting in the countertransference*. New York: Taylor & Francis.

Isaacs Russell, G. (2015). *Screen relations: The limits of computer-mediated psychoanalysis and psychotherapy*. London: Karnac.

Jackson, M. (2007). *Distracted: The erosion of attention and the coming dark age*. New York: Prometheus Books.

Kulwin, N. (2018). One has this feeling of having contributed to something that's gone very wrong. *New York Magazine*. Retrieved from http://nymag.com/selectall/2018/04/jaron-lanier-interview-on-what-went-wrong-with-the-internet.html

Kurzweil, R. (2010). *The singularity is near*. London: Gerald Duckworth & Co.

Lanier, J. (2011). *You are not a gadget: A manifesto*. New York, NY: Vintage.

Lanier, J. (2018). *Ten arguments for deleting your social media accounts right now*. New York, NY: Henry Holt and Company.

Lakoff, G., & Johnson, M. (2003). *Metaphors we live by* (2nd ed.). Chicago, IL: University of Chicago Press.

Lemma, A. (2017). *The digital age on the couch: Psychoanalytic practice and new media*. New York, NY: Routledge.

Little, S. (2015). Between silence and words: The therapeutic dimension of quiet. *Contemporary Psychoanalysis, 51*(1), 31–50.

Lombard, M., & Ditton, T. (1997). At the heart of it all: The concept of pres-ence. *Journal of Computer-Mediated Communication, 3*(2). Retrieved from http://onlinelibrary.wiley.com/doi/10.1111/j.1083-6101.1997.tb00072.x/full.

Mantovani, G., & Riva, G. (1999). "Real" presence: How different ontologies generate different criteria for presence, telepresence, and virtual presence. *Presence: Teleoperators and Virtual Environments, 8*(5), 538–548.

Meissner, W. W. (1998). The self and the body: IV. the body on the couch. *Psychoanalysis and Contemporary Thought, 21*, 277–300.

Ogden, T. H. (2004). The analytic third: Implications for psychoanalytic theory and technique. *Psychoanalytic Quarterly, 73*(1), 167–195.

Parsons, M. (2014). *Living psychoanalysis*. East Sussex: Routledge.

Riva, G. (2006). Being-in-the-world-with: Presence meets social and cognitive neuroscience. In G. Riva, M. T. Anguera, B. K. Wiederhold, & F. Mantovani (Eds.), *From communication to presence: Cognition, emotions and culture towards the ultimate communicative experience. Festschrift in honor of Luigi Anolli* (pp. 47–80). Amsterdam: IOS Press.

Riva, G. (2009). Is presence a technology issue? some insights from cognitive sciences. *Virtual Reality, 13*, 159–169. doi:10.1007/s10055-009-0121-6.

Riva, G., Anguera, M. T., Wiederhold, B. K., & Mantovani, F. (Eds.). (2006). From communication to presence: Cognition, emotions and culture towards the ultimate communicative experience. *Festschrift in honor of Luigi Anolli.* Amsterdam: IOS Press.

Riva, G., & Waterworth, J. (2003). Presence and the self: A cognitive neuro- science approach. *Presence-Connect, 3*(3). Retrieved September 29, 2012, from www.informatik.umu.se/~jwworth/Riva-Waterworth.htm

Riva, G., Waterworth, J., & Waterworth, E. (2004). The layers of presence: A biocultural approach to understanding presence in natural and mediated environments. *Cyber Psychology & Behavior, 7*(4), 402–416.

Riva, G., Waterworth, J., Waterworth, E., & Mantovani, G. (2009). From intention to action: The role of presence. *New Ideas in Psychology, XXX*, 1–14. doi:10.1016/j.newideapsych.2009.11.002

Ruhleder, K., & Jordan, B. (1999). Meaning-making across remote sites: How delays in transmission affect interaction. In S. Bodker, M. Kyng, & K. Schmidt (Eds.), *Proceedings of the sixth European conference on computer-supported cooperative work, 12–16 September 1999* (pp. 411–429). Copenhagen: Kluwer Academic.

Ruhleder, K., & Jordan, B. (2001). Co-constructing non-mutual realities: Delay-generated trouble in distributed interaction. *Computer Supported Cooperative Work, 10*(1), 113–138.

Sax, D. (2016). *The revenge of the analogue.* New York, NY: Public Affairs.

Scharff, J. S. (2013). *Psychoanalysis online: Mental health, teletherapy, and training.* London: Karnac.

Scharff, J. S. (2015). *Psychoanalysis online 2: Impact of technology on development, training, and therapy.* London: Karnac.

Scharff, J. S. (2017). *Psychoanalysis online 3: The teleanalytic setting.* London: Karnac.

Sletvold, J. (2014). *The embodied analyst: From Freud and Reich to relationality.* New York, NY: Routledge.

Stern, D. N. (1985). *The interpersonal world of the infant: A view from psychoanalysis and developmental psychology.* New York, NY: Basic Books.

Tronick, E. Z. (1989). Emotions and emotional communication in infants. *American Psychologist, 44*, 112–126.

Trub, L., & Magaldi, D. (2017). Left to our own devices. *Psychoanalytic Perspectives, 14*(2), 219–236.

Turkle, S. (2011). *Alone together.* New York, NY: Basic Books.

Turkle, S. (2015). *Reclaiming conversation.* New York, NY: Penguin.

Turkle, S. (2016). The empathy gap: Digital culture needs what talk therapy offers. *Psychotherapy Networker.* Retrieved from www.psychotherapynetworker.org/magazine/article/1051/the-empathy-gap

Turkle, S., Essig, T., & Russell, G. I. (2017). Afterword: Reclaiming psychoanalysis: Sherry Turkle in conversation with the editors. *Psychoanalytic Perspectives*, *14*(2), 237–248.

Turkle, S., & Tippett, K. (2012, November 15). Alive enough? Reflecting on our technology. *On Being Broadcast*. Retrieved July 7, 2018, from https://onbeing.org/programs/sherry-turkle-alive-enough-reflecting-on-our-technology/

Waterworth, J. A., & Waterworth, E. L. (2003). The meaning of presence. *Presence-Connect 3*. Retrieved from www.informatik.umu.se/~jwworth/PRESENCE-meaning.htm

Winnicott, D. W. (1955). Metapsychological and clinical aspects of regression within the psycho-analytical set-up. *International Journal of Psychoanalysis*, *36*, 16–26.

Winnicott, D. W. (1958). The capacity to be alone. *International Journal of Psychoanalysis*, 39, 416–420.

Winnicott, D. W. (1965). *The maturational processes and the facilitating environment: Studies in the theory of emotional development*. London: Hogarth Press.

Appendix

The following is a suggested document for distributing to patients prior to the first remote session, either on paper or via pdf if necessary. It is a useful tool for setting a frame appropriate for remote sessions.

Remote session guidelines

A remote session is not the same as that which happens when we meet in person. And, at the same time, it is not the same as a typical phone conversation, SKYPE, or FaceTime call. Listed below are some guidelines for how to get the most from remote sessions. Each guideline is a way to try to make a remote session as "session-like" as possible.

1. The most important feature is privacy. Please do everything possible to make sure you are in a private space where it is unlikely you will be heard or interrupted.
2. Try to make yourself comfortable, but not too comfortable. If you can, settle into a nice, comfortable chair. Avoid lying in bed or on your TV-watching couch as well as sitting on the floor or walking around the house or office.
3. Put a box of tissues next to where you are sitting. If you want, pour yourself a glass of water. But avoid having a snack or meal even though you may be reasonably close to your kitchen.
4. Leave yourself an additional 15 minutes both before and after the session. Fifteen minutes before the session, take a walk outside, even if it is just down the block or around the corner. It is not a good idea to leave a meeting or end a call and then immediately call in to start a session. You need time to clear your head and get ready for the work we are about to do. Similarly, after the session is over, take the same

walk in the opposite direction. This will give time for the session to resonate before jumping back into the day's activities. Plus there is evidence that simply walking to and from a place helps with memory and deepening an experience.

5   Turn off all devices other than the one you are using to make the call. If using a smartphone or computer, do your best to quit all programs other than the one we are using, and turn off all notifications if you can. It is best to leave your hands free by using headphones. If we are using audio only, then be sure to put your phone screen side down. If using a computer, please either turn off your monitor or completely darken your screen.

6   Consistency is important. Do your best to have a session from the same place each time. When this is not possible, take a moment at the beginning of the session to describe where you are. I will do the same. And if you find yourself curious about where I am, please feel free to ask, just as you would be able to see me when we meet in person.

I recognize that these guidelines make remote sessions a little less convenient. But the benefit will be more than worth the additional effort.

Index

Note: Page numbers in *italic* indicate a figure and page numbers followed by an "n" indicate a note on the corresponding page.

Adelphi University 140
adolescence 76, 88–92
aesthetics 90, 92–95, 96n10, 97n23
affordances 230–231, 232
aggression 17, 23, 141, 162–163
alcohol 9, 208; *see also* self-medication; substance use disorders (SUD)
American Psychoanalytic Association 137, 144, 155
anaclitic personality style 212, 217, 220–221
Apartheid 61, 63
Apollon, Willy 5, 75–77, 79–80, 96n9, 96n11; and aestheticism 93–94, 96n17; and anthropology 81–83; and sex 87
archetypes 56, 64, 66
attachment 164
attention 237–238

bad faith 108–109
beautiful, the 93–94; *see also* aesthetics
beliefs 85–86
Benjamin, Jessica 179
Bergeron, Danielle 5, 75
borders 79
brain laterality 121–125; *see also* right brain
Brenner, Charles 11, 36; *see also* compromise formations
bridge theory 173
Butler, Judith 200–201, 203

Cantin, Lucie 5, 75
castration 145
Catholicism 34–35

celebrity culture 68
censorship 85–86, 90, 122
child abuse 154–155, 192
choice 113–116
climate change 79
cocaine 220
collective unconscious *65*
communion 34
complexes 58–60
complexity theory 8
complex theory 57–58; *see also* cultural complexes
compromise formations 4, 11, 19, 36
conceptual self 128
continuous partial attention 238
core conflictual relationship theme method (CCRT) 208
countertransference 30–36, 138–139, 142, 145; *see also* interpersonal theory
creativity 129–131
critical rationalism 8, 183
cultural complexes 52–53, 57–58; and individuals 60–66; and nations 66–73
cultural unconscious 5, 55–57, 59, *65*

death-drive 96n13
defenses 11, 161–162
depressive affect 18
desires: and emotions 112–113; prohibition of 20
disillusionment 53–55
dissociation 124, 166, 173
Dostoevsky, Fyodor 204
drives 16, 25, 78, 83–85, 87, 92, 223

drugs of choice 210–211; see also self-medication
dysphoric affects 11

econiche 166
ecstasy 220
Edelman, Gerald 153, 164–167
embodiment 179–180, 231, 233, 238, 242–243
emotions 7, 56, 63, 70–71, 110–113
empathic listening 160–161
enactment 174, 176–177
environment 47–48
ethical subjectivity 200–204
existentialism 144
existential psychoanalysis 6, 100–105, 116–117; and choice 113–116; and emotions 110–113; and psychic reality 105–106; and the unconscious 106–110

facilitating environments 235–236
fallibilism 196, 199
fantasies: and Freud, Sigmund 105–106; of punishment 11–12, 24–25
fear 46
feminism 144–145
field theory 142
fixation 26, 28–29
freedom 113–116
free-floating attention 237
Freud, Sigmund 53, 105, 191; and adolescence 89; and choice 114; and existentialism 102–103; and neuropsychoanalysis 122; and neuroses 29; and *Project* 119–120, 131–132; and psychic reality 105–106; structural model of 11; and world-formation 95n1; see also fixation; regression; Wolf Man; working through
Freudian theory 44–45
Fromm, Erich 143, 146

gambling 9
gender 87, 178–181; see also sex; women
Gifric 75–78; and adolescence 89; and aestheticism 93–94; and anthropology 81–83; see also Apollon, Willy; world-formation
globalization 6, 75, 77–80
global warming see climate change
grammar 201
Greenberg, Jay 127, 140, 153–155, 172

group spirit 68–69
guilt 40

hallucinations 83
harm reduction psychotherapy 223
Harris, Adrienne 179
Heidegger, Martin 102, 107
Heisenberg, Werner 142
Hemingway, Ernest 103
hemispheric asymmetry 7
Henderson, Joseph 55–57, 59; see also cultural unconscious
heroin 214–215
Hitler, Adolf 71
Hobbes, Thomas 204
holding environments 235–236
Holocaust 203–204
homosexual desires 13, 15, 17–19, 27–28, 179
homosexuality 219

immigrants 56, 79
individuals 60–64
infants 96n13
innovation 75–76, 228–230, 232, 245
integration 23–24, 41, 48–49, 50n1, 178; see also synthesis
integrative self 128
internalization 11–12, 21, 24
interpersonal theory 8, 137–149
interpretations 42, 44
intersectionality 178–181
intersubjective systems theory 8
intersubjectivity 184n1, 192–199
intersubjectivity theory 9, 108, 149n3
intrapsychic conflict 4, 11, 23
introjective personality style 212, 216–217, 221

Jews 55
jouissance 83–84
Jung, Carl 5, 52, 53–55, 57–58, 177; see also complexes

Kaplinsky, Catherine 61, 64–66
Khantzian, Edward 209; see also self-medication
Klein, Melanie 5, 44–45, 100
Kohut, Heinz 8, 156–162

Lacanian theory 5, 81
Laing, R.D. 104–105

language 82–85, 96n14, 129–130
left brain 121, 124, 129–131
Levenson, Edgar 146
Levinas, Emmanuel 202
limitations 242
listening 159–160
literature 3
local therapy 9, 228–232; and clinical practice 241–245; and clinical process 235–241; and presence 228–235
loss 242

Manhattan Institute for Psychoanalysis, The 140
meditation artifacts 239
memory 238–239
mental representations 82–83
Merleau-Ponty, Maurice 107
methadone 214–218
migrations 79
Mitchell, Stephen 172–173
mobile cathesix 16
Mondialisation see world-formation
mutual enactment 139–140, 147
mutual influence 149n1, 182–183
mutual recognition 193–194

narcissism 66–68, 71–72
narratives 85, 86, 90–91, 142, 146, 197
nations 66–73
Nazism 54–55, 160, 203–204
neuropsychoanalysis 5, 120–121
Ngwekazi, Rosie 61–64
Nietzsche, Friedrich 102

object-representations 4, 12, 14–15, 19–24
obsessive-compulsive disorder 12–15
Oedipal complex 15; overstimulation of 27; and regression 29; and synthesis 12, 18–19, 23
opiates 210, 212–213

parental desires 21
participant-observations 139
penis envy 144–145
personality style 9, 222–224
phantasies 5, 39–43, 45; *see also* fantasies
pharmacospecificity hypothesis 221–222
phenomenology 9, 165; and ethical subjectivity 200–204; and intersubjectivity 192–199; and postmodernism 191–192; and trauma 199–200

philosophy 2–3, 191–192
Popper, Karl 8, 183
postmodernism 5, 48–49, 100–101, 191–192
posttraumatic stress disorders (PTSD) 211, 212, 214, 215, 218–220
pre-conscious mind 125
presence 228–235
process generalizations 165–166
projection 39–40, 45
psychic reality 105–106
punishment fantasies 11–12, 24–29

Québec school 5, 75–76, 78, 91

race 178–181
racism 61
Racker, Heinrich 32
refugees 56
regression 28–29
regulation theory 119–121
relational analysis 100–101, 183–184; critique of 181–183; and disclosure 174–177; and enactment 176–177; and intersectionality 178–181; origins of 172–174; and trauma 177–178
relational theory 8, 138–140, 149n2, 153–154, 156–157, 166–167
remote therapy 9, 228–232; and clinical practice 241–244; and clinical process 235–241; guidelines for 250–252; and presence 228–235
repression: and adolescence 90; neurobiology of 124
resistance 30–36
response of the self 209
reverie 237, 238
Ricoeur, Paul 107
right brain 119–121, 131–134; and psychoanalytic theory 121–125; and psychotherapy 125–131
rituals 12–16

sado-masochistic fantasies 13
Sartre, Jean-Paul 6, 102–103, 105; and emotions 110–113; on the unconscious 106–110
Searles, Harold 140, 143, 145, 147
secondary process 16–19
self 157
self-cohesion 158
self-critique 175

self-disclosure 174–177
self-experience 162
self-medication 9, 208–211; cases of 212–222; empirical research on 211–212; and personality style 222–224
selfobject function 158–159
self-psychology 8, 153–154; and brain research 164–166; and Kohut, Heinz 156–164
self-representations 4, 12, 14–15, 19–24
September 11, 2001 213, 219
sexuality 87, 141, 178–181; *see also* gender; women
signal anxiety 18
silent-disclosure 174–177
Singer, Erwin 146
Socrates 117n1
South Africa 61–62
speech 83–84
spirit 84–85
splitting 39–40
subjectivity 174–177
sublime 93–94, 97n23, 97n25
substance use disorders (SUD) 9, 208, 211–212
Suchet, Melanie 180
Sullivan, Harry Stack 141–142, 149n3, 149n5
superego 11, 19–24
symbol 94
synthesis 4; failures of 12–16; and punishment fantasies 24–25; and secondary process 16–19

technological unconscious 239–240
technology 9, 228–229, 237, 241, 244; *see also* remote therapy
telepresence 236–237
therapeutic presence 127, 234–235
Thompson, Clara 144–145
transference 30–36, 41, 44, 138–139, 142, 145, 149n5; and core conflictual relationship theme method (CCRT) 208–209; and personality style 222;

and postmodernism 48; *see also* interpersonal theory
trauma 5, 9, 47, 84; and brain research 166; and choice 115; neurobiology of 124; and phenomenology 199–200; and race 180; and relational analysis 177–178
traversal of castration 92
triangle of conflict 209
Trump, Donald 53, 66–68, 69–72

uncertainty 154–155
unconscious, the 195–196; and brain laterality 131–132; and complexes 64–66; and Freud, Sigmund 105–106; and language 96n14; and neurobiology 122–124; and right brain 125–126; and Sartre, Jean-Paul 106–110; and world-formation 81–87; *see also* collective unconscious; cultural unconscious
United States 66–72
unit status 235
urbanization 79

victimization 13, 15, 17–18
vulnerability 182

Wilde, Oscar 81
William Alanson White Institute 140
wishes 11
Wolf Man 32
Wolstein, Benjamin 145
women 41, 80, 87, 145, 203; *see also* gender; sexuality
working memory 124
working through 32, 196, 198; *see also* Freud, Sigmund
world-formation 6, 75–77, 95n1, 96n4; and adolescence 88–92; and aesthetics 92–95; and globalization 77–80; and the unconscious 81–87
World War I 54, 102
World War II 104, 203–204
Wotan 54

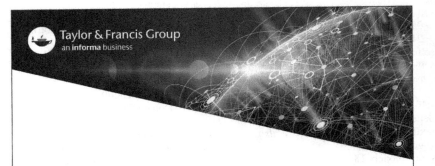